Cooperative and Distributed Intelligent Computation in Fog Computing

Hoa Tran-Dang • Dong-Seong Kim

Cooperative and Distributed Intelligent Computation in Fog Computing

Concepts, Architectures, and Frameworks

 Springer

Hoa Tran-Dang
Department of IT Convergence
Engineering
Kumoh National Institute of
Technology (KIT)
Gumi, Korea (Republic of)

Dong-Seong Kim
Department of IT Convergence
Engineering
Kumoh National Institute of
Technology (KIT)
Gumi, Korea (Republic of)

ISBN 978-3-031-33922-6   ISBN 978-3-031-33920-2   (eBook)
https://doi.org/10.1007/978-3-031-33920-2

This Springer imprint is published by the registered company Springer Nature Switzerland AG
The registered company address is: Gewerbestrasse 11, 6330 Cham, Switzerland

Preface

This book is meant to serve as a reference for those working in the field of fog computing, including educators, researchers, professionals, and developers.

The Internet of Things (IoT) paradigm has been expanded rapidly as a key pillar to realize the smart concept in various domains such as smart cities, smart grids, and smart factories since it enables the interconnection and interoperability of IoT-enabled physical and virtual entities to create smart services and informed decision-making for monitoring, control, and management purposes. The underlying principle of realization involves a set of activities that includes collecting, processing, analyzing, and getting insights from IoT data generated constantly by the IoT devices. Traditionally, the cloud computing platform plays an essential role in the realization process since it provides rich and powerful resources in terms of storage, computation, networking to handle an enormous amount of IoT data (big data) efficiently. However, more stringent requirements of IoT service provisioning such as (ultra)low delay expose crucial limitations of the cloud-based solutions because the delivery of data from the IoT devices to the centralized cloud computing servers seriously affects the performance in processing, analyzing data and results in network congestion issues and excessive delay as an ultimate consequence. This fact context leads to a strong push of fog computing integration into the IoT-cloud systems since it puts computing, storage, communication, and control closer to the IoT devices to meet the prescribed QoS requirements. Technically, the fog computing platform that is placed between the physical IoT devices and the cloud servers can handle a majority of service requests on behalf of the cloud servers to improve the system performance in terms of service delay, workload balancing, and resource utilization.

This book firstly provides an overview of innovative concepts of fog computing, and then proposes important methodologies to develop frameworks for performing intelligent distributed computation operations in the fog-enabled IoT systems. Concretely, the book discusses topics such as the basics of fog computing to help readers understand the technology from the ground up, details about the infrastructure and the integration of IoT, fog and cloud computing to help readers in gaining deeper insights into the technology. The book also includes the use of intelligent and optimal algorithms and emerging technologies like swarm intelligence and reinforcement learning with fog computing. Fundamentally, this book will be a readily accessible source of information for researchers in the area of distributed computing as well as for professionals who want to enhance their security and connectivity knowledge in IoT systems.

This book contains ten chapters, which are organized in a proper manner so that a beginner can follow and benefit from this material without any prior knowledge about the fog computing technology.

Chapter 1 is about "Fog Computing: Fundamental Concepts, Recent Advances in Architectures and Technologies." Fog computing has been introduced and designed to support the specific needs of latency-critical applications such as augmented reality, and Internet of Things (IoT) and cyber-physical systems (CPS) applications which produce massive volumes of data that are impractical to send to faraway cloud data centers for analysis. However, this also created new opportunities for a wider range of applications which in turn impose their own requirements on future fog computing platforms. This chapter summarizes the fundamental concepts of fog computing covering their objectives, characteristics, typical architectures, and enabling technologies associated to support and deliver the functionalities of fog computing paradigm for the future applications.

Chapter 2 discusses "Typical Applications of Fog Computing." In order to meet the unique requirements of latency-sensitive applications like augmented reality and industrial IoT, which generate enormous amounts of data that are prohibitive to transport to distant cloud data centers for processing, fog computing has been introduced and developed. Simultaneously, this also opened up potential possibilities for a larger range of applications, each of which places unique demands on developing fog computing platforms. This chapter aims at conducting a survey relating to these important applications that have been studied, proposed, and developed in the literature.

Chapter 3 presents "Cooperation for Distributed Task Offloading in Fog Computing Networks." Undoubtedly, fog computing enables data processing and storage close to IoT devices to provide the improved IoT services on behalf of the centralized cloud computing. The exploitation of fog computing resource is still ineffective, though, because these heterogeneous devices are distributed in space and time in many scenarios, thus causing an uneven load on the fog nodes. Many large tasks such as virtual reality, machine learning-based tasks must be executed by the remote cloud servers since the fog nodes have insufficient resource to handle them. However, these large tasks can be completed in distributed manner at various fog nodes if they can be divided into independent subtasks. The advances in technologies such as hardware, software, and in field of information and communication enable the different fog nodes to communicated together, thus potentially facilitating the distributed computing solution at fog. This chapter reviews proposed approaches to examine that the fog-fog cooperation can help to improve the performance of task offloading operations in the fog environment.

In Chap. 4, the authors propose and describe "FRATO: A Fog Resource Aware Framework for Adaptive Task Offloading in IoT Systems." This framework is developed for the IoT-fog-cloud systems to offer the minimal service provisioning delay through an adaptive task offloading mechanism. Fundamentally, FRATO is based on the fog resource to select flexibly the optimal offloading policy, which in particular includes a collaborative task offloading solution based on the data fragment concept. In addition, two distributed fog resource allocation algorithms, namely TPRA and MaxRU, are developed to deploy the optimized offloading solutions efficiently in cases of resource competition. Through the extensive simulation analysis, the FRATO-based service provisioning approaches show potential advantages in reducing the average delay significantly in the systems with high rate of service requests and heterogeneous fog environment compared with the existing solutions.

Chapter 5 deals with the dynamic nature of fog computing environment by proposing a dynamic task offloading strategy "DCTO: Dynamic Collaborative Task Offloading in Fog Computing Systems." This approach is based on the resource states of fog devices, to dynamically derive the task offloading policy. Accordingly, a task can be executed by either a single fog or multiple fog devices through the parallel computation of subtasks to reduce the task execution delay. Through extensive simulation analysis, the proposed approaches showed potential advantages in reducing the average delay significantly in systems with a high rate of service requests and heterogeneous fog environment compared with the existing solutions. In addition, the proposed scheme can be implemented online owing to its low computational complexity compared with the algorithms proposed in related works.

Chapter 6 presents "Matching Theory," which has been considered and applied in practical systems to handle the rational and selfish problems of agents, offering mutational benefits for them over time. This chapter presents the fundamental concepts of matching theory, describing the classified models, their structures, and distributed algorithmic aspects. The conventional applications of using matching theory is also reviewed and discussed.

Chapter 7 conducts a survey regarding the applications of "Matching Theory for Distributed Computation in IoT-Fog-Cloud Systems." In this chapter, the key solution concepts and algorithmic implementations proposed in the literature are highlighted and discussed thoroughly. Given the powerful tool of matching theory, its full capability is still unexplored and unexploited in the literature. We thereby discover and discuss existing challenges and corresponding solutions that the matching theory can be applied to resolve them. Furthermore, new problems and open issues for application scenarios of modern IFC systems are also investigated.

In Chap. 8, the authors propose "DISCO: Distributed Computation Offloading Framework for Fog Computing Networks." Designing an efficient offloading solution is still facing many challenges including the complicated heterogeneity of fog computing devices and complex computation tasks. In addition, the need for a scalable and distributed algorithm with low computational complexity can be unachievable by global optimization approaches with centralized information management in the dense fog networks. In these regards, DISCO framework is developed for offloading the splittable tasks using matching theory. Through the extensive simulation analysis, the proposed approaches show potential advantages in reducing the average delay significantly in the systems compared to some related works.

Chapter 9 features "Reinforcement Learning-Based Resource Allocation in Fog Networks." Reinforcement learning is a rising component of machine learning, which provides intelligent decision-making for agents to response effectively to the dynamics of environment. This vision implies a great potential of application of RL in the concept of fog computing regarding resource allocation for task offloading and execution to achieve the improved performance. This chapter presents an overview of RL applications to solve the resource allocation-related problems in the fog computing environment. The open issues and challenges are explored and discussed for further study.

Chapter 10 proposes an algorithm called "Bandit Learning and Matching-Based Distributed Task Offloading (BLM-DTO)" that allows each fog node (FN) to implement the task offloading operations in a distributed manner in the fog computing networks (FCNs). Fundamentally, BLM-DTO leverages the principle of matching game theory to achieve the stable matching outcome based on preference relations of two sides of the game. Due to the dynamic nature of fog computing environment, the preference relation of one-side game players is unknown a priori and achieved only by iteratively interacting with the other side of players. Thus, BLM-DTO further incorporates multi-armed bandit (MAB) learning using Thompson sampling (TS) technique to adaptively learn their unknown preferences. Extensive simulation results demonstrate the potential advantages of the proposed TS-type offloading algorithm over the ε-greedy and upper-bound confidence (UCB)-type baselines.

Gumi, Republic of Korea   Hoa Tran-Dang
                                                                                                    Dong-Seong Kim

Acknowledgments

We would like to express our gratitude to the publisher, Springer, for accepting this book as part of the series Computational Intelligence Methods and Application. In particular, we would like to thank Susan Evans, Senior Editor, for her editorial and production guidance.

Our acknowledgment goes to Dr. Tariq Rahim (Postdoctoral Research Fellow at Cardiff Metropolitan University, UK) and Dr. Arslan Musaddiq (Postdoctoral Research Fellow at Linnaeus University, Sweden), who contributed to the content of Chap. 9.

We specially would like to thank the department of IT convergence engineering and ICT Convergence Research Center (https://ictcrc.org/), Kumoh National Institute of Technology (KIT) in Gumi, Republic of Korea, which provides facilities and environment to realize the book. As one of the most educational institution in science and technology, we are grateful to be part of this visionary and innovative organization.

Finally, we would like to thank the funding agencies who are supporting constantly the authors to pursuing the academic and research works. They are the Ministry of Science and ICT (MSIT), Korea, under the Grand Information Technology Research Center support program (IITP) supervised by the IITP (Institute for Information & Communications Technology Planning & Evaluation), and Korea Research Fellowship Program through the National Research Foundation of Korea (NRF) funded by the Ministry of Science and ICT.

Contents

Abbreviations

5G	Fifth Generation
BN	Busy Node
CDN	Content Distribution Network
CPS	Cyber-Physical System
C-RAN	Cloud – Radio Access Network
D2D	Device-to-Device
DA	Deferred Acceptance
DRL	Deep Reinforcement Learning
DT	Digital Twin
FCN	Fog Computing Network
FN	Fog Node
F-RAN	Fog – Radio Access Network
HN	Helper Node
IaaS	Infrastructure-as-a-Service
IoT	Internet of Things
M2M	Machine-to-Machine
MAB	Multi-Armed Bandit
MTM	Many-to-Many
MTO	Many-to-One
NFV	Network Function Virtualization
OTO	One-to-One
PaaS	Platform-as-a-Service
PL	Preference List
RL	Reinforcement Learning
SaaS	Software-as-a-Service
SDN	Software-Defined Network
TS	Thompson Sampling
UCB	Upper Bound Confidence
VM	Virtual Machine
VN	Vehicular Network

Chapter 1
Fog Computing: Fundamental Concepts and Recent Advances in Architectures and Technologies

Fog computing has been introduced and designed to support the specific needs of latency-critical applications in the Internet of Things (IoT) and cyber-physical systems (CPS) in which all data with massive volume and complex structure constantly generated by the end devices are impractical to send to faraway cloud data centers for computation and analysis. This context also creates new opportunities for a wider range of fog-based applications, which in turn impose their own requirements on future fog computing platforms. This chapter summarizes the fundamental concepts of fog computing covering their objectives, characteristics, typical architectures, and enabling technologies associated to support and deliver the functionalities of fog computing paradigm for future applications.

1.1 Introduction

Computing paradigms have developed over time, moving from distributed to parallel to grid to cloud computing. Scalability, on-demand resource allocation, decreased administrative efforts, a flexible pricing mechanism (pay-as-you-go), and simple application and service provisioning are just a few of the inherent benefits of cloud computing [1]. It includes the infrastructure-as-a-service (IaaS), platform-as-a-service (PaaS), and software-as-a-service (SaaS) service models (SaaS). The virtualized resources, including computation, storage, and networking, are offered via IaaS. Software environments are provided by the PaaS for the creation, deployment, and administration of programs. The SaaS offers end users and other applications software applications and composite services.

Cloud computing is a type of computing that relies on sharing computing resources rather than having local servers or personal devices to handle applications. Cloud computing becomes an essential element of IoT and CPS systems; however, it exposes many limitations in practices. For example, although connectivity to the cloud is a prerequisite of cloud computing, it is not always available. Meanwhile,

© The Author(s), under exclusive license to Springer Nature Switzerland AG 2023
H. Tran-Dang, D.-S. Kim, *Cooperative and Distributed Intelligent Computation in Fog Computing*, https://doi.org/10.1007/978-3-031-33920-2_1

some IoT systems need to work even if the connection is temporarily unavailable. In addition, the available bandwidth to collect all the data from the IoT devices is not always sufficient, especially in industrial IoT applications. Moreover, some practical applications with latency-critical requirements are not fulfilled by cloud computing centralized solutions. Finally, data movement between the IoT layer and the distant cloud is vulnerable to attackers despite security mechanisms such as data encryption are applied in the cloud computing.

By bringing cloud computing and its services to the network's edge, the fog computing paradigm has arisen to address these problems with cloud computing-based solutions. Fog computing basically moves resources and processes to the edge of networks, frequently on network devices. As a result, processing times are shorter, and fewer resources are used [2]. In addition, fog computing enables achieving the green computing paradigm by optimized resource management and control mechanisms [3].

The Cisco System first used the phrase "fog computing" in January 2014 to describe a novel model for facilitating wireless data transfer to scattered devices in the IoT network paradigm. In addition, the OpenFog Consortium [4] is a group of global academic institutions and high-tech corporations with the goal of standardizing and advancing fog computing across a range of industries. According to the definition of this consortium, fog computing is "a system-level horizontal architecture that distributes resources and services of computing, storage, control, and networking anywhere along the continuum from cloud to Things". Summarily, the main features of fog computing include low service latency and location awareness, geographic distribution support, end device mobility, wireless access, real-time applications, and heterogeneity [5].

1.2   Fog Computing Architectures

Fog computing offers distributed architectures made up of several fog devices and tiny data centers that are located close to the sources of data creation such as sensors, cellphones, handheld devices, and machines. Basically, fog computing architecture is implemented in two predominant models, which are hierarchical architecture model and layered architecture.

1.2.1   Hierarchical Architecture Model

Serving as a middleware, fog computing is placed in the middle between the terminal layer and the remote cloud computing layer to create the service provisioning continuum along the thing-fog-cloud path. With this context, the hierarchical architecture model for fog computing is illustrated in Fig. 1.1.

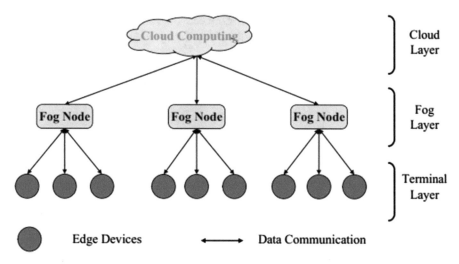

Fig. 1.1 The typical three-tiered architecture of fog computing paradigm

This model comprises of three layers: terminal layer, fog layer, and cloud layer, which are built on a tiered structure [6].

Terminal Layer

The terminal layer contains different physical edge devices such as smartcards, readers, sensors, actuators, smart vehicles, handheld devices, and mobile phones, which are distributed across different locations in the system coverage. Typically, the devices are categorized into a number of groups to serve specific roles. The primary functions of the terminal layer are data sensing and capture and then transmitting these data to the upper layer for further processing. In addition, the end devices are capable to process many tasks locally owing to the advancement of computing technology. In many IoT systems, the terminal layer can contain actuators which receive the commands and controls from the fog and cloud for making decisions [7].

Fog Layer

Fog nodes include a wide range of different devices including routers, gateways, access points, base stations, and certain fog servers. Fog nodes are deployed in a variety of places depending on the application, such as on the floor of a factory, atop a power pole, next to a railroad track, inside vehicles, on an oil rig, and so on. Fog nodes can be stationary (like those found in a bus terminal or coffee shop) or moving (like those installed inside a moving vehicle). Services are provided to the end devices through fog nodes. In addition, the data can be computed, transferred, and momentarily stored by fog nodes. The IP core networks are developed to enable fog nodes to connect and collaborate with the cloud to improve processing and storage capacity.

Cloud Layer

This layer comprises of computers and data servers with high performance and big storage capabilities. This layer carries out compute analysis and permanently stores data for users' backup and access. A cloud layer is composed of enormous data centers with high storage capacity and powerful processing and computing capabilities. Users may access all the fundamental elements of cloud computing through the data centers. The data centers offer scalable computational resources and do so on an as-needed basis. In a fog architecture, the cloud serves as a backup and offers persistent storage for data. Data that isn't needed close to the user is often cached and storage in the cloud layer.

It should be noted that, depending on the needs of the application, this architecture may be expanded to support more fog levels. For example, as illustrated in Fig. 1.2, the fog layer can be structured as a set of groups for supporting specific application domains with distributed computation perspectives [8]. This architecture can be used to build large-scale IoT and CPS systems to provide numerous types of services and applications. In this system, fog-fog communications are enabled to improve the system performance as well as the resource utilization of fog computing devices.

To support the processing the real-time tasks in the heterogeneous environment, a real-time heterogeneous hierarchical scheduling architecture-integrated fog-cloud architecture is introduced in [9]. As shown in Fig. 1.3, there are two tiers to build the architecture for fog computing networks.

In this model, the fog devices in tier-1 have a lower execution capacity than tier-2 fog devices. On the flip side, tier-2 fog devices are located at a greater geographical distance than tier-1 fog devices from the users. Thus, there exists an interesting tradeoff between execution capacity and propagation delay of tier-1 and tier-2 fog nodes.

This architecture is applied in the fog radio access networks (F-RANs), which recently emerged as an evolution of cloud radio access networks (C-RANs) to support new demands of users in the era of fifth-generation networking (5G) [10]. Figure 1.4 shows a typical structure of F-RAN with modified fog layer architecture. To fulfill the functions of F-RANs, the additional layer, termed by logical fog layer, is added to execute distributed communication and storage functions between the network layer and terminal layer. Global centralized communication and storage cloud layer, the centralized control cloud layer, the distributed logical communication cloud layer, and the distributed logical storage cloud layer are defined, which can make F-RANs take full advantage of fog computing, cloud computing, heterogeneous networking, edge cache, and edge artificial intelligence (AI).

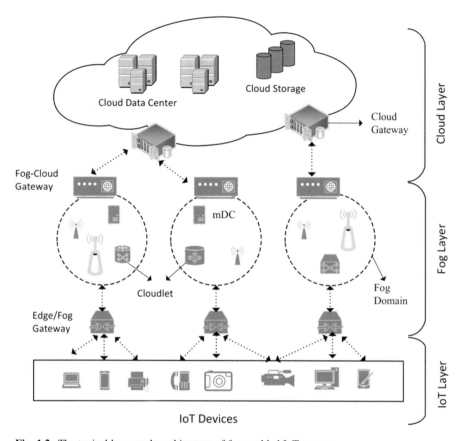

Fig. 1.2 The typical large-scale architecture of fog-enabled IoT systems

1.2.2 Layered Architecture Model

Fog computing architecture can be built on a layered structure form, which is composed of six layers, as shown in Fig. 1.5 [11].

Physical and Virtualization Layer

Generally, this layer includes physical devices, machines, and virtual nodes. The main function of the nodes, which are dispersed across the networks and systems, is data generation and collection. Sensing technology is often used by sensors to record their surroundings and gather information from the environment, which is then forwarded to higher layers via gateways for further processing and storage. A node might be a standalone device, such as a cell phone, or it can be an integrated component of a larger device, such as a temperature sensor installed inside vehicles, equipment, and machines.

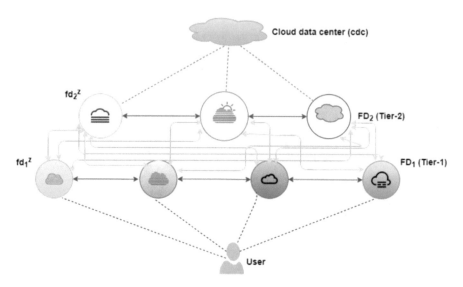

Fig. 1.3 Two-tiered architecture of fog computing to support real-time applications in the industrial IoT systems [9]

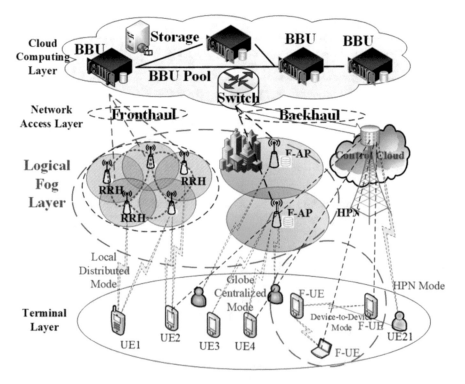

Fig. 1.4 Typical architecture of F-RAN proposed and introduced in [10]

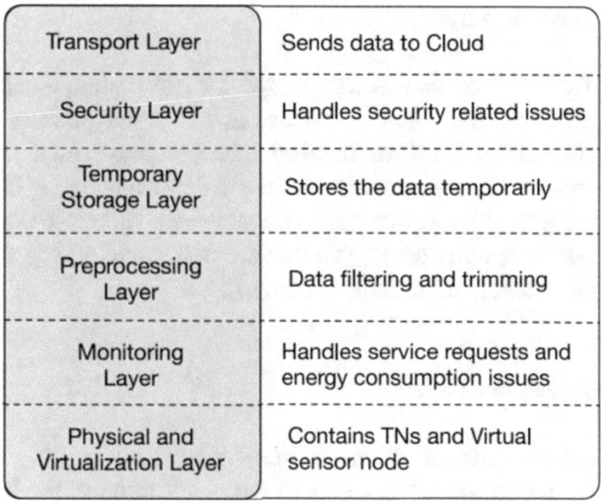

Fig. 1.5 Layered
architecture of fog
computing and layer
functionalities

Transport Layer	Sends data to Cloud
Security Layer	Handles security related issues
Temporary Storage Layer	Stores the data temporarily
Preprocessing Layer	Data filtering and trimming
Monitoring Layer	Handles service requests and energy consumption issues
Physical and Virtualization Layer	Contains TNs and Virtual sensor node

Monitoring Layer

Monitoring for various activities of fog computing is the core activity at this tier. The fog computing nodes can be observed for their duration of operation, their temperature and other physical characteristics, and their maximum battery life. The energy consumption of the fog nodes, or how much battery power they need while operating, is measured. In addition, applications' functionality as well as their current status are both tracked in real time for instant configuration.

Processing Layer

This layer executes a variety of data operations, primarily those involved in data analysis. Data is cleansed and examined for the presence of any undesirable data. Only meaningful data is gathered once data impurities have been eliminated. At this stage, data analysis may entail extracting useful information from the large amounts of data the end devices have gathered. One of the crucial aspects that must be considered before using data for a certain purpose is data analysis.

Temporary Storage Layer

All the pre-processed data will be cached and stored in this layer for further operations. Data distribution, replication, deduplication, and virtualization of storage are among the performance-enhancing tasks carried out here. Data replication and nonpermanent dissemination are related to this layer. In this layer, storage virtualization such as VSAN is utilized. Once data has been sent from this layer to the cloud, it is deleted from the temporary layer.

Security Layer

The received data is transmitted for processing, encryption, and decryption in this layer. Additionally, it guarantees that strict privacy and integrity regulations are adhered to. This layer handles data encryption and decryption as well as data privacy and integrity to ensure that the data is unaltered. Use-based privacy, data-based privacy, and location-based privacy are all possible types of privacy in the context of fog computing data. Data that are outsourced to fog nodes are protected and stored privately, thanks to the security layer.

Transport Layer

After receiving the data, the major goal of the transport layer is to upload pre-processed, secure data to the cloud through the fog-cloud gateways for further processing, computing, and long-term archival storage. The percentage of the data gathered and uploaded to the cloud server is optimized for the sake of efficiency achievement. In addition, because fog computing devices generally are limited by the amount of resources in terms of computation, networking, and storage, light-weight and effective communication methods between the fog and cloud servers should be developed and used. The advancement of technologies enables the fog computing nodes to advance their capabilities. For example, they can perform many tasks such as data communication and data computation in parallel as their processors are equipped with multiple cores.

1.3   Computation Offloading in Fog Computing–Based Systems

Computation offloading is a pivotal operation in the fog computing environment to help the systems to achieve improved performance such as reduced delay, balanced load, and better resource utilization.

However, designing efficient offloading solutions requires handling a set of complex challenges imposed by the natural feature of fog computing environment as well as various requirements of computational tasks. Based on the aforementioned architecture, the typical offloading model in the fog computing environment is illustrated in Fig. 1.6 [12].

There are many models introduced and implemented in the literature to perform computational offloading operations in fog-based systems. Depending on the application scenarios, the models are established appropriately to support the systems to achieve a single objective or multiple objectives simultaneously such as minimization of total energy consumption, minimization of offloading delay, maximization of resource utilization, and fairness and balance of workload. Fundamentally, an

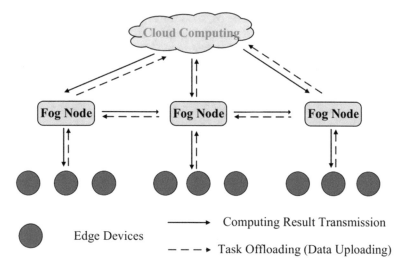

Fig. 1.6 The typical offloading operations between fog-fog and fog-cloud fog-end devices

offloading model takes into account multiple factors, including the system architecture, task properties to derive efficient algorithms that determine offloading locations, times to offload, and how a task is offloaded (how data of task is handled). In the following, we summarize and discuss these relevant aspects to highlight the key features of popular offloading models in the literature.

Regarding the offloading locations, there are two major classes of offloading models including intra-layer and inter-layer offloading. The former refers to models that the offloading operations take place in the same layer, whereas the the latter involve multiple layers (e.g., between IoT and fog layer, between fog and cloud). Concretely, the computational offloading processes can take place only within a stratum of systems where the computing devices in the same tier (e.g., the IoT, fog, and cloud tier) can share their available resources to handle the tasks cooperatively. Recently, the advance of technologies can equip modern IoT devices with more advanced features such as powerful resource and computing capability to process tasks locally. In combination with the emergence of device-to-device (D2D) communication technologies, the computational offloading between IoT devices will become pervasive in future fog-based systems. In the same sense, the tasks can be offloaded within the fog layer and cloud layer, mainly to balance the workload as well as improve resource utilization [13]. However, the heterogeneity of fog node (FN) types exposes a challenge of communication between them, which in turn makes fog-fog communication and task redistribution unavailable. To reverse the situations, it requires unified middleware and protocols to enable fog-to-fog communication and collaboration such as FRAMES developed in [14] enabling the collaborative fogs to jointly share and offload the tasks. Otherwise, FNs can communicate via a centralized agent such as fog service providers or brokers in their fog domains.

In most of the application scenarios, the offloading processes involve multiple layers. For example, as per [15], a task generated by an IoT device can be processed by itself locally or offload to a FN or the cloud finally. The associated analysis reveals that the offloading locations for tasks should be flexible with respect to the task type to get the benefit of offloading operations. Concretely, the heavy tasks should be offloaded to the cloud tier, while the medium tasks are processed by FNs. In addition, the light tasks can be computed locally by IoT devices if they have sufficient resource or offloaded to FNs, otherwise. As the tasks can be splitable, one part of the task can be processed by the IoT node and the other by the fog or cloud. Finally, there exist several application scenarios, in which the upper layers require the lower layers to execute the task. These uncommon offloading models include cloud offloading to fog/IoT and end user devices, fog offloading to the IoT, and end user devices for specific purposes of applications [16].

The determination of times to offload tasks is an important aspect of the offloading models. Generally, offloading is needed when TNs are unable to process the tasks locally, or processing them may not satisfy the QoS requirements. Although modern IoT devices and end user equipment can process some types of tasks locally, the majority of tasks (e.g., complex and heavy tasks, and sporadic tasks emergency cases) generated in the IoT layer are offloaded to the upper layers. However, the task offloading incurs additional costs, such as communication delay and energy consumption. Therefore, the offloading model requires the inclusion of mechanism to monitor the system performance, traffic flow rates, and network conditions that can support making the offloading decisions appropriately. For example, the FOGPLAN framework in [17] can provide dynamic offloading strategies to adapt to the dynamic change of QoS requirements. By observing and analyzing the task processing queue of FNs constantly, tasks currently resided in the processing queues of these FNs must be offloaded to HNs if the predicted processing delays are no longer to meet the deadlines of tasks. Network reliability is also a concern in the fog networks since it directly impacts the communication delay of offloading processes [18].

The offloading models also specify how the input data of tasks is offloaded and processed. Generally, a full offloading method is applied for a task when its whole data is indivisible and processed by a single HN. Conversely, as a divisibility of task is enabled, a partial offloading scheme can be used to offload a fractional part of task to HNs, while the other part of task is processed locally by TN. In most studies, a task is assumed to be decomposed into two subtasks; thus, there needs only one HN to offload the subtask. As subtasks are totally independent, the task division is an effective technique employed in the offloading models to cope with the heterogeneity of computing device resources and simultaneously improve the performance of computing operations. For example, according to the FEMTO model in the work [19], each task is divided into two subtasks with different data sizes, which are then processed by the IoT node and offloaded to the fog entity, respectively. This method contributes to minimizing the energy consumption of task offloading while achieving workload fairness among the fog nodes and satisfying the deadline constraints of tasks. Similarly, partial offloading is utilized in the task offloading models for the

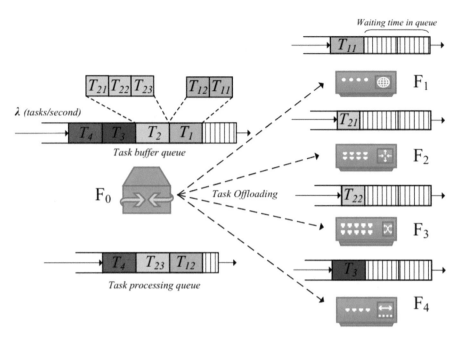

Fig. 1.7 A dynamic computation offloading model is proposed in [21] that integrates partial and full offloading to balance the workload in the fog layer

heterogeneous fog networks to reduce the task execution delay [20]. Dividing a task into multiple (more than two) subtasks is also considered in [21] to exploit the parallel computation of subtasks at different FNs. As analyzed in [20], compared to the full offloading model, partial offloading offers more advantages in terms of delay reduction, energy saving, resource utilization, and workload balancing. The independence of subtasks enabling the parallel processing of subtasks is obviously a key to achieving these advantages. However, in practice, some or all subtasks of a tasks can exist a data dependency relation. For example, the output of a subtask can be an input data for another subtask. Thus, completing the task requires a subtask scheduling plan with respect to the subtask processing order. This in turn can impact the performance of partial offloading models. For instance, as evaluated and analyzed in [22], a number of subtasks for a task can be optimized depending on the system context. In addition, not all tasks should be divided because more subtasks can probably lead to a coupling resource problem. An offloading framework in FRATO is then introduced based on many factors such as the FN resource status (e.g., queue status, computing capability), task request rates, and task properties (e.g., divisibility) to offer a dynamic offloading policy.

As illustrated in Fig. 1.7, FRATO dynamically applies the partial offloading and full offloading modes for the tasks based on the queue status of FNs. In this way, FRATO is able to significantly reduce the offloading delay as well as improve resource utilization, especially in cases of high rate of task requests. A similar investigation is presented in [14] that considers three models of task processing, in which the subtasks can be executed in sequential, parallel, and mixed processing order.

1.4 Key Technologies for Future Fog Computing Architectures

Fog computing contributes to create next-generation classes of intelligent computing systems in which fog computing nodes are able to process the requests of users for local computation and data processing on an autonomous and independent basis. With the capabilities of providing efficient, intelligent, and low-latency services, fog computing has been increasingly integrated in cyber-physical systems as well as IoT networks. However, the resource constrains in terms of energy, storage, communication, and networking are still a current limitation of fog computing preventing it from achieving the full potential of benefits in the integrated systems. The advance of hardware and software technologies will tackle this kind of challenges to assist the deployment and implementation of fog computing in various specific applications. This section discusses these kinds of technologies to advance the functionalities and capabilities of fog computing.

1.4.1 Communication and Networking Technologies

In the fog computing environment, a large number of geo-distributed devices (including EU devices, routers, switches, and access points) form "mini-cloud" at the edge of the network. Unlike the remote centralized data centers in traditional cloud computing, these connected devices manage themselves in a distributed way to upload/download data to/from core network as in traditional cloud computing as well as obtaining data from other users. In addition, the edge devices in fog network (FogNet) [23, 24] can share some of their resource like computing and storage capacity to support the demands of their neighbors. Only the task that is not well handled by the edge devices is sent to the remote cloud side for further processing. To enable these interactions, common wired and wireless communication networks such as 3G, 4G, Wi-Fi, Wireless Local Area Networks (WLAN), ZigBee, and Bluetooth are utilized [25].

The recent advanced communication and networking technologies including 5G enable the edge devices, fog computing nodes, and data center to interact through direct links, such as device-to-device (D2D) communication [26] and adjacent Small Cell (SC) networks [27]. This technology enables many challenging applications and services with resource-limited mobile terminals [28]. For fog computing, especially mobile fog computing, the bottleneck of resource limitations might be broken by 5G technology, which could provide mobile customers an increasing number of resource-intensive services [29]. Additionally, it may satisfy the requirements for low-latency services, high-quality wireless communication, and high-speed data applications. A fog computing-based radio access network is proposed in [30] to incorporate fog computing into a heterogeneous cloud radio access network, as a promising paradigm for 5G system to provide high spectral and energy efficiency. It effectively addresses the limitations of the typical cloud radio access network in the centralized baseband unit pool and confined front haul. At the edge devices, this paradigm can offer real-time collaborative radio signal processing and adaptable cooperative radio resource management.

1.4.2 Virtualization Technologies

Fog computing is a highly virtualized platform [11] that offers standard cloud computing services such as compute, storage, and networking between the end devices and the centralized data centers. Virtualization technologies emerged to overcome the limitations of hardware in the fog and edge devices.

Network virtualization is implemented using software-defined networking (SDN), an emerging paradigm in computing and networking. To provide flexible network traffic control, this design divides the control plane and data plane. A centralized server handles control, and it also determines the connection channel for each node [31]. It features scalability, programmability, and flexibility qualities. There is no requirement to rely on underlying network components (such as routers, switches, and firewalls), and the distinction from the heterogeneous underlying network components may be erased. SDN can aid in the effective administration of heterogeneous fog networks in fog computing [32]. Combining the SDN paradigm with fog computing might help resolve various problems including erratic connection, collisions, and high packet loss rates. For instance, SDN-based architecture in vehicular networks (VNs) based on fog computing may effectively address the aforementioned difficulties and meet the expectations of future vehicular networks applications. VNs allow cars and equipment to work together to offer network services, with cloud computing often providing value-added services. Fog computing may be used in this situation to satisfy user demands with the least amount of assistance from the Internet infrastructure by being placed closer to the users. Large-scale fog-enabled VN services could be used with the assistance of SDN [33].

Network function virtualization (NFV) is another important virtualization technology used to improve the flexibility of telecommunication service provisioning [34]. The core concept of NFV is to use virtualization and device abstraction technologies to separate the network function from the specialized physical network hardware. As a result, resources may be used completely and flexibly to facilitate the quick development and rollout of new services. NFV will help fog computing in many ways, including the ability to virtualize and install firewalls, switches, and gateways on fog nodes. In the diverse and extensively geo-distributed fog network, it may facilitate the smooth administration of resources (such as computation, storage, and communication) and orchestration of capabilities. Depending on the real needs, the new application may be extended easily and automatically deployed. The performance of virtualized network devices is a key consideration for NFVs' use in fog computing. To achieve low latency and high throughput, virtualized network devices are combined with effective instantiation, placement, and migration methods [35].

A new digital technology called a "digital twin" (DT) uses a digital representation of real-world objects to create a mixed-reality virtual environment [36]. In addition to offering an energy-efficient method of analysis and training the network management module's decision-making abilities, DT can capture the key functions of edge clouds. DT is another virtualization technology that can assist the fog computing to implement the task computation efficiently [37, 38]. By predicting the statuses of edge servers and giving DRL agent training data, DTs aid in the choice to offload mobile workloads.

1.4.3   Storage Technologies

Content distribution network (CDN) is a network of Internet-based cache servers that places CDN proxy servers at the edge of the network. The CDN system distributes the relevant materials to the CDN proxy server close to the users by carefully taking into account the information including connection state, load, and user distance of each node. Users can get the information they need, shorten the time it takes for content to download from distant sites, and speed up response times [39, 40]. Fog computing's features suggest that CDN technology can aid in reducing bandwidth consumption, network congestion, increasing content accessibility, and lowering expenses. Fog computing powered by CDNs, particularly when combined with context-aware technologies, can quickly deliver the most requested services to end users.

Pre-cache technology may be used to satisfy the requirements of low-latency property in fog computing. In advance, fog nodes choose the most popular contents to cache in the geo-distributed nodes based on their analysis of user demand. By doing so, the time it takes for material to download from faraway datacenters may be greatly decreased, and fog apps can fully utilize the storage resources to offer consumers the best services [41]. A proactive caching paradigm in 5G wireless networks is proposed in [42] to proactively pre-cache the desirable information before users request it. The premise for prediction was the popularity of the files and linkages between user and file usage patterns. Also used to proactively store strategic material were social networks and device-to-device conversations. By anticipating user requests and actively caching at base stations and edge devices, peak traffic demands may be significantly minimized. This pre-cache technique and framework are adaptable and support fog computing. Additionally, the storage capacities of edge devices are typically constrained. Therefore, storage expansion technology has a significant impact on boosting fog computing's total service capabilities. In [43], the authors suggested using personal storage for mobile devices as a solution for secure and effective storage growth. To provide a distributed storage service and increase storage capacity, it combined all of a user's personal storage space using fog networking.

1.4.4 Privacy and Data Security Technologies

Fog computing devices are typically used in some locations where protection and monitoring are relatively poor since they are near to end users [44]. For example, one possible method of data hijacking is the man-in-the-middle attack [45]. Fog node devices may be fictitiously used or changed in this assault. Methods of encryption and decryption can be used to address this issue.

In addition, multi-level collaboration creates a variety of security and privacy issues, chief among them identity management, authentication and authorization, resource access control, securely distributed decision enforcement and collaboration, information sharing policies, quality of security and service, and a host of others [46]. In order to facilitate secure cooperation and interoperability across different user-requested resources, the authors in [47] developed policy-based resource management and access control in fog ecosystem. Recently, F-RAN has been seen as a possible option to reduce the stress of rising traffic on present and future wireless networks because it moves processing and caching capabilities from faraway clouds to the network edge. However, it also increases the risk. To fix this problem, the authors in [48] propose a secure yet trustless blockchain-based F-RAN (BF-RAN). It takes advantage of the main characteristics of blockchain, such as decentralization, tamper-proof, and traceability, to enable a huge number of trustless.

1.5 Conclusions

This chapter summarizes the fundamental concepts of fog computing paradigm, which is increasingly integrated in the IoT systems and cyber-physical systems as an essential component. Depending on the specific applications of IoT systems, the architectures of fog are different. Through the literature review, we briefly present typical architectures to deploy fog computing. In addition, the main task offloading models are reviewed deeply to show the characteristics and capabilities of fog computing in improving the systematic performance in terms of latency, energy, workload balancing, and bandwidth saving. The enabling technologies to support the offloading operations and deployment of fog computing are described toward future applications.

References

1. Zhang Q, Cheng L, Boutaba R (2010) Cloud computing: state-of-the-art and research challenges. J Internet Serv Appl 1(1):7–18
2. Dastjerdi AV, Buyya R (2016) Fog computing: helping the internet of things realize its potential. Computer 49(8):112–116
3. Qureshi R, Mehboob SH, Aamir M (2021) Sustainable green fog computing for smart agriculture. Wirel Pers Commun 121(2):1379–1390
4. IEEE standard for adoption of OpenFog reference architecture for fog computing. 2018
5. Bonomi F, Milito R, Zhu J, Addepalli S (2012) Fog computing and its role in the internet of things. In: Proceedings of the first edition of the MCC workshop on Mobile cloud computing, pp 13–16
6. Sabireen H, Neelanarayanan V (2021) A review on fog computing: architecture, fog with IoT, algorithms and research challenges. ICT Express 7(2):162–176
7. Gupta H, Dastjerdi AV, Ghosh SK, Buyya R (2017) iFogSim: a toolkit for modeling and simulation of resource management techniques in the internet of things, edge and fog computing environments. Softw Practice Experience 47(9):1275–1296
8. Tran-Dang H, Kim D-S (2022) A survey on matching theory for distributed computation offloading in IoT-fog-cloud systems: perspectives and open issues. IEEE Access 10:118353–118369
9. Kaur A, Auluck N, Rana O (2022) Real-time scheduling on hierarchical heterogeneous fog networks. IEEE Trans Serv Comput:1–10
10. Peng M, Zhao Z, Sun Y (2020) System architecture of fog radio access networks. In: Fog radio access networks (F-RAN), Wireless networks. Springer, Cham. https://doi.org/10.1007/978-3-030-50735-0_2
11. Aazam M, Huh E-N (2016) Fog computing: the cloud-IoT/IoE middleware paradigm. IEEE Potentials 35(3):40–44
12. Zhu Q, Si B, Yang F, Ma Y (2017) Task offloading decision in fog computing system. China Commun 14(11):59–68
13. Contreras-Castillo J, Zeadally S, Guerrero-Ibanez JA (2017) Internet of vehicles: architecture, protocols, and security. IEEE Internet Things J 5(5):3701–3709
14. Al-khafajiy M, Baker T, Al-Libawy H, Maamar Z, Aloqaily M, Jararweh Y (2019) Improving fog computing performance via fog-2-fog collaboration. Futur Gener Comput Syst 100:266–280
15. Yousefpour A, Ishigaki G, Gour R, Jue JP (2018) On reducing IoT service delay via fog offloading. IEEE Intern Things J 5(2):998–1010
16. Aazam M, Zeadally S, Harras KA (2017) Offloading in fog computing for IoT: review, enabling technologies, and research opportunities. Futur Gener Comput Syst 87:278–289
17. Yousefpour A, Patil A, Ishigaki G, Kim I, Wang X, Cankaya HC, Zhang Q, Xie W, Jue JP (2019) FOGPLAN: a lightweight QoS-aware dynamic fog service provisioning framework. IEEE Internet Things J 6(3):5080–5096
18. Yao J, Ansari N (2019) Fog resource provisioning in reliability-aware IoT networks. IEEE Internet Things J 6(5):8262–8269
19. Zhang G, Shen F, Liu Z, Yang Y, Wang K, Zhou M (2018) Femto: fair and energy-minimized task offloading for fog-enabled IoT networks. IEEE Internet Things J 6(3):4388–4400
20. Liu Z, Yang Y, Wang K, Shao Z, Zhang J (2020) Post: parallel offloading of splittable tasks in heterogeneous fog networks. IEEE Internet Things J 7(4):3170–3183
21. Tran-Dang H, Kim D-S (2021) FRATO: fog resource based adaptive task offloading for delay-minimizing IoT service provisioning. IEEE Trans Parallel Distrib Syst 32(10):2491–2508
22. Tran-Dang H, Kim D-S (2021) Impact of task splitting on the delay performance of task offloading in the IoT-enabled fog systems. In: 2021 IEEE international conference on information and communication technology convergence (ICTC)

23. Vaquero LM, Rodero-Merino L (2014) Finding your way in the fog: towards a comprehensive definition of fog computing. ACM SIGCOMM Comput Commun Rev 44(5):27–32
24. Aryafar E, Keshavarz-Haddad A, Wang M, Chiang M (2013) Rat selection games in hetnets. In: 2013 proceedings IEEE INFOCOM, pp 998–1006
25. Hu P, Dhelim S, Ning H, Qiu T (2017) Survey on fog computing: architecture, key technologies, applications and open issues. J Netw Comput Appl 98:27–42
26. Feng D, Lu L, Yuan-Wu Y, Li GY, Feng G, Li S (2013) Device-to-device communications underlaying cellular networks. IEEE Trans Commun 61(8):3541–3551
27. Wildemeersch M, Quek TQ, Kountouris M, Rabbachin A, Slump CH (2013) Successive interference cancellation in heterogeneous networks. IEEE Trans Commun 62(12):4440–4453
28. Chen M, Zhang Y, Li Y, Mao S, Leung VC (2015) EMC: emotion-aware mobile cloud computing in 5G. IEEE Netw 29(2):32–38
29. Amendola D, Cordeschi N, Baccarelli E (2016) Bandwidth management VMs live migration in wireless fog computing for 5G networks. In: 2016 5th IEEE international conference on cloud networking (Cloudnet), pp 21–26
30. Peng M, Yan S, Zhang K, Wang C (2016) Fog-computing-based radio access networks: issues and challenges. IEEE Netw 30(4):46–53
31. Nunes BAA, Mendonca M, Nguyen X-N, Obraczka K, Turletti T (2014) A survey of software-defined networking: past, present, and future of programmable networks. IEEE Commun Surv Tutor 16(3):1617–1634
32. Kim H, Feamster N (2013) Improving network management with software defined networking. IEEE Commun Mag 51(2):114–119
33. Nobre JC, de Souza AM, Rosario D, Both C, Villas LA, Cerqueira E, Braun T, Gerla M (2019) Vehicular software-defined networking and fog computing: integration and design principles. Ad Hoc Netw 82:172–181
34. Mijumbi R, Serrat J, Gorricho J-L, Bouten N, Turck FD, Boutaba R (2015) Network function virtualization: state-of-the-art and research challenges. IEEE Commun Surv Tutor 18(1): 236–262
35. Han B, Gopalakrishnan V, Ji L, Lee S (2015) Network function virtualization: challenges and opportunities for innovations. IEEE Commun Mag 53(2):90–97
36. Wang F-Y, Qin R, Li J, Yuan Y, Wang X (2020) Parallel societies: a computing perspective of social digital twins and virtual–real interactions. IEEE Trans Comput Soc Syst 7(1):2–7
37. Sun W, Zhang H, Wang R, Zhang Y (2020) Reducing offloading latency for digital twin edge networks in 6G. IEEE Trans Veh Technol 69(10):12240–12251
38. Protner J, Pipan M, Zupan H, Resman M, Simic M, Herakovic N (2021) Edge computing and digital twin based smart manufacturing. IFACPapersOnLine 54(1):831–836
39. Papagianni C, Leivadeas A, Papavassiliou S (2013) A cloud-oriented content delivery network paradigm: modeling and assessment. IEEE Trans Depend Secure Comput 10(5):287–300
40. Coileain DO, O'mahony D (2015) Accounting and accountability in content distribution architectures: a survey. ACM Comput Surv (CSUR) 47(4):1–35
41. Luan TH, Gao L, Li Z, Xiang Y, Wei G, Sun L (2015) Fog computing: focusing on mobile users at the edge. arXiv preprint arXiv:1502.01815
42. Bastug E, Bennis M, Debbah M (2014) Living on the edge: the role of proactive caching in 5G wireless networks. IEEE Commun Mag 52(8):82–89
43. Hassan MA, Xiao M, Wei Q, Chen S (2015) Help your mobile applications with fog computing. In: 2015 12th annual IEEE international conference on sensing, communication, and networking-workshops (SECON workshops), pp 1–6
44. Hu P, Ning H, Qiu T, Song H, Wang Y, Yao X (2017) Security and privacy preservation scheme of face identification and resolution framework using fog computing in internet of things. IEEE Internet Things J 4(5):1143–1155

45. Lee K, Kim D, Ha D, Rajput U, Oh H (2015) On security and privacy issues of fog computing supported internet of things environment. In: 2015 6th international conference on the network of the future (NOF), pp 1–3
46. Yaakob N, Khalil I, Kumarage H, Atiquzzaman M, Tari Z (2014) By-passing infected areas in wireless sensor networks using BPR. IEEE Trans Comput 64(6):1594–1606
47. Dsouza C, Ahn G-J, Taguinod M (2014) Policy-driven security management for fog computing: Preliminary framework and a case study. In: Proceedings of the 2014 IEEE 15th international conference on information reuse and integration. IEEE IRI, pp 16–23
48. Wang Z, Cao B, Liu C, Xu C, Zhang L (2022) Blockchain-based fog radio access networks: architecture, key technologies, and challenges. Digit Commun Netw 8(5):720–726

Chapter 2
Applications of Fog Computing

In order to meet the unique requirements of latency-sensitive applications like augmented reality and industrial IoT, which generate enormous amounts of data that are prohibitive to transport to distant cloud data centers for processing, fog computing is increasingly integrated in the IoT and CPS systems. Simultaneously, the integration of fog computing in these systems also opened up potential possibilities for developing a larger range of applications, each of which places unique demands on developing fog computing platforms. This chapter aims at conducting a survey relating to these important applications that have been studied and proposed in the literature.

2.1 Introduction

Fog computing is a development of cloud computing that deals with the nonviable part of the cloud in most IoT systems. This part usually causes the inability to meet customers' demands—to process data in a matter of milliseconds and deliver decision-making in real time. Practically, the use of fog computing in enterprises has steadily increased as a result of data being the crucial element in achieving sustainability in modern IoT systems. In 2015, the OpenFog Consortium was established by representatives from Cisco, Dell, Intel, Microsoft, ARM, and Princeton University [1]. Its objective is to provide an open reference architecture that promotes and standardizes fog computing across sectors.

However, there is a tough obstacle that fog computing researchers must overcome: there isn't yet a large-scale, all-purpose fog computing platform that is accessible to the general public. In addition, they must fully comprehend the types of applications that will employ fog computing technologies and the demands they will place on the underlying fog platforms in order to create effective fog computing platforms. On the other hand, until these platforms already exist, few (if any)

H. Tran-Dang, D.-S. Kim, *Cooperative and Distributed Intelligent Computation in Fog Computing*, https://doi.org/10.1007/978-3-031-33920-2_2

developers will invest a lot of effort in creating apps that make use of the features of fog computing platforms.

This chapter is based on the review of literature for examining a sample group of fog applications that have either already been put into practice or are only being considered for future development. The objective is not to summarize a list of all proposed applications for fog computing, but rather to identify a representative sample of typical usages of fog computing paradigm. Consequently, we intend to describe the applications of fog computing in five major sectors including healthcare, smart cities, logistics and supply chains, smart grid, and smart factories. The functional and nonfunctional needs for a general-purpose fog computing platform are then discussed using this set of reference applications to solve a number of important issues. We demonstrate the wide range of fog applications and the needs that go along with them, and we emphasize the particular characteristics that fog platform builders may wish to include in their systems to enable particular types of applications.

2.2   Typical Applications of Fog Computing

2.2.1   Healthcare

The healthcare industry can fully leverage the IoT paradigm to bring unprecedented benefits for all parties involved, including patients, doctors, hospitals, and health insurance companies [2, 3]. To enhance its services and solutions, the healthcare sector frequently relies on innovative technologies. In addition to other technical developments, fog computing has been used to the advantage of the healthcare sector [4].

eHealth is one of the most important uses of fog computing in the medical field. The eHealth platform, available online and in print, gracefully leads healthcare stakeholders through the trajectory of healthcare, which frequently undergoes intriguing changes as a result of growing technological involvement and other structural changes. Fog computing makes it easier to diagnose and evaluate patients since experts may access electronic medical records (EMR) that include findings from tests like X-rays, ultrasounds, CT scans, and MRIs. Additionally, it secures the data in a private cloud [5].

Rapid patient data retrieval is essential in healthcare monitoring systems, and the Internet of Things (IoT) has made it possible to install such systems. However, because IoT nodes' computing and storage capabilities are constrained, addressing the resource constraint issue is a must for quick patient data retrieval. Fog nodes in fog computing have strong computation and lots of storage resources, so they can process, cache, and send data quickly compared to IoT nodes. These contexts are therefore driven to use fog computing to get over IoT node resource constraints and present a fog-assisted healthcare IoT system. This system takes advantage of in-network caching and request aggregation of the content-centric networking to reduce patient data retrieval latency and accomplish quick patient data retrieval [6]. In addition, the systems for remote and automated healthcare monitoring are designed to identify patient health emergencies and symptoms as soon as possible so that prompt and efficient treatment may be administered.

Regarding mobile health and remote patient monitoring, Internet of Things (IoT) technology offers a competent and organized method for handling service delivery components of healthcare. Cloud computing can process the tremendous amount of data that IoT creates. However, the latency introduced by transmitting data to the cloud and back to the application is intolerable for real-time remote health monitoring systems. In light of this, fog computing is integrated at the smart gateway of systems to provide remote patient health monitoring in smart homes [7]. The suggested paradigm makes advantage of cutting-edge methods and services, including distributed storage, notification systems, and embedded data mining. To handle the patient's real-time data at the fog layer, an event triggering-based data transfer approach is used. By determining the patient's temporal health index, the temporal mining concept is employed to assess the adverse occurrences. Health data from 67 patients in an IoT-based smart home environment were systematically produced for 30 days to assess the validity of the system. Results show that, in comparison to previous classification algorithms, the proposed Bayesian belief network classifier-based model has excellent accuracy and reaction time in predicting the status of an event. The suggested system's value is further increased by decision-making based on real-time healthcare data.

The evolution of wearables is introduced by technological progress and IoT. From a watch that tells the time and date to a smartwatch that does more than that by providing users with other data, such as their health status. The wearables are also used on hospital patients to continuously provide information on their vital signs, blood sugar levels, and other things. These devices benefit from fog computing because it guarantees timely data delivery in emergency situations. An effective architecture for IoT-based healthcare systems that is built on fog is introduced in [8] in order to efficiently execute the body sensor network and medical IoT devices data. Then, in order to prevent security breaches, the system developed an identity management user authentication approach. The output token for the user authentication method is created using the Elliptic Curve Cryptography method.

eWALL is an intelligent home environment that offers individualized context-aware apps based on fog computing and enhanced sensing on the front and cloud solutions on the back, as described by Kyriazakos [9]. The eWALL platform is an example of how ICT may help people live longer, be more independent, and have a higher quality of life while also lowering expenses for national health systems. The uniqueness of eWALL, which aims to establish a home care environment, is based on its sophisticated sensing capabilities, together with a high level of customization and wise decision-making, which are obtained from an inventive service-oriented architecture (SOA) implemented in the fog and cloud computing sites.

Health Fog, a framework that uses fog computing as an intermediary layer between end users and the cloud, was introduced by Ahmad [10]. Particularly, the framework integrates ensemble deep learning in edge computing devices and implemented it for a practical application of autonomous heart disease analysis. Using IoT devices, HealthFog provides healthcare as a fog service and effectively maintains user-requested cardiac patient data. To implement and verify the performance of the suggested model in terms of power consumption, network bandwidth, latency, jitter, accuracy, and execution time, FogBus, a fog-enabled cloud framework, is employed. HealthFog may be configured to operate in a variety of ways that, depending on the situation and the needs of the user, offer the optimum quality of service or forecast accuracy. In addition, health Fog's architecture effectively lowers the additional communication expense, which is often considered in similar systems.

2.2.2   Smart Cities

Practically, rapid development of urbanization exposes more significant issues such as environmental deterioration, sanitation issues, traffic congestion, and thwarting urban crime. In such context, adoption of advanced ICT solutions in the supervision and management of public affairs has been recognized as a potential response to tackle these issues through realizing the concept of smart cities [11]. Fundamentally, smart cities rely on smart technologies, especially IoT technology to collect the required data and analyze them for informed actions in real time [56]. Concretely, with advanced sensing and computation capabilities by IoT-enabled infrastructure (e.g., building, traffic lights, and vehicles), data is gathered and evaluated in real time to extract the information, which is further converted to usable knowledge and smart services. This will enhance the decision-making with respect to the monitoring, control, and management of the city and citizens [12]. Basically, the vision of smart cities enables benefits in following city-related aspects transportation, surveillance, and environment protection, which rely heavily on fog computing to realize their objective functions [13].

Surveillance

The most crucial components of situational awareness (SAW)—efficient information abstraction and speedy decision-making—remain challenging in the IoT-based smart city models owing to the enormous volume of dynamic input and the strict processing time limits. Because the servers are positioned distant from the sensing platform, which is a need for many urban surveillance duties, strong cloud technology cannot ensure a connection in an emergency. As a result, on-site data processing, information fusion, and decision-making are necessary (i.e., near the data collection locations). The deployment of fog computing for real-time urban surveillance can be viable for detecting fast vehicles [14]. In addition, a fog computing prototype can be created by using a drone to keep an eye on the driving automobiles for on-the-ground, continuous, online urban surveillance tasks.

The architecture given by fog computing as proposed in [15] may be used to create distributed surveillance systems that are inexpensive, real-time, and latency-sensitive in order to solve privacy issues in open environments. Additionally, fog computing also enables real-time tracking, anomaly detection, and insights from data collected over long periods of time [16]. Using urban traffic surveillance as an example, a dynamic video stream processing scheme is proposed in [14] to meet the needs of real-time information processing and decision-making.

Congestion Control

Traffic management is one of the most prominent uses of fog computing in smart cities. In order to gather information on vehicle movement on the road, sensors are put in traffic lights and road barriers. Real-time data analysis made possible by fog computing enables the traffic signal to be adjusted in response to the flow of traffic [17]. In addition, vehicle fog computing [18] is a smart traffic management tool that is increasingly developed to warn other vehicles to take alternate routes when traffic is heavy [19, 20].

Smart Transportation

The development of inter-fog communication enables the prototype of the smart transportation application based on fog computing, which is suggested in [21]. With real-time traffic data, the inter-fog communication in the smart transportation system may guarantee that the edge nodes managing the traffic signals and the street light control are handled locally by the corresponding fog nodes. When traffic is heavy, it can also recommend other routes. The growing number of parking spots cannot keep up with the growing number of automobiles. Employing the smart parking system allows for early notification of cars before they enter the parking space, preventing annoyance [22, 23].

Energy Consumption

The safety and energy consumption issues in smart cities can be solved by smart street lamps (SSLs), according to [24]. The following SSL is capable of using this suggested approach: (i) every street lamp may be operated individually, which makes for good administration; (ii) all street lamps can also be changed dynamically for brightness; and (iii) they can all sound an autonomous warning in the event of an aberrant condition, such as a broken or stolen lamp.

Big Data Analytics

The widespread deployment of various types of sensors in smart cities is the biggest difficulty in data-intensive analysis. Due to the inherent nature of geo-distribution, a new computer paradigm is needed to provide location awareness, latency sensitivity, and intelligent control. This need is met by fog computing, which takes computation to the network's edge [25]. To allow the integration of a sizable number of infrastructure elements and services in future smart cities, a hierarchical distributed fog computing architecture is required. A fog computing architecture as proposed in [26] incorporates intelligence in order to execute data representation and feature extraction, recognize anomalous and dangerous occurrences, and provide the best possible reactions and controls.

2.2.3 Smart Grid

By integrating the communication, sensing, monitoring, and regulating technologies in the conventional grid, smart grids offer automated, secure, and affordable electrical services [27]. According to European Commission in 2012, a smart grid initially is defined as an electricity network allowing devices to communicate between suppliers to consumers, allowing them to manage demand, protect the distribution network, save energy, and reduce costs [28]. The rapid development of IoT technologies including advanced sensing [29], ultra-low and reliable communication, and data processing, computing, and analyzing [30–32] have made them driving forces to accelerate the realization of smart grid concept. In converging with the smart cities, smart girds nowadays also include IoT-based solutions to monitor, control, and manage the utility usage of smart cities including electricity, gas, and water through smart metering and smart billing system [33].

Fog computing is examined to be practical for smart grid architecture [34]. An edge-centered fog computing model is constructed based on the key needs of an idealized smart grid infrastructure to achieve the processing and computational goals of smart grids. In order to enable the creation of novel real-time and latency-free applications, the model constantly interacts with core-centered cloud computing infrastructure through a fog service-oriented architecture (SOA). Smart meters and fog computing work together to control the amount of power used in houses, giving owners access to real-time data that they can use to make the best decisions [35, 36]. By analyzing data from the smart grid via fog computing, the burden on cloud servers is reduced [37]. To further reduce the latency and make judgments in real time, 5G networking services can be combined with fog computing [38].

2.2.4 Industrial Robotics and Automation in Smart Factories

Due to delays, security concerns, and the need for structured data to be transmitted over the Internet to online services and the cloud, most tasks in the industrial process must be completed locally. Between the industrial environment and the cloud/web services, middleware assistance is needed to complete this task. Fog computing is a potential middleware in this context that might be quite helpful for various industrial applications. Actuators and robotics in the manufacturing sector can receive local processing help from fog with tolerable latency. Furthermore, because industrial big data is frequently unstructured, it can be locally cut and polished by the fog before being sent to the cloud. An architectural model integrating the fog computing to the industrial IoT systems is proposed in [39] to support the local task computation in the Industry 4.0 environment.

Fog computing can host industrial applications in a way that is similar to the cloud thanks to its low latency and availability of resources on demand. Robotics is one industrial sector that could gain from the capabilities of fog computing. However, creating and putting in place a robotic system based on fog presents a variety of difficulties, which are typically represented by resource virtualization, memory interference control, real-time communication, and system scalability, dependability, and safety. The authors in [40] propose a fog-based robotic system at the factory level to provide such capabilities.

By meeting futuristic needs like flexible and improved processing, storage, and networking capability closer to the field devices, the Fog computing paradigm utilizing several technologies is predicted to play a significant role in a variety of industrial applications. While the Fog paradigm's performance-related components have gained most of the attention from researchers, safety-related aspects have not yet gotten enough attention. In order to improve safety in industrial automation settings, the authors in [41] address different safety concerns associated to the Fog paradigm and offer particular safety design considerations. With this design, a distributed mobile robotics could benefit from the deployment of the fog model consequently.

The architecture of conventional control systems, like industrial robotic systems, must change to suit the demands of future automation systems. Although cloud-based systems offer on-demand services like computing resources, they are unable to meet the real-time performance demands of control applications. A promising new architectural paradigm called fog computing addresses the shortcomings of the cloud-based platform to complement it. In [42], the authors examine the design of the current robot systems and suggest a fog-based approach to industrial robotic systems that takes into account the requirements of upcoming automation systems. In this design, using Time-Sensitive Networking (TSN) services is suggested for real-time communication and OPC-UA for information modeling.

2.2.5 Agriculture

The growth in global population is pushing a change toward smart agriculture practices. This, together with the depletion of natural resources, the scarcity of arable land, and the rise in the unpredictability of weather, makes food security a top worry for most nations. As a result, the Internet of Things' disruption has had a significant impact on the agricultural and farming industries by boosting operational efficiency and production in the agriculture sector [43, 44].

For agricultural precision irrigation to increase crop output, lower costs, and promote environmental sustainability, smart freshwater management is crucial. The intensive use of technology provides a way to provide plants the precise amount of water they require. Despite the fact that there is still work to be done in the integration of many technologies to make the Internet of Things (IoT) function effortlessly in practice, it is the obvious choice for smart water management applications. The SWAMP project uses a practical approach based on four pilots in Brazil and Europe to develop an IoT-based smart water management platform for precision irrigation in agriculture. As scalability is a major concern for IoT applications, this paper presents the SWAMP architecture, platform, and system deployments that highlight the platform's ability to be replicated [45]. It also includes a performance analysis of the FIWARE components used in the Platform because scalability is a major concern. Results indicate that it is capable of offering the SWAMP pilots an appropriate level of performance, but it necessitates specifically designed configurations and the re-engineering of some components to offer increased scalability while utilizing fewer computational resources.

Pests and crop diseases have continued to pose a danger to both the quality and quantity of crop production. Their precise and on-time forecasts may lessen both negative environmental effects and global economic losses. For the purpose of preventing excessive use of cloud resources and lowering operational loads, fog computing tries to move processing capabilities closer to the target customers [46]. All agricultural land management techniques and the developing field of precision agriculture can benefit from the fog computing methodology. It is necessary to develop a forecasting technique that can correctly anticipate crop disease given the observed symptoms.

The fog computing paradigm is a relatively new development in the field of computing that successfully complements cloud computing with more environmentally friendly technology. Fog computing's low carbon footprint makes it a key contributor to the development of smart agriculture [47]. In this study, we offer a green fog-based architecture for processing data from IoT sensors, specifically for the agricultural sector, using single board computers as low-power fog nodes. By incorporating renewable energy sources, the suggested system may easily meet its low energy needs and become more sustainable. The suggested green fog-based architecture would contribute to the development of a green environment for various application areas in addition to the smart agriculture sector.

2.2.6 Logistics and Supply Chains

A large amount of data has been generated as a result of the rapid spread of RFID devices in global supply chain management. This data will need to be stored and promptly retrieved in order to enable real-time decision-making. This is crucial for the supply chain of perishable goods, such as fruits and pharmaceuticals, which have high asset values attached to them and could lose all of their value if they are not stored in precisely controlled and cool settings. While cloud-based RFID technologies are used to monitor and track goods as they move from the producer to the retailer. In addition, fog computing is necessary to improve efficiency and lower waste in the supply chain for perishable products. Using blackberry fruit as a case study, the authors in [48] use fog computing in perishable product supply chain management. In the process, the system takes advantage of the suggested fog nodes for the purposes of real-time monitoring and actuation in the supply chain for blackberries.

Supply chain performance, operational expenses, and the environment have all suffered as a result of increased competition and customer demands. The risk to quality, safety, traceability, and transparency has multiplied. Fog computing technology as a cloud extension aids supply chain operations by optimizing resource usage, enhancing performance, lowering hazards, and reducing identification, bandwidth usage, tracking, energy consumption, and most importantly real-time monitoring. Otherwise, all of these supports are challenging due to the diversity of accessible platforms and technologies. Through cooperation and interoperability among stakeholders, innovative fog, IoT, and cloud computing infuse unique techniques to assimilate, store, and distribute transactional data. Cloud-based data centers can communicate and work with edge-stored data. With the aid of applications that require quick response times, fog computing offers real-time data processing [49].

Today's global economy presents logistic organizations with significant problems, including those related to evolving customer needs, complex business models, and rising environmental, social, and regulatory concerns. Among the most important challenges that logistics systems have increasingly taken into account in recent years are supply chain efficiency and sustainability. The authors in [50] suggest a cloud-fog architecture in this context to satisfy the updated needs of logistic networks built on the Physical Internet (PI) model. This study compares two scenario models: the "cloud-only" model and the "cloud-fog" model in order to evaluate supply chain performance in terms of time and cost-effectiveness. The A-star (A*) pathfinding algorithm and the real-time processing capabilities made possible by the Internet of Things (IoT) and fog computing are the foundations of the method chosen. The suggested approach enables optimal physical routing at a fair price and in a timely manner. Along the entire supply chain, enhanced visibility and traceability are also accomplished.

2.3 Summary and Conclusions

In combination with cloud computing, fog computing increasingly is integrated in IoT systems to provide IoT services continuously with improved QoS. The wide variety of fog computing applications logically imposes a wide range of constraints on the fog computing platforms created to serve them. Currently, there is no general-purpose fog platform that can claim to meet all of these needs.

Fog nodes are inherently more suited for some tasks, whereas clouds are better suitable for others. In other words, depending on specific applications, tasks can be scheduled appropriately to be processed in the fog or cloud in order to meet the QoS requirements. If the network state changes in any of the following areas, processor loads, link bandwidths, storage capacity, fault occurrences, security risks, cost objectives, etc., this segmentation might be planned but could also alter dynamically.

A general fog platform that may be used for any vertical market or application is described in the OpenFog RA. This architecture can be used in a wide range of industries, including, but not limited to, those in transportation, agriculture, smart cities, smart buildings, healthcare, hospitality, financial services, and more. It offers business value for IoT applications that need network constraints, low latency, real-time decision-making, and improved security.

This chapter is based on the review of literature for examining a typical group of fog applications that have either already been put into practice or are only being considered for future development. The objective is not to summarize a list of all proposed applications for fog computing, but rather to identify a representative sample of typical usages of fog computing paradigm. Consequently, we intend to describe the applications of fog computing in six major sectors including healthcare, smart cities, logistics and supply chains, smart grid, smart factories, and smart agriculture. The functional and nonfunctional needs for a general-purpose fog computing platform are then discussed using this set of reference applications to solve a number of important issues. We demonstrate the wide range of fog applications and the needs that go along with them, and we emphasize the particular characteristics that fog platform builders may wish to include in their systems to enable particular types of applications.

References

1. IEEE standard for adoption of OpenFog reference architecture for fog computing, 2018
2. Islam SR, Kwak D, Kabir MH, Hossain M, Kwak K-S (2015) The internet of things for health care: a comprehensive survey. IEEE Access 3:678–708
3. Laplante PA, Laplante N (2016) The internet of things in healthcare: potential applications and challenges. IT Prof 18(3):2–4
4. Kraemer FA, Braten AE, Tamkittikhun N, Palma D (2017) Fog computing in healthcare—a review and discussion. IEEE Access 5:9206–9222
5. Zhang L, Cao B, Li Y, Peng M, Feng G (2020) A multi-stage stochastic programming-based offloading policy for fog enabled IoT-eHealth. IEEE J Select Areas Commun 39(2):411–425

6. Wang X, Li Y (2020) Fog-assisted content-centric healthcare IoT. IEEE Internet Things Magaz 3(3):90–93
7. Verma P, Sood SK (2018) Fog assisted-IoT enabled patient health monitoring in smart homes. IEEE Internet Things J 5(3):1789–1796
8. Awaisi KS, Hussain S, Ahmed M, Khan AA, Ahmed G (2020) Leveraging IoT and fog computing in healthcare systems. IEEE Internet Things Magaz 3(2):52–56
9. Kyriazakos S, Mihaylov M, Anggorojati B, Mihovska A, Craciunescu R, Fratu O, Prasad R (2016) eWALL: an intelligent caring home environment offering personalized context-aware applications based on advanced sensing. Wirel Pers Commun 87(3):1093–1111
10. Ahmad M, Amin MB, Hussain S, Kang BH, Cheong T, Lee S (2016) Health fog: a novel framework for health and wellness applications. J Supercomput 72(10):3677–3695
11. Schaffers H, Komninos N, Pallot M, Trousse B, Nilsson M, Oliveira A (2011) Smart cities and the future internet: towards cooperation frameworks for open innovation. In: The future internet assembly. Springer, Berlin, pp 431–446
12. Zanella A, Bui N, Castellani A, Vangelista L, Zorzi M (2014) Internet of things for smart cities. IEEE Internet Things J 1(1):22–32
13. Hajam SS, Sofi SA (2021) IoT-fog architectures in smart city applications: a survey. China Commun 18(11):117–140
14. Chen N, Chen Y, Ye X, Ling H, Song S, Huang C-T (2017) Smart city surveillance in fog computing. In: Studies in big data. Springer, Heidelberg, pp 203–226
15. Sicari S, Rizzardi A, Coen-Porisini A (2022) Insights into security and privacy towards fog computing evolution. Comput Secur 120:10–22
16. Sarkar I, Kumar S (2019) Fog computing based intelligent security surveillance using PTZ controller camera. In: 2019 10th IEEE international conference on computing, communication and networking technologies (ICCCNT)
17. Tang C, Xia S, Zhu C, Wei X (2019) Phase timing optimization for smart traffic control based on fog computing. IEEE Access 7:84217–84228
18. Hou X, Li Y, Chen M, Wu D, Jin D, Chen S (2016) Vehicular fog computing: a viewpoint of vehicles as the infrastructures. IEEE Trans Vehic Technol 65(6):3860–3873
19. Huang C, Lu R, Choo K-KR (2017) Vehicular fog computing: architecture, use case, and security and forensic challenges. IEEE Commun Magaz 55(11):105–111
20. Ning Z, Huang J, Wang X (2019) Vehicular fog computing: enabling real-time traffic management for smart cities. IEEE Wirel Commun 26(1):87–93
21. Shaikh R, Modak M (2022) Smart transportation using fog computing. In: Lecture notes in electrical engineering. Springer, Singapore, pp 363–369
22. Tang C, Wei X, Zhu C, Chen W, Rodrigues JJPC (2018) Towards smart parking based on fog computing. IEEE Access 6:70172–70185
23. Aliedani A, Loke SW, Desai A, Desai P (2016) Investigating vehicle-to-vehicle communication for cooperative car parking: the CoPark approach. In: 2016 IEEE international smart cities conference (ISC2)
24. Jia G, Han G, Li A, Du J (2018) SSL: smart street lamp based on fog computing for smarter cities. IEEE Trans Industr Inform 14(11):4995–5004
25. Zhang W, Zhang Z, Chao H-C (2017) Cooperative fog computing for dealing with big data in the internet of vehicles: architecture and hierarchical resource management. IEEE Commun Magaz 55(12):60–67
26. Tang B, Chen Z, Hefferman G, Pei S, Wei T, He H, Yang Q (2017) Incorporating intelligence in fog computing for big data analysis in smart cities. IEEE Trans Industr Inform 13(5):2140–2150
27. Fang X, Misra S, Xue G, Yang D (2011) Smart grid – the new and improved power grid: a survey. IEEE Commun Surv Tutor 14(4):944–980
28. Kylili A, Fokaides PA (2015) European smart cities: the role of zero energy buildings. Sustain Cities Soc 15:86–95

29. Morello R, Mukhopadhyay SC, Liu Z, Slomovitz D, Samantaray SR (2017) Advances on sensing technologies for smart cities and power grids: a review. IEEE Sensors J 17(23): 7596–7610
30. Li Y, Cheng X, Cao Y, Wang D, Yang L (2018) Smart choice for the smart grid: narrowband internet of things (NB-IoT). IEEE Internet Things J 5(3):1505–1515
31. Chin W, Li W, Chen H (2017) Energy big data security threats in IoT-based smart grid communications. IEEE Commun Magaz 55(10):70–75
32. Samie F, Bauer L, Henkel J (2018) Edge computing for smart grid: an overview on architectures and solutions. In: IoT for smart grids. Springer, pp 21–42
33. Bera S, Misra S, Rodrigues JJ (2014) Cloud computing applications for smart grid: a survey. IEEE Trans Parallel Distrib Syst 26(5):1477–1494
34. Hussain MM, Alam MS, Beg MMS (2019) Feasibility of fog computing in smart grid architectures. In: Proceedings of 2nd international conference on communication, computing and networking, Springer, Singapore, pp 999–1010
35. Moghaddam MHY, Leon-Garcia A (2018) A fog-based internet of energy architecture for transactive energy management systems. IEEE Internet Things J 5(2):1055–1069
36. Chen Y-D, Azhari MZ, Leu J-S (2018) Design and implementation of a power consumption management system for smart home over fog-cloud computing. In: 2018 3rd IEEE international conference on intelligent green building and smart grid (IGBSG)
37. Bhattarai BP, Paudyal S, Luo Y, Mohanpurkar M, Cheung K, Tonkoski R, Hovsapian R, Myers KS, Zhang R, Zhao P, Manic M, Zhang S, Zhang X (2023) Big data analytics in smart grids: state-of-the-art, challenges, opportunities, and future directions. IET Smart Grid 2(2):141–154
38. Kumari A, Tanwar S, Tyagi S, Kumar N, Obaidat MS, Rodrigues JJPC (2019) Fog computing for smart grid systems in the 5G environment: challenges and solutions. IEEE Wirel Commun 26(3):47–53
39. Aazam M, Zeadally S, Harras KA (2018) Deploying fog computing in industrial internet of things and industry 4.0. IEEE Trans Industr Inform 14(10):4674–4682
40. Shaik MS, Struhr V, Bakhshi Z, Dao V-L, Desai N, Papadopoulos AV, Nolte T, Karagiannis V, Schulte S, Venito A, Fohler G (2020) Enabling fog-based industrial robotics systems. In: 2020 25th IEEE international conference on emerging technologies and factory automation (ETFA), vol 1, pp 61–68
41. Desai N, Punnekkat S (2019) Safety of fog-based industrial automation systems. In: Proceedings of the workshop on fog computing and the IoT. ACM. https://doi.org/10.1145/3313150.3313218
42. Salman SM, Struhar V, Papadopoulos AV, Behnam M, Nolte T (2019) Fogification of industrial robotic systems. In: Proceedings of the workshop on fog computing and the IoT. ACM. https://doi.org/10.1145/3313150.3313225
43. Gia TN, Qingqing L, Queralta JP, Zou Z, Tenhunen H, Westerlund T (2019) Edge AI in smart farming IoT: CNNs at the edge and fog computing with LoRa. IEEE Africon:1–6
44. Elijah O, Rahman TA, Orikumhi I, Leow CY, Hindia MN (2018) An overview of internet of things (IoT) and data analytics in agriculture: benefits and challenges. IEEE Internet Things J 5(5):3758–3773
45. Kamienski C, Soininen J-P, Taumberger M, Dantas R, Toscano A, Cinotti TS, Maia RF, Neto AT (2019) Smart water management platform: IoT-based precision irrigation for agriculture. Sensors 19(2):276–286
46. Roy C, Das N, Rautaray SS, Pandey M (2022) A fog computing-based IoT framework for prediction of crop disease using big data analytics. In: AI, edge and IoT-based smart agriculture. Elsevier, London, pp 287–300

47. Qureshi R, Mehboob SH, Aamir M (2021) Sustainable green fog computing for smart agriculture. Wirel Pers Commun 121(2):1379–1390
48. Musa Z, Vidyasankar K (2017) A fog computing framework for blackberry supply chain management. Proc Comput Sci 113:178–185. https://doi.org/10.1016/j.procs.2017.08.338
49. Gupta R, Singh A (2022) Fog computing framework: mitigating latency in supply chain management. In: Fog computing. Chapman and Hall/CRC, pp 205–211. https://doi.org/10.1201/9781003188230-15
50. Mededjel M, Belalem G, Neki A (2021) A cloud-fog architecture for physical-internet-enabled supply chain. Supply Chain Forum 23(3):307–322. https://doi.org/10.1080/16258312.2021.1996861

Chapter 3
Cooperation for Distributed Task Offloading in Fog Computing Networks

Undoubtedly, fog computing enables data processing and storage close to IoT devices to provide improved IoT services on behalf of centralized cloud computing. The exploitation of fog computing resources is still ineffective, though, because these heterogeneous devices are distributed in space and time in many scenarios, thus causing an uneven load on the fog nodes. Many large tasks such as virtual reality and machine learning-based tasks must be executed by the remote cloud servers since the fog nodes have insufficient resources to handle them. However, these large tasks can be completed in a distributed manner at various fog nodes if they can be divided into independent subtasks. The advances in technologies such as hardware, software, and in the field of information and communication enable the different fog nodes to communicate together, thus potentially facilitating the distributed computing solution at fog. This chapter reviews proposed approaches to examine that fog-fog cooperation can help to improve the performance of task offloading operations in the fog environment.

3.1 Introduction

As a solution to extend the cloud-like services to the edge of network, fog computing ensures the continuum along the cloud to objects by providing processing, storage, control, and networking operations nearby the IoT data generation sources. It enables a group of close-by end user, network edge, and access devices to work together to complete resource-demanding activities. As a result, a variety of tasks that were previously intended for the cloud can now be successfully finished at the edge by nearby fog computing resources. In this way, fog computing allows low-latency, high-reliability, location-aware, and privacy-preservation services since it performs a sizable portion of data storage, computation, and communication close to end users [1].

A major problem in fog computing is how to efficiently assign computation tasks to a collection of accessible heterogeneous fog nodes (FNs) [2] to achieve these performance benefits. Some researches have been done with the goal of reducing the end-to-end service delay as the majority of tasks are offloaded in the fog layer. For example, most of existing work emphasizes on the vertical interaction between the fog and cloud to optimize the service placement (FSPP) as introduced in [3, 4]. In these models, the fog landscape is divided into fog colonies, each of which includes a centralized fog control node and other distributed fog cells. Additionally, each fog cell represents a visualized fog node (e.g., router, gateway, or a cyber-physical system) with computational, network, and storage capabilities that coordinate a group of terminal IoT devices including sensors and actuators. Following a sense-process-actual model, each IoT application in this scenario typically comprises of three corresponding services, namely, sensing, processing, and actuating. To optimally place the requested services onto the fog cells, the FSPP optimization is formulated taking into account QoS constraints (i.e., prescribed deadlines of applications). In this way, the optimal solution ensures the requirement satisfaction of applications while improving the fog resource utilization and reducing the execution cost.

As per [5], a framework FOGPLAN is introduced for QoS-aware dynamic service provisioning. In this scheme, to ensure the QoS requirement of delay-sensitive IoT applications, the fog service controllers constantly monitor their task execution performance and the service request rate to dynamically decide whether to deploy a new request or to release a queued request from the queues. This key mechanism enables the fog node to remove the queued tasks, which no longer violate the prescribed delay requirement. As a result, the percentage of services satisfying the QoS constraints is increased significantly while reducing the overall cost. However, the resources of fogs are not made full use of in these works since a majority of heavy tasks is likely processed by the cloud servers.

To deal with the large tasks in the system, one potential solution is to divide the tasks into subtasks that are then processed by different computing nodes (i.e., edge, fog, and cloud) in a distributed manner. For example, the task division concept is employed in the work [6] to minimize the energy consumption of task offloading while achieving workload fairness among the fog nodes. The studied scenario divides the task into two subtasks with different sizes, which are processed locally by the IoT node and the fog layer, respectively. In this model, the subtasks are assumed to be independent; thus, the delay reduction is beneficial from the parallel task execution.

Although the vertical combination of fog and cloud helps in improving the task offloading performance, the fog computing resource is not utilized effectively due to the lack of fog-fog interaction. Conventionally, the heterogeneity of fog nodes in terms of hardware, software, and functionalities serves as a barrier to their horizon interaction. However, the advances in technology such as network function virtualization [7, 8] and software-defined network [9] can remove the barrier and allow fogs to communicate together. As a result, fogs can share the computing resource for offloading tasks. In addition, offloading can be more efficient if a task can be processed in parallel by different fog nodes with available resources. This mechanism is feasible when the computation task can be divided into independent subtasks. Thus, in this case, the fog-fog cooperation can be applicable to further improve the offloading performance. In these regards, this chapter conducts a survey to investigate the impact of cooperation on the overall performance of system.

3.2 System Model

3.2.1 Fog Computing Networks

A general architecture of fog-enabled IoT system consists of three main layers: IoT layers with IoT-connected physical devices, fog layer, and the remote cloud layer with a set of data centers, which are connected by LAN and WAN to provide various services for IoT-connected users such as computing, caching, storage, and networking services as illustrated in Fig. 3.1.

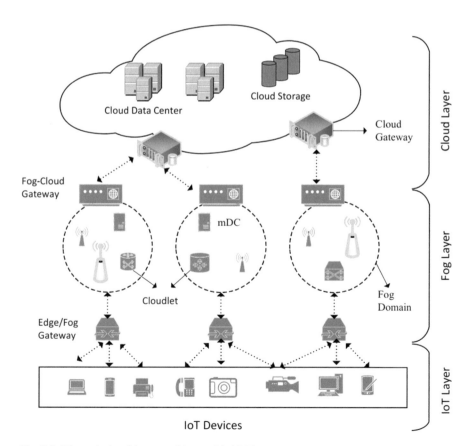

Fig. 3.1 The typical architecture of fog-enabled IoT systems

The IoT layer is recorded by a set $I = \{d_1, d_2, \ldots, d_{|I|}\}$ of IoT nodes, which generate computation tasks recorded in a set $T = \{T_1, T_2, \ldots, T_{|T|}\}$. Similarly, $F = \{F_1, F_2, \ldots, F_{|F|}\}$ and $C = \{C_1, C_2, \ldots, C_{|C|}\}$ represent the sets of fog nodes (FNs) and cloud servers, respectively. In practical applications, FNs are grouped into clusters, and each provides a set of specific IoT applications for the end users (EUs). Generally, FNs in each domain are deployed in a distributed manner. In some scenarios, there is a presence of centralized fog controllers such as fog service providers (FSPs) to manage the fog resources in the domains as well as security-related issues. In many scenarios, the cloudlets [10] and micro data centers (mDCs) [11, 12] serving as mini-servers are added to the fog domains to enhance the computing capability. The fog-fog communication is enabled in the scenarios; thus, the fog domains can communicate together to share resources and perform cooperative task offloading operations.

3.2.2 Computation Tasks

Each computing task T_k can be described with a tuple $T_k = \langle A_k, O_k, B_k, D_k \rangle$, where A_k and O_k represent the input and output data size (bits) of task, B_k is the computational resource demands to execute the task, and D_k is the deadline to process T_k. The input data sizes of tasks can be ranged from kilobytes to terabytes depending on the specific applications [13]. Based on this feature, the tasks can be classified into light, medium, and heavy tasks [14, 15].

Task divisibility is also investigated in offloading cases. As a task is indivisible, its entire data is definitely processed by a single computing device (e.g., FN, cloud, or even powerful IoT node). In many scenarios, a single task can be divided into multiple subtasks based on data size and data type. Such task division is employed to get benefit from parallel computing since the subtasks can be processed by different devices simultaneously [16, 17].

Regarding the resources needed for computation offloading operations, some of the existing works just only consider B_k as the number of central processing units (CPU cycles) [18]. In another scenario, GPU and memory requirements are considered during resource allocation for executing heavy and complex tasks such as the AI and ML ones [19].

3.2.3 Computation Offloading Modes

Depending on many factors such as specific requirements of systems and characteristics of tasks, there are three modes for performing the computation offloading in fog computing environments. They are full offloading, partial offloading, and hybrid offloading combining the first two modes dynamically. Figure 3.2 shows the three task offloading models derived by IoT devices.

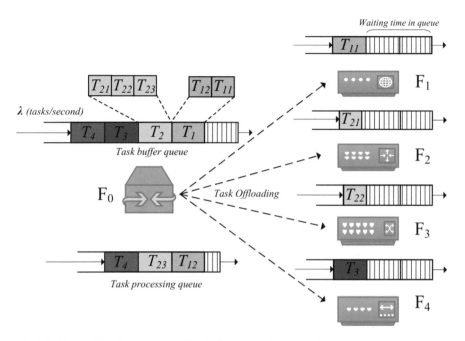

Fig. 3.2   Three offloading modes used in the fog computing networks

Full Offloading

In the full offloading mode, all tasks are assumed to be indivisible. In this sense, a single task must be executed completely by a single computing node (i.e., a fog node or cloud). Therefore, only cooperation between fog-fog interactions can be exploited to perform the offloading operation such as task T_3 is offloaded completely by F_4.

Partial Offloading

In contrast to the full offloading mode, partial offloading is applicable in the systems where all tasks can be divided into subtasks, and these subtasks can be executed in parallel by different computing nodes. In these cases, both parallelism and cooperation are employed to handle the computation offloading. As illustrated in Fig. 3.3, task T is processed partially by different fog computing nodes when it can be divided into four subtasks ST_1, ST_2, ST_3, and ST_4, which then are executed by F_1, F_2, F_3, and F_4, respectively. The main benefit of partial offloading is to help the system to improve fog resource utilization as some fog nodes are unable to process a single task due to lack of resources. This also leads to improve system performance in terms of delay thanks to the employment of parallel processing of subtasks.

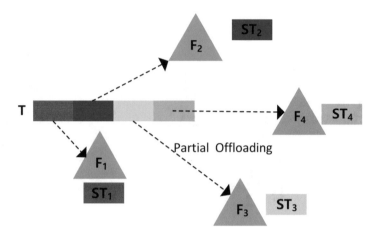

Fig. 3.3 An example of partial offloading

Hybrid Offloading

In many scenarios, the systems may have a wide range of task types, which are characterized by different features. Some types of tasks are divisible, and others are indivisible. In these cases, hybrid offloading mode is used to offload the tasks dynamically in many fog-based computing systems where some tasks can be processed by full offloading and others are offloaded by partial offloading methods.

3.3   Cooperation-Based Task Offloading Models

This section describes typical studies that focus on the application of fog-fog cooperation to improve system performance through computation offloading. The description covers the used context scenarios, system architectures, and proposed algorithms, and feature techniques developed to realize the predefined objectives of systems.

Building a common communication protocol for fog nodes is proposed first in [20]. In addition, a novel load balancing technique called the Fog Resource Management Scheme (FRAMES) is proposed as a new Fog-2-Fog (F2F) collaboration model that encourages offloading incoming requests across fog nodes in accordance with their load and processing capabilities. FRAMES studies three types of service processing: sequential processing, parallel processing, and mixed processing as illustrated in Fig. 3.4.

The technological viability of F2F collaboration has been demonstrated through a set of tests and the formulation of a formal mathematical model of F2F and FRAMES. When compared to other load-balancing models, the suggested fog load-balancing approach performs better.

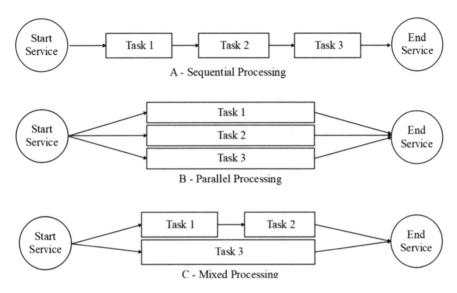

Fig. 3.4 Three types of services processed in FRAMES [20]

Another FSPP is formulated and examined in [21] to place software components of distributed IoT applications onto a set of fog nodes to minimize the average response time of applications. In the model, the low delay of fog-to-fog communication is exploited for collaborative task offloading in order to reduce the total response time of application provisioning. The suggested method, which is based on a backtrack search algorithm and accompanying heuristics, may effectively make placement decisions that meet the goal of reducing the reaction time of deployed apps while handling large-scale issues.

FRATO framework [17] inherits the advantage features from the optimal service placement to further reduce the service delay by exploiting the low fog-fog communication delay to reduce the service transfer time. Figure 3.5 shows the mechanism to exploit the fog-fog cooperation to implement the distributed task offloading in the fog networks. In this framework, based on the resource state of fog neighbors, each service (task) is dynamically divided into fragments, which are offloaded by different neighbor fog nodes optimally.

The letter [22] studied the problem of scheduling offloaded tasks in the fog network as the tasks are delay-bounded. The work proposed a scheduling policy for the task queues of fogs based on Lyapunov drift-plus-penalty function to maximize the number of completed tasks within their deadlines as well as maintaining the stability of fog queues. The fog-fog communication is enabled to share the load between the fogs in order to meet the deadlines of tasks.

Offloading multiple tasks to different fog resources can be formulated by multi-objective optimization problems to achieve the efficient tradeoff of fog-based offloading systems in terms of energy consumption, delay, and execution cost [23, 24]. The limitation of works is just to model a single fog node without

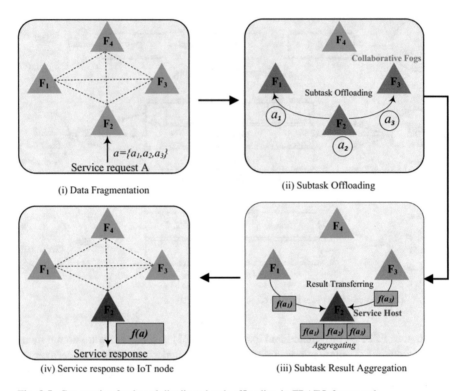

Fig. 3.5 Cooperative fog based distributed task offloading in FRATO framework

considering the large-scale deployment of fog environment in which the fog nodes are required to interact to realize some tasks practically.

The authors in [25] formulate a latency-driven task data offloading problem taking into account the transmission delay from fog to the cloud and service rate that includes the local processing time and waiting time at each fog node in order to jointly optimize the amount of tasks offloaded to the neighboring fog nodes and communication resource allocation for the offloaded tasks to the remote cloud. For parallel task data offloading, they evaluated vertical cooperation with the faraway cloud and horizontal collaboration with several fog nodes. Finally, the optimization problem is expressed as quadratic programming with quadratically constrained variables and using semidefinite relaxation to solve it.

In [26, 27], the authors take into account networks of cooperative fog nodes, which might work together to offload burden from cloud data centers. To further enhance the quality of experience for its users, they suggest a novel cooperative technique called offload forwarding, in which each fog node can pass some or all of its unprocessed workload to its nearby fog nodes in addition to depending on cloud data centers to process it.

Offloading multiple tasks of fog nodes (FNs) to multiple neighbor FNs (i.e., helper nodes (HNs)) to minimize the average service delay of tasks in a distributed manner is referred to as the multitask multihelper (MTMH) problem, which is studied recently in some works [28–30], Accordingly, a paired offloading of multiple tasks (POMT) in heterogeneous fog networks in [28] is modeled as a strategic game between the FNs and HNs for deciding which tasks are offloaded to which HNs to achieve the reduced delay. The associated algorithm is developed to obtain the Nash Equilibrium point (NE) for the POMT game to make the suboptimal offloading strategy decisions. However, this model does not consider performing complex computing tasks, which probably require multiple sparse fog nodes instead of single fogs. To deal with this concern, a parallel offloading of splittable tasks (POST) mechanism is proposed in [29]. By adopting the similar method used in their previous work (i.e., POMT), POST explores the benefits of task division in reducing service delay. On a similar basis of partial task offloading, a certain number of studies in the literature proposed the fog-to-fog (F2F) collaboration strategies to improve the performance of fog computing systems in terms of delay such as [20, 27]. In this framework, a single task can be divided up into two subtasks to deal with the heterogeneity of fog resources. Accordingly, a subtask was processed by the primary fog locally, and the other was offloaded to the best neighbor fog or the cloud. The main objective of F2F collaboration policies is to decide when or where to offload the subtasks so that the average delay is minimized. Particularly, these works simply assumed that all the subtasks are independent and the delay of original task execution is derived from the most time-consuming subtask. Therefore, the delay reduction is benefited from the associated parallel computing of subtasks. Such a limited assumption is studied intensively in our general framework, which also takes into account the process of aggregating subtask processing results in calculating the delay. In addition, the system performance is thoroughly investigated in cases of increasing the service request rate, which is a lack of the existing study. Furthermore, different tasks can be executed efficiently by adaptive offloading manners, such as tasks should be divided or not, how many subtasks should be optimized, and so on, that are not addressed in the POST scheme [29].

The most recent literature studies the application of matching theory to offer distributed computation in fog computing networks [31, 32]. In these papers, a single task is divided into multiple subtasks, which are executed by different helper nodes and clouds in parallel. To map each subtask to a fog computing node, the matching algorithm is applied and developed such that the outcome (matching result) is stable. The fundamental of matching-based algorithm is to resolve the individual rational and selfishness of fog computing nodes that only maximize their own objectives without considering the overall performance of systems. The matching-based algorithms based on the classical deferred acceptance mechanism ensures that the matching is stable and distributed and can be achieved in a polynomial time complexity.

3.4 Open Research Issues

Fog computing is to be an essential component of the next-generation IoT systems to address various demands of users for service provision issues. The advent of technology promises to advance fog computing capabilities in terms of networking, communication, storage, and computing. At the same time, new requirements of network and internet users expose new issues for the systems to provide the services efficiently that may not be solved efficiently by current proposed solutions. This potentially links to a call for advanced techniques, algorithms, and frameworks to deal with these problems. This section scraps and discusses promising issues for development and research.

3.4.1 Data Fragmentation

As evaluated in the simulation results, the data division is a key approach contributing in reducing the delay in the complicated heterogeneous fog environment. However, the diversity of input data structure in practical application requires alternative division solutions for improving or optimizing the system performance. For instance, as the data dependency constraints among the subtasks are taken into account in the associated workflow model, the collaborative task offloading mechanism must be adapted to such a change accordingly. In addition, the data can be divided according to different features such as by size explicitly. In this way, an optimization can be formulated to find the optimal number of data subsets and associated sizes of data subset for optimizing the system performance.

3.4.2 Distribution of Fog Networks

The distribution of heterogeneous fogs also affects the performance of algorithms. This current work assumed a uniform distribution of fogs in the operating region; thus, workload can be balanced. However, the task imbalance can be a significant issue when the fogs are placed in a nonuniform manner. Therefore, the offloading solutions must be redesigned to deal with such change. In addition, the mobility of fog nodes and/or the end user, which strongly impacts on the fog resource status, must be taken into account in designing the algorithms.

3.4.3 Advances of Distributed Algorithms

Although the aforementioned heuristic algorithms proposed in the existing literature are efficient for offloading different context applications, there is still limitation regarding solving the offloading problems in the general point of view. Applying advanced technologies such as machine learning, reinforcement learning, and digital twins is promising to rise the high level of systematic performance. For example, machine learning-based algorithms can be used to analyze the data representing the state of the entire system, thus ensuring to derive the optimal offloading policies [33]. In addition, reinforcement learning is an efficient technique to provide intelligent decision-making for agents to respond effectively to the dynamics of fog computing environment [34]. Currently, digital twin is emerging to be enabling technology for industry 4.0, aiming to provide the modeling, simulation, and centralized controls for every IoT system. In the context of fog computing, it can be used to enhance the offloading decisions [35].

3.4.4 Comprehensive Performance Analysis

Finally, the other potential studies include a comprehensive evaluation of system performance in terms of energy consumption, bandwidth utilization, and overall cost to use the fog and cloud services.

3.5 Conclusions

This chapter provides a discussion regarding the cooperation for distributed task offloading in fog computing networks. The heterogeneity of fog computing devices such as gateways, switches, and routers is the main factor causing the barrier of fog-fog communication, thus limiting resource sharing in the fog layer. As a result, there are available resources in some fog devices, which are underutilized. This issue promotes the need for fog-fog interaction for facilitating resource management. The advances in hardware and software technologies enable to realize fog-fog communication in the future fog-enabled IoT networks. In this context, the cooperation between fogs becomes essential contributing to the performance improvement of task offloading operation.

A survey is conducted in this chapter to present the key architecture, algorithms, and frameworks leveraging the fog-fog cooperation for task offloading in the fog computing networks. Based on the evaluation results associated with the proposed researches, the cooperation between fogs is beneficial in many aspects such as low service response latency, energy consumption reduction, efficient resource utilization, and load balancing.

The ever-increasing demands of IoT-connected users expose new problems that need the service provisioning to be more flexible and dynamic. In these regards, this chapter sketches out many important directions for future researches. One of the typical examples is to integrate new technologies in the field of machine learning, artificial learning, block chain, and digital twin to optimize the task offloading in the fog computing networks.

References

1. Bonomi F, Milito R, Zhu J, Addepalli S (2012) Fog computing and its role in the internet of things. In: Proceedings of the first edition of the MCC workshop on Mobile cloud computing, pp 13–16
2. Chiang M, Zhang T (2016) Fog and iot: an overview of research opportunities. IEEE Internet Things J 3(6):854–864
3. Skarlat O, Nardelli M, Schulte S, Borkowski M, Leitner P (2017) Optimized iot service placement in the fog. SOCA 11(4):427–443
4. Skarlat O, Nardelli M, Schulte S, Dustdar S (2017) Towards QoS-aware fog service placement. In: 2017 IEEE 1st international conference on fog and edge computing (ICFEC), pp 89–96
5. Yousefpour A, Patil A, Ishigaki G, Kim I, Wang X, Cankaya HC, Zhang Q, Xie W, Jue JP (2019) Fogplan: a lightweight qos-aware dynamic fog service provisioning framework. IEEE Internet Things J 6(3):5080–5096
6. Zhang G, Shen F, Liu Z, Yang Y, Wang K, Zhou M-T (2018) Femto: fair and energy-minimized task offloading for fog-enabled iot networks. IEEE Internet Things J 6(3):4388–4400
7. Wu J, Dong M, Ota K, Li J, Yang W, Wang M (2019) Fog-computing-enabled cognitive network function virtualization for an information-centric future internet. IEEE Commun Mag 57(7):48–54
8. Li J, Jin J, Yuan D, Zhang H (2017) Virtual fog: a virtualization enabled fog computing framework for internet of things. IEEE Internet Things J 5(1):121–131
9. Baktir AC, Ozgovde A, Ersoy C (2017) How can edge computing benefit from software-defined networking: a survey, use cases, and future directions. IEEE Commun Surv Tutorials 19(4): 2359–2391
10. Satyanarayanan M, Bahl P, Caceres R, Davies N (2009) The case for VM-based cloudlets in mobile computing. IEEE Pervasive Comput 8(4):14–23
11. Bahl V (2015) Emergence of micro datacenter (cloudlets/edges) for mobile computing. In: Microsoft devices & networking summit 2015, vol 5
12. Bilal K, Khalid O, Erbad A, Khan SU (2018) Potentials, trends, and prospects in edge technologies: fog, cloudlet, mobile edge, and micro data centers. Comput Netw 130:94–120
13. Ahmed A, Arkian H, Battulga D, Fahs AJ, Farhadi M, Giouroukis D, Gougeon A, Gutierrez FO, Pierre G, Souza PR Jr et al (2019) Fog computing applications: taxonomy and requirements. arXiv preprint arXiv:1907.11621
14. Yousefpour A, Ishigaki G, Gour R, Jue JP (2015) On reducing iot service delay via fog offloading. IEEE Internet Things J 5(2):998–1010
15. Liu Z, Yang X, Yang Y, Wang K, Mao G (2018) Dats: dispersive stable task scheduling in heterogeneous fog networks. EEE IoT J 6(2):3423–3436
16. Tran-Dang H, Kim D-S (2021) FRATO: fog resource based adaptive task offloading for delay-minimizing IoT service provisioning. IEEE Trans Parallel Distrib Syst 32(10):2491–2508
17. Tran-Dang H, Kim D-S (2021) Frato: fog resource based adaptive task offloading for delay-minimizing iot service provisioning. IEEE Trans Parallel Distrib Syst 32(10):2491–2508

18. Guo K, Sheng M, Quek TQS, Qiu Z (2019) Task offloading and scheduling in fog-RAN: a parallel communication and computation perspective. IEEE Wireless Commun Lett 9(2): 215–218

19. Bian S, Huang X, Shao Z, Yang Y (2019) Neural task scheduling with reinforcement learning for fog computing systems. In: 2019 IEEE global communications conference (GLOBECOM), pp 1–6

20. Al-khafajiy M, Baker T, Al-Libawy H, Maamar Z, Aloqaily M, Jararweh Y (2019) Improving fog computing performance via fog-2-fog collaboration. Futur Gener Comput Syst 100:266–280. Available: https://doi.org/10.1016/j.future.2019.05.015

21. Xia Y, Etchevers X, Letondeur L, Coupaye T, Desprez F (2018) Combining hardware nodes and software components ordering-based heuristics for optimizing the placement of distributed iot applications in the fog. In: Proceedings of the 33rd annual ACM symposium on applied computing, pp 751–760

22. Mukherjee M, Guo M, Lloret J, Iqbal R, Zhang Q (2019) Deadline-aware fair scheduling for offloaded tasks in fog computing with inter-fog dependency. IEEE Commun Lett 24(2): 307–311

23. Liu L, Chang Z, Guo X, Mao S, Ristaniemi T (2017) Multiobjective optimization for computation offloading in fog computing. IEEE Internet Things J 5(1):283–294

24. Yao J, Ansari N (2019) Fog resource provisioning in reliability-aware iot networks. IEEE Internet Things J 6(5):8262–8269

25. Mukherjee M, Kumar S, Mavromoustakis CX, Mastorakis G, Matam R, Kumar V, Zhang Q (2020) Latency-driven parallel task data offloading in fog computing networks for industrial applications. IEEE Trans Industr Inform 16(9):6050–6058

26. Xiao Y, Krunz M (2017) QoE and power efficiency tradeoff for fog computing networks with fog node cooperation. In: IEEE INFOCOM 2017 – IEEE conference on computer communications

27. Masri W, Ridhawi IA, Mostafa N, Pourghomi P (2017) Minimizing delay in IoT systems through collaborative fog-to-fog (f2f) communication. In: 2017 IEEE ninth international conference on ubiquitous and future networks (ICUFN)

28. Yang Y, Liu Z, Yang X, Wang K, Hong X, Ge X (2019) Pomt: paired offloading of multiple tasks in heterogeneous fog networks. IEEE Internet Things J 6(5):8658–8669

29. Liu Z, Yang Y, Wang K, Shao Z, Zhang J (2020) Post: parallel offloading of splittable tasks in heterogeneous fog networks. IEEE Internet Things J 7(4):3170–3183

30. Pang A-C, Chung W-H, Chiu T-C, Zhang J (2017) Latency-driven cooperative task computing in multi-user fog-radio access networks. In: 2017 IEEE 37th international conference on distributed computing systems (ICDCS), pp 615–624

31. Liu Z, Yang X, Yang Y, Wang K, Mao G (2018) DATS: dispersive stable task scheduling in heterogeneous fog networks. IEEE Internet Things J 6(2):3423–3436

32. Tran-Dang H, Kim D-S (2022) A survey on matching theory for distributed computation offloading in iot-fog-cloud systems: perspectives and open issues. IEEE Access 10:1–19

33. Abdulkareem KH, Mohammed MA, Gunasekaran SS, Al-Mhiqani MN, Mutlag AA, Mostafa SA, Ali NS, Ibrahim DA (2019) A review of fog computing and machine learning: concepts, applications, challenges, and open issues. IEEE Access 7:153123–153140

34. Tran-Dang H, Bhardwaj S, Rahim T, Musaddiq A, Kim D-S (2022) Reinforcement learning based resource management for fog computing environment: literature review, challenges, and open issues. J Commun Netw 24(1):83–98

35. Sun W, Zhang H, Wang R, Zhang Y (2020) Reducing offloading latency for digital twin edge networks in 6g. IEEE Trans Veh Technol 69(10):12240–12251

Chapter 4
Fog Resource Aware Framework for Task Offloading in IoT Systems

In IoT-based systems, fog computing allows the fog nodes to offload and process tasks requested from IoT-enabled devices in a distributed manner instead of the centralized cloud servers to reduce the response delay. However, achieving such a benefit is still challenging in the systems with high rate of requests, which implies long queues of tasks in the fog nodes, thus exposing probably an inefficiency in terms of latency to offload the tasks. In addition, a complicated heterogeneous degree in the fog environment introduces an additional issue that many single fogs cannot process heavy tasks due to lack of available resources or limited computing capabilities. Particularly, this chapter introduces FRATO (Fog Resource Aware Adaptive Task Offloading)—a framework for the IoT-fog-cloud systems to offer minimal service provisioning delay through an adaptive task offloading mechanism. Fundamentally, FRATO is based on the fog resource to select flexibly the optimal offloading policy, which in particular includes a collaborative task offloading solution based on the data fragment concept. In addition, two distributed fog resource allocation algorithms, namely, TPRA and MaxRU, are developed to deploy the optimized offloading solutions efficiently in cases of resource competition. Through the extensive simulation analysis, the FRATO-based service provisioning approaches show potential advantages in reducing the average delay significantly in the systems with high rate of service requests and heterogeneous fog environments compared with the existing solutions.

4.1 Introduction

The Internet of Things (IoT) paradigm has been recognized as a key driving force to realize the smart concept in various domains such as smart cities [1], smart grids [2], and smart factories [3] since it enables the interconnection and interoperability of IoT-enabled physical and virtual entities to create smart services and informed decision-making for monitoring, control, and management purposes [4, 5]. The

© The Author(s), under exclusive license to Springer Nature Switzerland AG 2023
H. Tran-Dang, D.-S. Kim, *Cooperative and Distributed Intelligent Computation in Fog Computing*, https://doi.org/10.1007/978-3-031-33920-2_4

underlying principle of realization involves a set of activities that include collecting, processing, analyzing, and getting insights from IoT data perceived by IoT devices. Traditionally, the cloud computing platform plays an essential role in the realization process since it provides rich and powerful resources (i.e., storage, computation, networking) to handle an enormous amount of IoT data (big data) efficiently [6]. However, more stringent requirements of IoT service provisioning, such as (ultra)low delay, expose crucial limitations of the cloud-based solutions because the delivery of data from the IoT devices to the centralized cloud computing servers seriously affects the performance in processing and analyzing data and results in network congestion issues and excessive delay as an ultimate consequence. This fact context leads to a strong push of fog computing integration into the IoT-cloud systems since it puts computing, storage, communication, and control closer to the IoT devices to meet the prescribed QoS requirements [7–9]. Technically, the fog computing platform that is placed between the physical IoT devices and the cloud servers can handle a majority of service requests on behalf of the cloud servers to improve the system performance in terms of service delay, workload balancing, and resource utilization. This technique often called task offloading in the literature involves task-sharing mechanisms and resource allocation (i.e., which fog node is responsible for executing which task) in tandem to achieve the ultimate goal of applications [10].

The mutual benefits gained from the combination of fog and cloud enable the resulting IoT-fog-cloud systems to provide uninterrupted IoT services with various QoS requirements for the end users along the things-to-cloud continuum. However, employing fog computing raises another concern regarding decisions on whether the tasks should be processed in the fog or in the cloud. There are many factors impacting on the offloading decision policies such as offloading criteria and application scenarios [10]. Basically, in most existing offloading techniques, the tasks are probably offloaded to the best surrogate nodes called offloadees, which have the most ample resources (e.g., large storage capacity, high speed processing) and reliable communication network conditions in terms of delay, bandwidth between them and their neighbors, the IoT devices, and even the cloud servers. However, such fog offloading solutions face significant challenges regarding the workload distribution among the complicated heterogeneous fog devices characterized by different computation resources and capabilities. The challenge is further amplified by increasing the rates of service requests, which probably makes the task queues of resource-rich fog nodes longer. As a result, the requirements of latency-sensitive applications can be violated because of excessive waiting time of long queues. Furthermore, the reliance of remote cloud servers to fulfill the tasks may not help in improving the situation due to high communication delay or networking-related disturbance.

These issues exposed from the above use cases do urge the need to develop an adaptive offloading mechanism that is capable of the fog resource awareness to make the best context-aware offloading decisions. One possible solution to overcome these issues is to divide the tasks into subtasks, which can be executed in parallel by the different limited-resource fog nodes to reduce the overall processing delay.

Practically, this advantage feature of divide and conquer concept has been widely inherited and adopted in parallel computing [11], grid computing [12], or in service-providing systems [13, 14]. However, a few of existing works intensively examine the potential advantages of mentioned techniques in the context of IoT computing service provisioning. For example, the micro-service and micro-task concept was adopted in the work [15] to develop an offloading decision policy for mobile fog computing. In this technique, the micro-service is probed to unknown devices that are in the vicinity of mobile node to predict the resource consumption required to complete the larger tasks. Based on the analysis done on this approach, predictions of when to offload tasks based on micro-tasks have been more than 85% correct.

In this chapter, we present a Fog Resource-aware Adaptive Task Offloading (FRATO) framework, which is used to support the offloading decision-making in the IoT-fog-cloud systems. Fundamentally, on the basis of fog resource awareness, FRATO investigates and optimizes three feasible offloading policies including full task offloading in the fogs, full task offloading in the cloud, and collaborative task offloading in the fogs enabled by the task division. In addition, the optimization problem of the FRATO framework is solved by particle swarm optimization (PSO)-based method. Furthermore, based on the optimized offloading solutions, two distributed resource allocation mechanisms are developed to allocate the fog resources for executing the computing tasks. In conclusion, the main contributions of the chapter are summarized as follows:

- A framework, namely, FRATO, is formulated to analyze the offloading policies and then to adaptively select the optimal offloading solution based on the system context.
- Two distributed fog resource allocations, namely, TPRA and MaxRU, are developed to derive the task-fog resource mappings based on the obtained offloading policies.
- We conduct extensive simulation scenarios to examine the impact of the FRATO approach on the performance of fog-based IoT systems, especially in cases with high rate of requests and complicated level of heterogeneity of fog environment.

4.2 Related Works

This section highlights related offloading techniques to minimize the service delay in the IoT-fog-cloud systems. Similar to the partial task offloading concept, the fog service placement problem (FSPP) has been studied in the existing literature [16, 17]. The models introduced in these works employ the clustering concept to partition the fog landscape into fog colonies, each of which includes a centralized fog control node and other distributed fog cells. Additionally, each fog cell represents a visualized fog node (e.g., router, gateway or a cyber-physical system) with computational, network, and storage capabilities that coordinate a group of terminal IoT devices including sensors and actuators. Following a sense-process-actual model, each IoT application in this scenario typically comprises of three corresponding services, namely, sensing, processing, and actuating. To optimally place the requested services onto the fog cells, the authors formulate and address the optimization fog service placement problem (FSPP), which takes into account QoS constraints (i.e., prescribed deadlines of applications). In this way, the found solutions ensure the requirement satisfactions of applications while improving the fog resource utilization and reducing the execution cost. By inheriting the advantage features from this optimal service placement, our work can further reduce the service delay by exploiting the low fog-fog communication delay to reduce the service transfer time, which has not been uncovered in the existing works. In addition, our work provides a general framework to deal with undivided tasks, which through the proposed adaptive offloading mechanism can be offloaded by the best neighbor offloadees or to the cloud as the final solution.

Another FSPP is formulated and examined in [18] to place software components of distributed IoT applications onto a set of fog nodes. With respect to the required resources of components and the fog capacities, the problem may have multiple solutions. However, only one is selected among these mapping solutions to minimize the average response time of applications through an associated optimization problem. The work further develops two placement backtrack algorithms and two heuristics to accelerate the placement decision-making process. Although the low fog-to-fog communication is exploited in the proposed approach to reduce the total response time of application provisioning, the IoT-to-Fog communication is not addressed. In addition, there is a significant lack to investigate the queue status of fog infrastructure, which should be taken into account in the analytical model of service delay, especially in practical cases with high request rates or high heterogeneity of fog resources. Our framework considers the problem from a general standpoint, which covers these existing limitations to remodel and evaluate the service delay in an intensive methodology.

The task division concept is employed in the work [19] to minimize the energy consumption of task offloading while achieving workloadness fair among the fog nodes. The studied scenario divides the task into two subtasks with different sizes, which are processed locally by the IoT node and offloaded to the fog entity, respectively. The result from processing the subtask at the fog is then transmitted back to the terminal node. Similar to the FSPP model, however, the subtasks are assumed to be independent, even in their processing results. Thus, the total task delay is defined as the maximum value of all the subtask delays. Such a limited assumption is impractical in some IoT services, which are created eventually by aggregating all the processing results of subtasks. In addition, the transmission time of processing result from the fogs to the IoT nodes is neglected in this approach due to the processing result, which is just a small packet-like control signal [20–22]. That point can make sense in some scenarios, in which the task can be divided into small subtasks. Our approach covers and overcomes these limitations of existing work by accounting for heavy subtasks and aggregation of subtask processing results in calculating the overall task delay.

The authors in the study [23] formulated a multi-objective optimization problem as a general framework to achieve the efficient tradeoff of fog-based offloading systems in terms of energy consumption, delay, and execution cost. The limitation of the work is just to model a single fog node without considering the large-scale deployment of fog environment in which the fog nodes are required to interact to realize some tasks practically. Similarly, the authors in [24] studied an inherent tradeoff between the cost of renting the fog resources (i.e., virtual machines (VMs)) for executing requesting tasks and the reliability of VMs in the fog-aided IoT networks. A multi-objective fog resource provisioning optimization problem was constructed to minimize the rental cost and simultaneously maximize the reliability. On the contrary, our study models a single optimization problem, which aims at minimizing the service provisioning delay with respect to a general sense of both heterogeneous fog environment and characteristics of requesting services.

The work in [25] proposed an offloading policy for fog nodes to minimize the averaged delay for providing the IoT services to the IoT nodes in the IoT-fog-cloud application scenarios. The policy to offload the tasks in the fog layer or forward them to the cloud is decided based on an intensive analytical delay model, which takes into account the IoT-to-cloud and fog-to-cloud communication delay. In particular, the fog-to-fog communication is exploited to reduce the service delay through an efficient task-sharing mechanism, which accounts for not only the queue length status of fog nodes but also the types of IoT service requests (i.e., light and heavy tasks). In conclusion, the service provisioning tasks are dynamically assigned to be processed in the fog landscape or in the cloud by an optimized manner. Also concerning the performance of fog computing systems, the work [26] developed a decentralized algorithm for allocating the tasks among the neighboring fog nodes and the edge cloud. The algorithm was designed based on the game's theoretical formulation, which can solve the problem of minimizing completion time as the equilibrium of game strategy reaches. The extensive simulation results have shown the advantage of the proposed methods in improving the performance of fog computing systems in terms of response delay as compared with the myopic best responsive algorithm.

As per [26], a framework FOGPLAN is introduced for QoS-aware dynamic service provisioning. In this scheme, to ensure the QoS requirement of delay-sensitive IoT applications, the fog service controllers constantly monitor their task execution performance and the service request rate to dynamically decide whether to deploy a new request into or to release a queued request from the queues. This key mechanism enables the fog node to remove the queued tasks, which no longer violate the prescribed delay requirement. As a result, the percentage of services satisfying the QoS constraints is increased significantly while reducing the overall cost. Generally, these two approaches add to the existing collection that commonly reveals the capability of fog computing paradigm in supporting the delay-sensitive IoT applications. However, the resources of fogs are not made full use of in these works since a majority of heavy tasks are likely processed by the cloud servers. Our approach probably alleviates such a situation by employing the task division concept, which enables the collaborative fogs to accomplish complex tasks instead of forwarding them to the cloud.

The latter [27] studied the problem of scheduling offloaded tasks in the fog network as the tasks are delay-bounded. The work proposed a scheduling policy for the task queues of fogs based on the Lyapunov drift-plus-penalty function to maximize the number of completed tasks within their deadlines and to maintain the stability of fog queues. Our work also takes into account the state of task queues to allocate the fog resources for executing the tasks. In particular, unlike the aforementioned work that just offloaded entire tasks to the fogs, our proposed scheme explored the task division concept to handle the imbalance of workload distribution among fog nodes caused by the complicated heterogeneity of fog environment in terms of computational capability, storage, and communication. Recently, in a few existing works, both horizontal (fog to fog) and vertical (fog to cloud) collaborations are jointly considered during the computational resource allocation to minimize the task execution time [28–31]. These works considered both the communication delay between fogs and between fogs with cloud and the waiting time in queues of fogs to derive the optimal offloading decisions. In addition, the task division was examined to deal with the resource limitation of some fogs, which is insufficient to process the entire input data of tasks. However, none of these works studied the scenarios, in which the large input data of tasks (i.e., machine learning data) contain multiple types of data (i.e., text, image, audio, video), and a portion of fog devices can only process some of these data types. More importantly, the data sets of some subtasks can be dependent, thus requiring a predefined order during execution. This constraint must be taken into account in designing the schedule because it impacts directly on the delay of whole task execution.

Offloading multiple tasks of fog nodes (FNs) to multiple neighbor FNs (i.e., helper nodes (HNs)) to minimize the average service delay of tasks in a distributed manner is referred to as the multitask multi-helper (MTMH) problem, which is studied recently in some works [32–34]. Accordingly, a paired offloading of multiple tasks (POMT) in heterogeneous fog networks in [32] is modeled as a strategic game between the FNs and HNs for deciding which tasks are offloaded to which HNs to achieve the reduced delay. The associated algorithm is developed to obtain the Nash Equilibrium point (NE) for the POMT game based on a series of handshaking procedures between FNs and HNs to make the offloading strategy decisions. Although the proposed solution can obtain the near-optimal offloading performance in terms of average delay, it raises notable concerns in cases where accomplishing complex computing tasks probably requires multiple sparse fog nodes instead of single fogs. In addition, the work assumed that all tasks are not divisible. To deal with these two concerns, a parallel offloading of splittable tasks (POST) mechanism is proposed in [33]. By adopting the similar method used in their previous work (i.e., POMT), POST explores the benefits of task division in reducing service delay.

On the similar basis of partial task offloading, a certain number of studies in the literature proposed the fog-to-fog (F2F) collaboration strategies to improve the performance of fog computing systems in terms of delay such as [35–37]. In this framework, a single task can be divided up into two subtasks to deal with the heterogeneity of fog resources. Accordingly, a subtask was processed by the primary fog locally, and the other was offloaded to the best neighbor fog or the cloud. The main objective of F2F collaboration policies is to decide when or where to offload the subtasks so that the average delay is minimized. Particularly, these works simply assumed that all the subtasks are independent and the delay of original task execution is derived from the most time-consuming subtask. Therefore, the delay reduction is benefited from the associated parallel computing of subtasks. Such a limited assumption is studied intensively in our general framework, which also takes into account the process of aggregating subtask processing results in calculating the delay. In addition, the system performance is thoroughly investigated in cases of increasing the service request rate, which is a lack of the existing study. Furthermore, based on the solutions of optimization problem, different computing tasks can be executed efficiently by adaptive offloading manners, such as tasks should be divided or not, how many subtasks should be optimized, and so on, which are not addressed in the POST scheme [33]. In particular, the task-resource mapping problem is resolved in our study by workflow-based lightweight algorithms.

4.3   System Model and Problem Formulation

4.3.1   System Model

The work considers an IoT-fog-cloud system, as illustrated in Fig. 4.1, which basically comprises of three layers, namely, IoT, fog, and cloud layer to provide IoT services. The first layer includes all IoT-enabled devices that generate IoT data and/or primarily process the data and periodically reports the raw and/or pre-processed data to the fog or cloud for further advanced processing and computing (i.e., data streaming applications). In addition, the IoT devices submit requests to the upper layers for providing computing services due to their limited computation resources. The fog nodes (e.g., router, switches, and gateways) and servers distributed in the fog layer and cloud layer, respectively, are responsible for receiving, processing, and responding to the IoT service requests sent from the IoT layer.

For readability, important terminologies used in this paper are defined and clarified as following definitions:

Definition 4.1
An IoT service A typically is an application, which is implemented and provided by an IoT-fog-cloud domain vertically connected by a domain C of x cloud servers ($C = \{C_1, ..., C_x\}$), domain F of y fog nodes ($F = \{F_1, ..., F_y\}$) and domain I of z IoT devices ($I = \{I_1, ..., I_z\}$). Therefore, a certain service request can be denied to be served if it does not belong to the application domain of service providers (e.g., fogs or cloud servers), which receive the request.

In this work, an IoT service A is modeled as a tuple $A = (ID_A, ID_I, a, R_a, f(a))$, where ID_A is identifier number of service A; ID_I is identifier number of IoT node, which sent the service request A; a is input data size needed to be processed; R_a represents required resources for processing a; and $f(a)$ is the expected output data

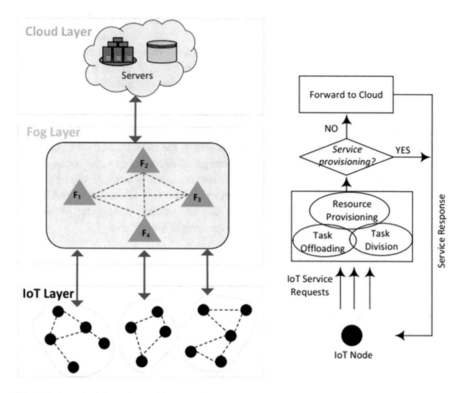

Fig. 4.1 A typical three-tier architecture of IoT-Fog-Cloud system, which provides specific kinds of IoT services through either

size of processing. Practically, the tuple can contain a predefined deadline of service in some use cases that imposes an intensive-delay requirement. However, the work is to examine the IoT-fog-cloud system featured especially by the heterogeneity of fog environment in providing as best as possible the service (i.e., minimized service provisioning delay).

Definition 4.2
The service provisioning delay D_A is defined as the time interval elapsed from when a fog receives the service request A (i.e., the input data a) until the requesting IoT node receives the response (i.e., the output of input data processing f(a)).

In our IoT-fog-cloud system, the IoT nodes primarily submit the service requests to their closest connected fogs. However, the services can be handled and served by either the fog nodes or the cloud based on the QoS requirements and context of system.

Definition 4.3
Provisioning an IoT service to a requesting IoT device is modeled as a workflow, which includes a set T_A of m tasks, $T_A = \{t_1, ..., t_m\}$.

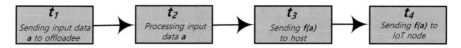

Fig. 4.2 A general workflow for service provisioning processes includes possibly four tasks, which are executed sequentially

Basically, there are two types of tasks in the set: data communication and data processing tasks. The first type refers to tasks for sending and receiving the data through communication channels, while the second type is for executing the data by dedicated algorithms and software. Depending on the characteristics of input data and the employed service provisioning methods, there exists a data dependency or independence for each pair of tasks. For example, as the input data is not divided, the processing orders of tasks follow a linear topology. Figure 4.2 illustrates such an overall workflow, in which each task is sequentially executed, with output data as the input of its subsequent task [38].

In addition, the final task t_n is to send the computing result $f(a)$ to the requesting IoT node. To describe the parametric context of each task, we define a tuple $B_i = (ID_i$ i, $type_i$, a_i, $f(a_i))$ to model a task t_i, where ID_i is identifier number of task t_i, $type_i$ indicates type of task (e.g., communication or processing), a_i and $f(a_i)$ are the input and output data size, respectively. In addition, $\gamma_{ti} = f(a_i)/a_i$ represents the input-output data ratio of task t_i, which is dependent on the types of tasks and the associated task execution methods [39]. For example, $\gamma_{ti} = 1$ for the data communication tasks, which just send and receive same amounts of data. Notably, some tasks may have no input data since they just aim to gather data from a dedicated set of IoT nodes or retrieve historical data from the server.

Since no orchestration mechanism (i.e., no centralized fog controller) is employed in the fog environment in this work, the optimal offloading decision for each requesting service is made by primary host in a distributed manner, which is a fog node receiving the request. As the service can be processed either by the primary host or by its neighbor fogs through offloading mechanisms. However, neither of these two solutions may be feasible in the systems featured by a highly heterogeneous fog environment. For example, Fig. 4.3 illustrates such potential use cases in IoT-fog-cloud systems, in which the primary host F_2 cannot process the whole input data of service request A due to lack of resources. Meanwhile, offloading the task to the fog neighbors F_1 and F_3 may lead to an extensive delay since there are high workloads in queues of these fog nodes. In this work, we propose and examine a collaborative task offloading method to potentially cope with the situation, which is based on a data fragmentation concept to enable a distributed offloading by a set of neighbor heterogeneous fog nodes.

Definition 4.4
Task division refers to a process of dividing the data of task into portions (subtasks) with smaller data sizes for facilitation of processing.

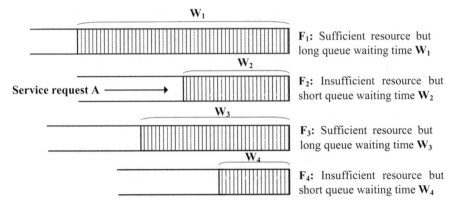

W₁

F₁: Sufficient resource but long queue waiting time **W₁**

W₂

Service request A ⟶

F₂: Insufficient resource but short queue waiting time **W₂**

W₃

F₃: Sufficient resource but long queue waiting time **W₃**

W₄

F₄: Insufficient resource but short queue waiting time **W₄**

Fig. 4.3 The heterogeneity and unbalanced workload of fog environment in the IoT-fog-cloud systems expose issues in providing

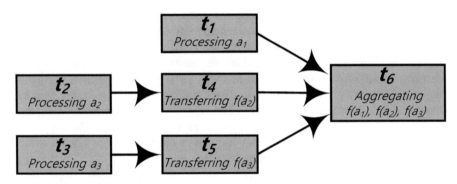

Fig. 4.4 Based on the data fragmentation concept, processing the input data (a) includes a set of tasks, which process the data subsets a_1, a_2, a_3 before completing the whole task by jointly processing the output data $f(a_1)$, $f(a_2)$, and $f(a_3)$ to achieve $f(a)$

In this work, we employ this concept to partition an IoT input data of a service request into subsets, which are assumed to be independent. This assumption is reasonable in practical use cases since the large set of input IoT data in heavy computation applications can be various in forms, which can be classified and divided into multiple groups, such as text, image, audio, and video or temperature, humidity, and a few to name for processing facilitation. In this context, a full task referring to the computation process of the whole input data can be divided into corresponding subtasks, which can process the corresponding data subsets by different fogs. Figure 4.4 illustrates the main subtasks for computing the input data a as it can be divided into three independent subsets $\{a_1, a_2, a_3\}$. In particular, the outputs of subtasks (i.e., $f(a_1)$, $f(a_2)$, $f(a_{13})$) are collected and jointly processed in the final stage to achieve the desired outcome (i.e., $f(a)$).

Definition 4.5

We define a fog colony of a primary host for each request A as a set C_A of fog nodes including the primary host and its neighbor fog nodes. In particular, all the fogs in this set are connected either by wired or wireless communication technologies. Figure 4.5 shows a colony of fog node F_2, which includes three additional neighbor fogs F_1, F_3, and F_4. Depending on the selected offloading policy, some additional fog nodes in the colonies can involve in executing the tasks of workflow. Such kinds of fogs are named as service hosts and collaborative fogs, which are defined as follows.

Definition 4.6

*A fog node is called **host** (or **service host**) of a service request A if it eventually takes charge of sending the computation result f(a) to the requesting IoT node.*

In addition, the host can accomplish some tasks before executing the final task such as: (i) it serves as an offloadee to process the whole input data by its own, (ii) it handles some tasks relating to some of data subsets (e.g., task t_2 or task t_3 in Fig. 4.4), and (iii) it only aggregates all the outputs of all the tasks (e.g., task t_6 in Fig. 4.4). Notably, the host may be different from the primary host, which purely receives the input data of request. In addition, the host can be the cloud as the fog infrastructure is unable to process the request efficiently. Figure 4.5 illustrates the example of host (the fog node F_1 or the cloud) and primary host (F_2).

Fig. 4.5 The host of service can be a neighbor of the primary host or the cloud

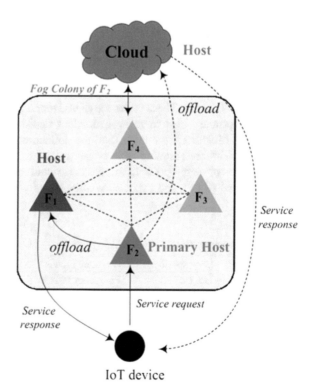

Definition 4.7
*Unlike the offloadees, which can process the whole input data due to its sufficient resource, **collaborative fogs** only handle the data subsets (i.e., subtask offloading tasks as t_1, t_2, and t_3 in Fig. 4.4) as the input data is fragmented.*

4.3.2   Problem Formulation

Concerning the responsive ability of IoT-fog-cloud systems in providing IoT (computing) services, this work aims at developing a general framework for supporting offloading decisions so that the service response delay is minimized. In many of the use cases, the complicated heterogeneity of fog environment represents a critical challenge for these systems to achieve the objective. Accordingly, the presence of limited resource fogs results in the imbalance of workload distribution among the fogs, which in turn impacts negatively on the performance of system in terms of delay. In addition, the high rate of requests potentially prolongs the task queues in the powerful fog nodes since the limited resource fog nodes with respect to the computational capability, and storage may be unable to process the whole input data of service. Furthermore, constrained by the cloud rental cost, the other objective of the proposed framework is to maximize the usage of fog resources, thus minimizing the reliance on the cloud. All these perspectives serve as a direction to explore the task division concept that potentially can help in reducing the task execution delay through parallel subtask executions of limited resource fogs. In this framework, each primary host is based on the available resources and workload state of its fog colony and characteristics of computing data to derive the optimal offloading policy, which provides the minimal service provisioning delay. Recall that each fog maintains its own neighbor resource table containing the updated information about the available resources of its colony. These tables are shared among the member of their colony to support the primary host to make offloading decisions, which ultimately aim at selecting the offloadees, the hosts, and the collaborative fogs. Table 4.1 shows an example of neighbor resource table stored by the fog node F_1, which records the resource states of neighbors with respect to residual memory (M_r), clock frequency, round-trip time (RTT), and expected waiting time in queue (W).

Table 4.1 Resource table of neighbors of fog node F_1

| Node ID | Fog specification and resource status | | | |
	M_r (MB)	Frequency (GHz)	RTT (ms)	W (ms)
F_2	200	10	2.5	350.2
F_3	100	5	3.1	500
F_4	400	2.5	4.8	239.1

4.4   FRATO Fog Resource Aware Task Offloading Framework

Fundamentally, FRATO is based on the awareness of available fog resources and the data characteristics of computing service to make the optimal offloading policy, which provides the minimal service provisioning delay. Fundamentally, FRATO examines three following offloading strategies to achieve the objective.

4.4.1   Offloading Strategies for Minimizing Service Provisioning Delay

Optimal Full Task Offloading in Fog (OFTO$_F$)

As there exists at least one fog node in the colony to host and process completely the whole input data, the OFTO mechanism is just to seek the best offloadee and/or the host in the colony such that the total delay is minimal. In this case, we refer to $D_A^{OFTO_F}$ as the minimized service delay obtained from the OFTO$_F$ strategy. Figure 4.6 illustrates a typical example of OFTO$_F$ strategy, in which $D_A^{OFTO_F}$ includes three components: offloading time (i.e., time to send the whole input data from the primary

Fig. 4.6 A typical optimal full task offloading mechanism in the fog layer involves selecting simultaneously the offloadee, the host, and associated reliable communication routes through an optimized manner

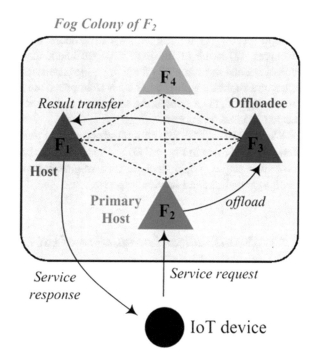

host to the offloadee), processing time (i.e., time used by the offloadee to process the data), and response time (i.e., time to transfer the computing results to the IoT node). Notably, the offloadee can be the service host unexpectedly in some cases to reduce the communication overhead.

Optimal Full Task Offloading in Cloud (OFTO$_C$)

Although some fogs in the colony are able to host and process the computing service request, forwarding the computing task to the cloud is probably efficient since these fogs have long queues of waiting tasks. Especially, as the request rate is increasing, the cloud-based solutions enable to share and balance the workload with the heterogeneous fog environment effectively. In this case, we refer to $D_A^{OFTO_C}$ as the minimized service delay obtained from the OFTO$_C$ strategy. Similar to OFTO$_F$, $D_A^{OFTO_C}$ includes the offloading time, the processing time in the cloud, and the response time. We assume that all servers at cloud in the application domain have the same resource capability. Thus, the total service delay heavily relies on the communication delays, that is, fog-to-cloud, cloud-to-fog, and fog-to-IoT communication delays.

Optimal Collaborative Task Offloading in Fog (OCTO$_F$)

The task division and associated subtask offloading strategy can be beneficial in multiple cases: (1) no fog nodes can process the full task due to insufficient resources, (2) some of the fogs have sufficient resources but have long waiting time of queued tasks, and (3) some fog nodes have sufficient resource to process one or several subtasks with smaller sizes to improve the resource utilization of system. As the input data of computing task can be divided into the subsets, the OCTO$_F$ mechanism can be applied.

We refer to $D_A^{OCTO_F}$ as the minimized service delay obtained from the OCTO$_F$ strategy. As shown in Fig. 4.7 $D_A^{OCTO_C}$ accounts for time intervals for completion of four main stages, which include data fragmentation, subtask offloading, subtask result aggregation, and service response.

4.4.2 Mathematical Formulation of FRATO

Generally, the mathematical model of FRATO is built on the associated workflow of offloading policy as described above. The problem is turned into resource and communication scheduling, which simultaneously maps appropriate resources (fogs and cloud) to process corresponding tasks and then establish an order to send the processing results to the host. Therefore, the first stage of FRATO modeling

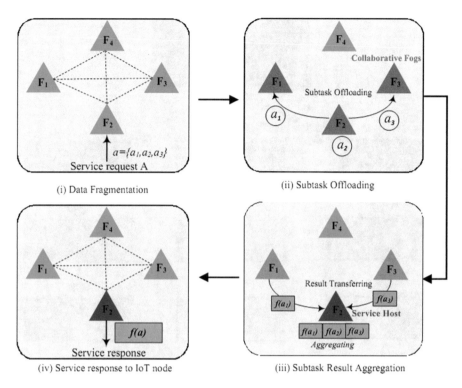

(i) Data Fragmentation   (ii) Subtask Offloading

(iv) Service response to IoT node   (iii) Subtask Result Aggregation

Fig. 4.7   Four main stages to implement the OCTO$_F$ mechanism

is to design the workflow, which specifies all the involved tasks and their possible processing orders (i.e., data dependency or independence). Figure 4.8 illustrates a workflow for the OCTO$_F$ offloading policy as the input data can be divided into three subsets. In particular, this workflow structure can be totally used for the OFTO$_F$ and OFTO$_C$ policies; however, the number of tasks is decreased considerably since the input data is not fragmented.

Based on the workflow, the second stage of FRATO is to find a schedule to execute the workflow on fog and cloud computing resources so that the makespan of schedule (i.e., service provisioning delay) is minimized. We define a schedule for each workflow of provisioning the service A as a tuple $S_A = (C_A^+, M_A, D_A)$, which include a set C_A^+ of fog and cloud resources ($C_A^+ = C_A \cup C$), a task-to-resource mapping M_A, and the total execution time of schedule (i.e., total service provisioning delay) D_A. Figure 4.9 shows an example of an optimal schedule generated by the OCTO$_F$ strategy for the workflow shown in Fig. 4.8. In this schedule, three resources F_1, F_2, and F_3 are collaborative fogs to execute all the tasks of workflow. Notably, since the data subset a_2 is processed by the primary host F_2, the tasks t_2, t_5, t_{11}, and t_{14} are removed. Meanwhile, the other data subsets a_1 and a_3 are outsourced by F_1 and F_3, respectively.

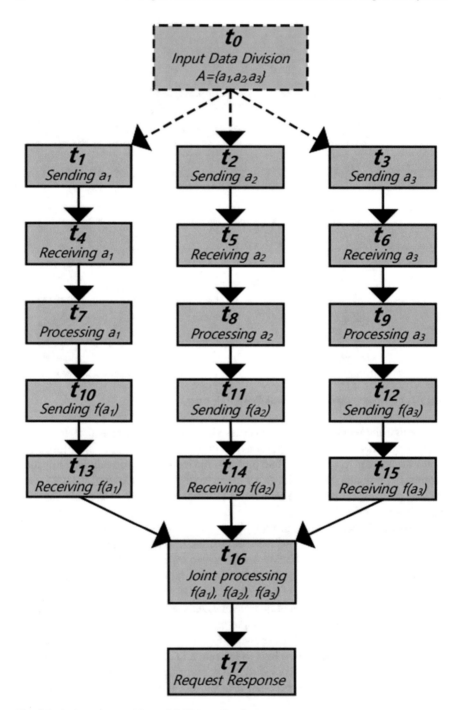

Fig. 4.8 An intensive workflow of OCTO$_F$ policy for heterogeneous fog environment as the input data of computing service request can be partitioned into three sets {a_1, a_2, a_3}

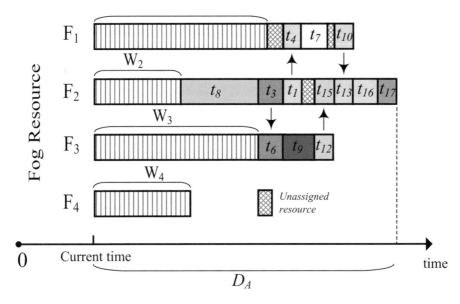

Fig. 4.9 Example of an optimal schedule generated by the OCTO$_F$ strategy for the workflow shown in Fig. 4.8

In each schedule, $C_A^+ = \{F_1, F_2, ..., F_n, C\}$ is the set of fogs in the colony of primary host and the cloud, which need to be assigned for executing the tasks. MA represents a task-resource mapping and is comprised of tuples of the form $m_{t_i}^{r_j} = (t_i, r_j, ST_{t_i}, ET_{t_i})$, one for each task of workflow. A mapping tuple $m_{t_i}^{r_j}$ implies that task t_i is scheduled to be processed by resource r_j and is expected to start executing a time ST_{t_i} and complete by time ET_{t_i}, where $t_i \in T_A$, and $r_j \in C_A^+$.

Fundamentally, concerning exclusively on the service provisioning delay, FRATO is to evaluate the three prescribed mechanisms (i.e., OFTO$_F$, OFTO$_C$, and OCTO$_F$) and then select the optimal solution, which provides the minimal delay. The deterministic policy space is denoted as $\Pi = \{OFTO_F, OFTO_C, OCTO_F\}$. The objective of the optimization is to find an optimal policy $\pi^* \in \Pi$ that minimizes the service provisioning delay that is PO: $\pi^* \in \operatorname{argmin}_{\pi \in \Pi} D_A^\pi$, s.t. *Constraints*.

On the other hand, as D_A^{FRATO} is defined as the delay obtained from FRATO strategy, it implies that $D_A^{FRATO} = \min\left\{D_A^{(*)}\right\}$, where $(*)$ indicates optimal offloading policies in the space Π and $D_A^{(*)}$ is obtained from optimization problem **P** modeled as follows:

$$\textbf{P}: \textbf{Min } D_A^{(*)}$$

s.t. Constraints

Objective Function

The objective function is to minimize the service provisioning delay D_A, which is calculated as follows:

$$D_A^{(*)} = ST_m + \sum_{j \in C_A^+} \alpha_{mj} T_{mj}^{\text{proc}} - T_{\text{cur}},$$

where ST_m is the start execution time of final task tm of workflow and $\alpha_{mj} = 1$ if the task t_m is processed by the resource r_j $(r_j \in C_A^+)$, T_{cur} is current time captured by the primary host as it receives the request A, and T_{mj}^{proc} is time to process the task t_m. Since tm is the final task of workflow, T_{mj}^{proc} is time to transfer the result $f(a)$ from the host r_j (i.e., a fog or cloud) to the requesting IoT node. We assume that there are l hops to connect the host r_j to the IoT nodes; thus, T_{mj}^{proc} is derived by:

$$T_{mj}^{\text{proc}} = \sum_l \frac{f(a)}{R_l} + T_{mj}^{\text{prop}},$$

where $f(a)$ is the output data size in bits, R_l is the data rate of lth link on the path to transmit $f(a)$ from r_j to the IoT node, and T_{mj}^{prop} is propagation time from a node m to a node j, which can be calculated from RTT (see Sect. 4.6).

Constraints

To execute a task, a resource must have sufficient resource available to process the input data of task. Since all requesting services may have different requirements on the kind of resource features (e.g., available storage, CPU processing capability, and/or their combinations) to process the input data, we use the operator $\succeq$ to indicate the sufficiency of resource. Thus, the constraints are modeled as follows:

$$\sum_{j \in C_A^+} \alpha_{ij} R_j^{\text{avai}} \geq R_{t_i}^{\text{req}}, \forall t_i \in T_A,$$

where R_j^{avai} is the current available state of resource r_j and $R_{t_i}^{\text{req}}$ is required resource to execute the task t_i. In this work, we use storage capability and computation capability of data type to verify the available state of fog resources. Accordingly, a fog should have a residual memory greater than the input data size of a task t as well as have supportive capability to process some types of data such as image and audio contained in the input data.

Thus, each task is processed only by a single resource that implies the following constraint.

$$\sum_{j \in C_A^+} \alpha_{ij} = 1, \forall t_i \in T_A.$$

With respect to the queued tasks, all start times of tasks must be greater than the current waiting times of queues of resources, which process the tasks:

$$ST_{t_i} - T_{\text{cur}}^{r_k} \geq \sum_{j \in C_A^+} \alpha_{ij} W_j, \forall t_i \in T_A,$$

where $T_{\text{cur}}^{r_k}$ is current time captured by a fog resource r_k, which is expected to process t_i .

Regarding the order of tasks, as a task t_i is finished completely before a task t_j is executed, their start times must satisfy the following condition:

$$\beta_{ij} \left(ST_{t_i} + \sum_{j \in C_A^+} \alpha_{ij} T_{ik}^{\text{proc}} \right) \leq ST_{t_j}, \forall \{t_i, t_j\} \in T_A,$$

where β_{ij} is defined as:

$$\beta_{ij} = \begin{cases} 1, & \text{if } O_{t_j} > O_{t_i}, \\ 0, & \text{Otherwise}. \end{cases}$$

Notably, the processing orders of tasks t_i (i.e., O_{t_i}) are dependent on the their data dependence and can be obtained based on the constructed workflow. Meanwhile, for the data processing tasks, the time required for a resource r_i to process a_k-bit data of task t_k is calculated as follows:

$$T_{ik}^{\text{proc}} = \frac{a_k \gamma_{ik}}{f_i},$$

where f_i is the computation capability of r_i, that is, the CPU frequency (in CPU cycles per second), and γ_{ik} is the processing density of r_i to process the data of task t_k (in CPU cycles per a data bit).

As a pair of tasks t_i, t_j involves sending and receiving a set of data, they are executed in parallel by a transmitter T_x and a receiver R_x, thus:

$$\sigma_{ij}\left(ST_{t_i} - ST_{t_{ij}}\right) = 0, \forall \{t_i, t_j\} \in T_A,$$

$$ET_{t_i} = ET_{t_j} = ST_{t_i} + T_{TxRx}^{com},$$

where T_{TxRx}^{com} is the communication delay to send data from T_x to R_x and σ_{ij} is defined and retrieved from the built workflow as follows:

$$\sigma_{ij} = \begin{cases} 1, \text{if } O_{t_j} = O_{t_i}, \\ 0, \text{Otherwise.} \end{cases}$$

Multitask single resource constraint: Unlike the general resource provisioning scheduling algorithms for scientific workflows on the cloud with multi-core servers as assumed in [40], the resource allocation for offloading mechanisms in the heterogeneous fog environment faces additional concerns regarding constraints on concurrent usage of resource and time. In this work, we suppose that no multiple tasks are executed in parallel by a single resource. On the other hand, as a task t_i and a task t_j are assigned to be executed by a resource r_k, their start times must respect to the following condition:

$$\left(\alpha_{ik}ST_{t_i} - \alpha_{jk}ET_{t_j}\right)\left(\alpha_{jk}ST_{t_j} - \alpha_{jk}ET_{t_i}\right) < 0, \forall \{t_i, t_j\} \in T_A.$$

4.4.3   Solution Deployment Analysis

In this work, we employed particle-swarm optimization (PSO) approach to resolve the proposed optimization problem **P**. PSO is an evolutionary computational technique, which models the behavior of animal flocks to move in an optimal position [41].

Fundamentally, PSO-based algorithm enables to derive a set of feasible solutions to the optimization problem in the search space, which includes an optimal one to offer minimal service delay. The optimal solution may not be deployed eventually due to the unavailability of expected task-resource mapping, which in turn is basically caused by unavailable resource of involved fogs (i.e., offloadees, collaborative fogs, and hosts), or unreliable communication dropping the resource allocation requests. To cope with this situation, we utilize an additional feasible solution (i.e., suboptimal solution) in the set as a backup solution. Suppose that a fog obtains a set $S_A^{FRATO} = \left\{S_A^*, S_A^1, \ldots, S_A^p\right\}$ of feasible solutions for offloading task A, which includes the optimal solution S_A^* and a number p of suboptimal solutions. We denote D_A^{k} $(k = 1,\ldots,p)$ as the expected service delay as the corresponding solution S_A^k is implemented. As the deadline of service is not considered in this work, the feasible solutions are selected such that their corresponding delay is less different, or

$\mid D_A^* - D_A^k \mid /D_A^* \le \gamma_{th}\%$, where γ_{th} is acceptable threshold of difference between delays obtained by any feasible solution and the optimal solution. To facilitate the selection of solution, the feasible solutions in the list are sorted in descending order according to the expected delay. In addition, as some solutions can offer nearly the same service delay, the overhead to deploy the solution is taken into account during the solution selection process. Fundamentally, the overhead is proportional to the number of tasks specified by the workflow of associated offloading policy. Therefore, solutions that use lower overhead are preferred to be selected as the offloading approach. In this way, the order of solution is used to represent the priority in the phase of decision-making.

Figure 4.10 shows the diagram describing the policy to select and deploy the solution.

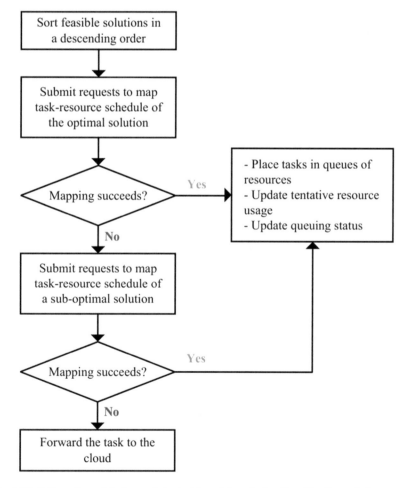

Fig. 4.10 Policy of a certain fog node to decide and then deploy the offloading solution

As feasible solutions are already sorted, fogs submit the resource allocation requests to the involved neighbor fogs (i.e., offloadees, collaborative fogs, service hosts) for implementing the optimal solution first. When the first solution is not deployed, the second solution in the set is attempted. If it fails, the service request is forwarded finally to the cloud.

4.5   Distributed Resource Allocation in Fog

A fog node can receive multiple resource allocation requests simultaneously in executing different tasks, some of which may expose an overlap of expected resource usage. As illustrated in Fig. 4.11, five task execution requests t_1, t_2, t_3, t_4, and t_5 cannot be served altogether by a fog node F_3 due to their mutual conflicts of some requesting resources (e.g., resource overlap between t_3 and t_5). Accordingly, the request t_2 totally is rejected since the resource is already allocated for processing t_1. Meanwhile, the three remaining tasks t_3, t_4, and t_5 must compete for usage of resource.

Due to the lack of global information, the fog nodes make decisions on which task requests are accepted to process in a distributed manner. In a simple way, the fog nodes can employ the first-come first-serve (FCFS) mechanism to handle the requests. However, it probably leads to degrade the overall system performance in terms of delay in the cases that the requests for implementing the optimal solutions are denied. In addition, deploying the backup solutions or the cloud-based solutions in the worst cases can attribute to an increased delay averagely. In this study, we propose and investigate two distributed resource allocation algorithms for the fog nodes to handle the resource allocation requests based on their own resource availability status and information contained in the requests, which include a task priority-based resource allocation (TPRA) and maximal resource utilization-based allocation (MaxRU).

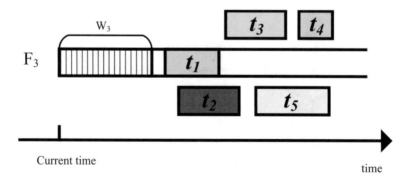

Fig. 4.11 Multiple requests for executing tasks expose possible conflicts of resource usage in fogs

Table 4.2 Main functions used in algorithms

Function	Description
REMOVE(t,T)	Remove a task t from the list T
INSERT(t,T)	Insert a task t into the list T
SORT$_x$(T)	Sort all elements (tasks) in the list T based on parameter x
RC_OVERLAP (t,T)	Return 0 if requesting resource for a task t overlap with any allocated resource for tasks in the list T (Using equation (13) to verify the condition). Return 1, otherwise
ALLOC_SOL (T)	Return feasible solutions to allocate the requesting tasks in the list T such that their resources are non-overlapping. Each solution is a set of the allocated tasks

Suppose that at instance τ of decision-making of resource allocation, a fog receives a set T^r of p requesting tasks, $T^r = \left\{ t_1^r, t_2^r, \ldots, t_p^r \right\}$ (e.g., tasks t_2, t_3, t_4, and t_5 in Fig. 4.11).

We denote T^a as a set of q allocated tasks, $T^a = \left\{ t_1^a, t_2^a, \ldots, t_q^a \right\}$ (e.g., task t_i in Fig. 4.11). In the following sections, we present TPRA and MaxRU algorithms used by fog nodes to respond to the requests.

The response messages specify if the resource allocation requests are accepted or not. In particular, fog nodes provide the already allocated tasks to avoid further conflict of resource usage if the execution of backup solutions involves them again.

For the sake of clarity, Table 4.2 summarizes the main functions used to implement the proposed algorithms.

4.5.1 Task Priority-Based Resource Allocation

In this work, the requests from fog nodes are classified into two types: non-priority (normal) and priority level. The type normal requests imply that they can be denied by the resource providers (i.e., fogs receiving the requests) since the backup solutions can offer efficient service provisioning delay. In contrast, the priority is set on the requests to specify the significance of success of these task-resource mappings. In other words, when these mappings are unsuccessful, the overall service provisioning delay can be prolonged considerably in cases of deployment of a backup solution or cloud-based one.

Algorithm 4.1: TPRA: Task Priority-Based Resource Allocation

Input: $T^r = \{t_1^r, t_2^r, ..., t_p^r\}$, $T^a = \{t_1^a, ..., t_q^a\}$
// Sets of p requesting tasks and q allocated tasks
Output: $Res = \{t_1^r.res, t_2^r.res, ..., t_p^r.res\}$, // Response to requests, $t_i^r.res = 1$: accepted; $t_i^r.res = 0$: rejected

1 **begin**
    // Rejecting tasks which violate the allocated tasks
2   **for** $t_i^r \in T^r$ **do**
3   **if** $RC\_OVERLAP(t_i^r, T^a) = 0$ **then**
4        $t_i^r.res \leftarrow 0$ // Rejecting t_i^r
5        $REMOVE(t_i^r, T^r)$ // Update T^r

    // Accepting tasks that their requesting resources do not overlap with that of the other tasks
6   **for** $t_i^r \in T^r$ **do**
7   **if** $RC\_OVERLAP(t_i^r, T^r \backslash \{t_i^r\}) = 1$ **then**
8        $t_i^r.res \leftarrow 1$ // Accepting t_i^r
9        $REMOVE(t_i^r, T^r)$ // Update T^r

    // Extracting priority and non-priority tasks
10   **for** $t_i^r \in T^r$ **do**
11   **if** $t_i^r.pri = 1$ **then**
12        $INSERT(t_i^r, T_{pri}^r)$ // List of priority requests
13   **else**
14        $INSERT(t_i^r, T_{non-pri}^r)$ // List of non-priority requests

    // Sort tasks in sets in a ascending order of delay and update task lists
15 $T_{pri}^r \leftarrow SORT_D(T_{pri}^r)$
16 $T_{non-pri}^r \leftarrow SORT_D(T_{non-pri}^r)$
    // Accepting the task with minimal delay
17 $t_{pri,1}^r.res \leftarrow 1$
    // Insert new allocated tasks to a new list
18 $INSERT(t_{pri,1}^r, T_{new}^a)$
    // Handle priority tasks
19 **for** $t_{pri,k}^r \in T_{pri}^r \backslash t_{pri,1}^r$ **do**
20   **if** $RC\_OVERLAP(t_{pri,k}^r, T_{new}^a) = 1$ **then**
21      $t_{pri,k}^r.res \leftarrow 1$
22      $REMOVE(t_{pri,k}^r, T_{pri}^r)$
23      $INSERT(t_{pri,k}^r, T_{new}^a)$
24   **else**
25      $t_{pri,k}^r.res \leftarrow 0$
26      $REMOVE(t_{pri,k}^r, T_{pri}^r)$
    // Handle non-priority tasks
27 **for** $t_{non-pri,k}^r \in T_{non-pri}^r$ **do**
28   **if** $RC\_OVERLAP(t_{non-pri,k}^r, T_{new}^a) = 1$ **then**
29      $t_{non-pri,k}^r.res \leftarrow 1$ $REMOVE(t_{non-pri,k}^r, T_{pri}^r)$
30      $INSERT(t_{non-pri,k}^r, T_{new}^a)$
31   **else**
32      $t_{non-pri,k}^r.res \leftarrow 0$
33      $REMOVE(t_{pri,k}^r, T_{non-pri}^r)$

In the TPRA mechanism, the priority attribute of requests is used to assist the decision-making on the acceptance or rejection of requests as their requesting resources overlap mutually. Accordingly, the requesting resources of priority requests are prioritized to be handled first. In addition, as multiple priority requests compete for resource usage, the estimated service provisioning delays (i.e., D_A) of associated offloading solutions are taken into account. Notably, D_A is embedded in the request messages. In this way, the requesting task that contains the minimal delay will be allocated to be executed. After handling the priority requests, the non-priority tasks are handled as the same way by prioritizing the tasks based on the delay. Algorithm 4.1 shows the key procedures of TPRA mechanism.

4.5.2 Maximal Resource Utilization-Based Allocation

In MaxRU scheme, some of received requests are accepted to be served by a certain fog so as the resource utilization of the fog is maximized. We denote T_i^r as a feasible allocation solution, which is a set of p_i possible maximum requesting tasks $(0 \leq p_i \leq p)$ such that their expected resources are nonoverlapping, $T_i^r = \left\{ t_1^{r'}, t_2^{r'}, \ldots, t_{p_i}^{r'} \right\}$. Notably, $t_j^{r'}$ is selected from the set T^r, $\forall j = 1, \ldots, p_i$, and the tasks in T_i^r is sorted in ascending order of start time (ST). As the allocation solution T_i^r is deployed in a certain fog, its resource utilization RU_i is defined and calculated by:

$$RU_i = \frac{\sum_j^{p_i} \left(ET_j - ST_j \right)}{ET_{p_i} - ST_1},$$

where ST_j and ET_j are start time and end time of execution of task $t_j^{r'}$, which are obtained from the optimization problem solutions.

Algorithm 4.2: MaxRU: Maximal Resource Utilization Based Allocation

---

Input: $T^r = \{t_1^r, t_2^r, \ldots, t_p^r\}$, $T^a = \{t_1^a, \ldots, t_q^a\}$
// Sets of p requesting tasks and q allocated tasks
Output: $Res = \{t_1^r.res, t_2^r.res, \ldots, t_p^r.res\}$ // Response to requests, $t_i^r.res = 1$: accepted; $t_i^r.res = 0$: rejected
1 **begin**
    // Rejecting tasks which violate the allocated tasks
2   **for** $t_i^r \in T^r$ **do**
3   **if** $RC\_OVERLAP(t_i^r, T^a) = 0$ **then**
4             $t_i^r.res \leftarrow 0$ // Rejecting t_i^r
5             $REMOVE(t_i^r, T^r)$ // Update T^r
    // Accepting tasks that their requesting resources do not overlap with that of the other tasks
6   **for** $t_i^r \in T^r$ **do**
7   **if** $RC\_OVERLAP(t_i^r, T^r \backslash \{t_i^r\}) = 1$ **then**
8             $t_i^r.res \leftarrow 1$ // Accepting t_i^r
9             $REMOVE(t_i^r, T^r)$ // Update T^r
    // Find $\bar{p}$ feasible allocation solutions
10    $\mathcal{T}_{sol} = \{T_1^r, \ldots, T_{\bar{p}}^r\} = ALLOC\_SOL(T^r)$
    // Sort tasks in an ascending order of ST
11   **for** $T_i^r \in \mathcal{T}_{sol}$ **do**
12       $T_i^r \leftarrow SORT_{ST}(T_i^r)$; // $t_i^r.ST \leq t_{i+1}^r.ST$ $\forall t_i^r \in T_s^r$
13   Calculate RU_i as Equation 14
14   **if** $RU_k = MaxRU$ **then**
15   T_k^r is selected to be deployed
16   **for** $t_j^r \in T_k^r$ **do**
17          $t_j^r.res \leftarrow 1$

Suppose that there exists a maximum $\bar{p}$ allocation solutions (i.e., $T_1^r, \ldots, T_{\bar{p}}^r$), thus the maximum resource utilization can be derived by MaxRU $= \max\{RU_k\}$. Consequently, in MaxRU mechanism, the allocation solution that offers the maximal resource utilization is selected to be deployed. Algorithm 4.2 summarizes key procedures to implement MaxRU mechanism.

4.6　Simulation and Performance Evaluation

4.6.1　Simulation Environment Setup

Characteristics of IoT Services

In this work, the input data of all the computing service requests includes four types: text, audio, image, and video. In addition, the variety of requests is characterized by the sizes of input data, which are determined by the size of each data type. We assume that the sizes are uniformly distributed as U[1–3] MB, U[2–5] MB, U[4–7] MB, and U[5–12] MB for type text, audio, image, and video data, respectively. Accordingly, the minimum data size of applications can be 12 MB, and the maximum one is 27 MB. We vary the service request rate of IoT nodes according to the list $\mu = \{0.01, 0.02, 0.03, 0.04, 0.05\}$ (requests per second) to investigate the performance of systems in the cases of increasing workload. The input-output ratio of data execution tasks is set to be 0.1 for all the types of data. In addition, we suppose that the output data of all tasks are in the text format.

System Configuration

The fog layer is composed of 25 heterogeneous fog nodes, which are characterized different configurations. In addition, the topology of fog landscape is generated randomly such that the average node degree is 4 for all the simulation scenarios. In this work, the heterogeneity of fog nodes is modeled according to the capability to process data types. We use a powerful (fog) node (e.g., mini data centers, cloudlet platforms) to represent a fog node, which is capable of processing the four types of data. Meanwhile, other fog nodes (i.e., less powerful fogs) are heterogeneous in terms of processing one, two, or three types of data that can play a role as spare computing resources for the powerful nodes. We configure four scenarios of fog deployment, in which each fog node can connect to exactly λ ($\lambda = \{1, 2, 3, 4\}$) powerful nodes in its colony, respectively. In this case, λ is used to represent the scarcity of powerful resources (i.e., powerful fogs), which is an additional dimension of complicated heterogeneity level of fog environment. Hence, as $\lambda = 4$, all the fogs are powerful nodes, which just are discriminated by the computation capability and CPU frequency. Such configuration is used to examine the load sharing capability of fog environment as well as the reliance of cloud. The data processing capability of fogs is featured by computation capability (i.e., CPU processing density) γ and CPU frequency f, which are assumed to be uniformly distributed in U[200, 2000] (cycles/bit) and U[1, 15GHz] (U[10^9, 15×10^9](cycles/s)), respectively [19]. We also assume that the computation capabilities of fogs are the same for processing all the data types. The memory and storage capacity are two other factors characterizing the heterogeneity of fog environment. For all studied scenarios, the powerful fogs have 1 GB of RAM and 6 GB of storage. Meanwhile, these two parameters of the least powerful fogs are randomly selected in the set $\{256, 512\}$ MB of RAM and $\{1, 2, 3\}$ GB of storage, respectively.

Communication Delay and Channel Capacity

The propagation delay can be estimated by having the round-trip time (RTT), which itself can be expressed as RTT(ms) = 0.03 × distance (km) + 5 [25, 42]. Thus, this work assumes that the propagation delay between the IoT nodes and the fog nodes, among fog nodes, and between fog nodes and the cloud servers are uniformly distributed between U[1, 2] (ms), U[0.5, 1.2] (ms), and U[15, 35] (ms) [25], respectively. Furthermore, the data rate between the IoT layer and fog layer is 54 Mb/s according to IEEE 802.11 a/g (i.e., Wi-Fi standard). Meanwhile, the transmission rate between the fog nodes is 100 Mb/s. We assume that there are six hops to connect any fog node to the cloud servers, and the data rate of each hop link is 1 Gb/s.

4.6.2 Comparative Approaches

To evaluate the performance of FRATO-based solutions in terms of average service provisioning delay, the following related approaches are used for the comparative study.

(a) *Optimal Offloading in the Cloud*: As similar to the existing works, forwarding all the requests to the cloud for processing is recognized as a worst-case (i.e., upper bound) approach for examining the role of fog computing in reducing the delay. We also simulate the OFTOC mechanism to observe the system performance.

(b) *Proposed Offloading Solutions:* We verify and evaluate two proposed offloading solutions based on the FRATO framework and the two corresponding resource allocation mechanisms. These two methods are abbreviated as TPRA and MaxRU to show in the figures.

(c) *Related Works:* We employed three offloading policies AFP, POMT, and POST, which are introduced in the related works [25, 32, 33], respectively, to analyze and compare with the performance of our proposed solutions in different scenarios. In AFP mode, deciding on processing the task offloading requests in the fog layer or the cloud servers is determined by two heuristic parameters, namely, fog offloading limit (e_M) and waiting time threshold (θ_{th}) of fogs. Meanwhile, in POMT algorithm, the helper nodes (i.e., role as offloadees in our study), which receive multiple offloading requests, rely on a cost function to make decisions on accepting or rejecting these requests. Accordingly, the cost function calculates the amount of time that a requesting task contributes to the total offloading time of helper nodes in a time slot. In contrast to our FRATO-based solutions and AFP policy, POMT and POST try to accomplish all the tasks in the fog layer without reliance on the cloud (Table 4.3).

Table 4.3 Summarizes all settings for simulation scenarios for comparison and evaluation analysis

Setting	System configuration	Comparative algorithms
#1	All tasks are processed by fogs and clouds. Tasks are splittable. $\lambda = \{1,2,3,4\}$, $\mu = \{0.1,0.2,0.3,0.4,0.5\}$	TPRA, MaxRU, AFP, OFTO$_C$, OFTO$_F$
#2	All tasks are processed by fogs. Tasks are splittable. $\lambda = \{1,2,3,4\}$, $\mu = \{0.1,0.2,0.3,0.4,0.5\}$	OFTO$_F$, TPRA, MaxRU, POMT, POST

4.6.3 Evaluation and Analysis

This section presents and analyzes the performance of systems with respect to the service provisioning delay as different offloading strategies are employed in different simulation scenarios. We conduct the first simulation scenario according to setting #1.

Figure 4.12 depicts the average service delay achieved by five comparative algorithms TPRA, MaxRU, AFP, OFTO$_F$, and OFTO$_C$ as the service request rate μ and the scarcity of powerful fog nodes λ are varied. As expected, the cloud-based solution (OFTO$_C$) totally incurs the longest delay, which resulted from the dominance of delays in communication tasks since the data are transmitted over long distances from the fog layer to the remote cloud server. Meanwhile, OFTO$_F$ utilizes the computing stations (fogs) nearby the data sources (IoT field sensors) to reduce the average delay compared to OFTO$_C$. However, the performance gain of these two offloading scheme is small in cases of high request rate (μ) and high degree of fog resource scarcity (λ) since these two parameters directly cause an increase the task queues of fogs. In parallel, the other fog-based offloading solutions (i.e., TPRA, MaxRU, and AFP) achieve a lower delay regardless the variations of μ and λ. Such result completely confirms the essential role of fog computing platforms in improving the system performance in terms of service delay as recognized in the existing literature. In particular, since the rate of service requests directly impacts on the queuing status of fog nodes, the performance gain obtained by the fog-supported computing systems gets larger in cases of lower μ.

As $\lambda = 4$, all the fogs can process the requesting tasks if they have sufficient resource capability. Such the setting of homogeneous fog environment was used in the related work [25] to verify the performance of AFP offloading policy. Notably, according to the size of tasks set in the simulations of AFP scheme, all requests in our work are heavy tasks; thus, they all can be processed by either the fogs or the cloud instead of the limited computing IoT nodes. Figure 4.12a shows that TPRA and MaxRU enable the system to provide the reduced delay IoT services as compared with AFP. In addition, as μ is higher, more workloads are computed by the cloud in the AFP scheme since the neighbor fog nodes probably have long queues of waiting tasks. Furthermore, the scarcity of powerful computing fogs (i.e., small value of λ) leads to a significant increase in the amount of tasks forwarded to the cloud server in the AFP policy. Therefore, as displayed in Fig. 4.12b–d the performance gap between (OFTO$_C$) and AFP is being narrowed when λ decreases and μ increases. The FRATO-based adaptive offloading mechanism enables more services hosted

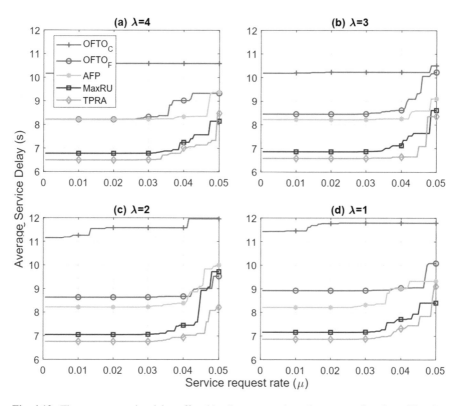

Fig. 4.12 The average service delay offered by the comparative schemes as a function of λ and μ

and processed by the fog landscape through the task division and associated efficient load balancing among the fogs. As a result, the average service delay offered by our proposed solutions is lower than that of AFP regardless of changes of λ and μ. Figure 4.13 supports such claim through the percentage of workload (P_{wl}^F), which is processed by the fog layer. As shown in this figure, as the rate of request is low, the task division mechanism is not significantly beneficial. However, the FRATO-based offloading solutions enable the fogs to serve up to 75% of IoT service requests at the highest request rate ($\mu = 0.05$), which implies approximately only 25% of requests needed to be processed by the cloud. Meanwhile, the comparative scheme (AFP) can handle a smaller percentage of requests (roughly 55%) in the fog layer, and thus, up to 45% requests are forwarded to the cloud.

As the request rates increase, the proposed FRATO-based solutions enable to achieve larger performance gain due to reliable schedules of computation and communication tasks among the involved fogs. In particular, as the scarcity of powerful fogs in the fog environment increase the benefit of task, division-based offloading obtains a significant reduction of service delay. As λ decreases (i.e., number of powerful fogs decreases), more workloads are likely processed by powerful nodes or the cloud if the waiting times in queues of powerful nodes

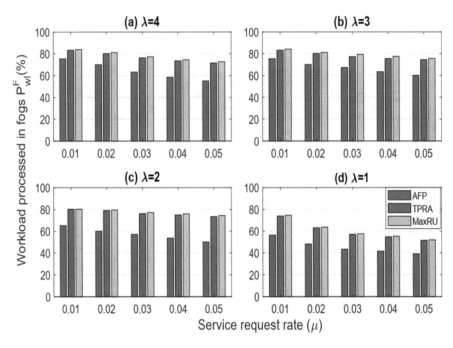

Fig. 4.13 Percentage of workload processed in the fog landscape as a function of λ and μ

overcome the threshold (θ_{th}). Regardless of the location where the requests are hosted, the AFP solution exposes a lack of a mechanism to cope with such a scarcity of complicated heterogeneous fog environment. On the contrary, by splitting the tasks into independent subtasks, less powerful fogs with available resources in TPRA and MaxRU are exploited effectively to process these subtasks. Figure 4.13b–d show the variation of P_{wl}^F in the presence of scarcity of powerful fogs (i.e., decreased values of λ). Basically, the increment of λ increase P_{wl}^F because more powerful fogs can host and share the load. Such result affects equally on all the algorithms. However, due to the adaptive subtask offloading, the FRATO-based offloading strategies enable the fog to process a higher amount of workload as compared with AFP. Practically, it would be the "best" solution to process the entire task locally by primary host, or by a best neighbor fog through offloading. However, since these two approaches are infeasible or not beneficial for the system improvement due to the limitation of heterogeneous fog resources, the task division or cloud is used.

As the cloud is not employed to assist the task offloading, all the service requests are served and processed only by the fog network. In this case, we use the setting #2 to conduct the simulation scenarios and compare the proposed solutions with $OFTO_C$, POMT, and POST. In addition, we modified the solution deployment policy as shown in Fig. 4.10 such that the full task is processed by the powerful fogs in the colony instead of the cloud if the first two task-resource mappings are

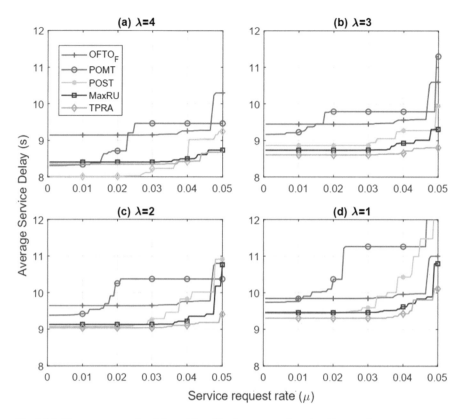

Fig. 4.14 The average service delay achieved by the comparative algorithms as the two parameters μ and λ are varied in the networks

unsuccessful. Furthermore, since transmitting the final computing result to the IoT node is not considered in POMT and POST, we remove the last task of workflow in our work during calculating the service delay. Since the optimal solution is infeasible in the MTMH problem, the fundamental of POMT and POST is to obtain a NE point of game theory through a number of iterations (i.e., decision slots). This point implies a suboptimal mapping between requesting tasks and fog resources at every time slot of task offloading. The simulation results as shown in Fig. 4.14a imply that POMT and POST achieve better performance than the proposed solutions (TPRA, MaxRU) in cases of low request rates because the NE points can be reached within a small number of decision slots. However, as μ is higher, TPRA and MaxRU enable the system to provide lower-delay services.

In particular, as the heterogeneity of fog landscape is added by the scarcity of powerful fog nodes (i.e., $\lambda < 4$), our FRATO-based offloading policies outperform both POMT and POST as illustrated in Fig. 4.14b–d. Additionally, the performance gap is getting larger as λ is smaller and μ is higher. Obviously, that is because neither the fog resource states (i.e., waiting queues (W), λ) nor the request rate (i.e., μ) is considered in both POMT and POST algorithms. Therefore, the increment of workload caused by increasing μ in combination with the lack of powerful nodes for load sharing leads to a larger number of decision slots required to achieve the NE points in POMT and POST. In addition, as studied intensively in [33], POST can offer the lower delay than POMT mainly due to the parallel offloading of subtasks. Although dividing the tasks into multiple independent subtasks is considered as an efficient method to exploit the benefit of parallel processing, it is not always beneficial. For example, in the cases of high request rate, the task division probably causes an increasing conflict of requesting resources. The complexity of conflict is further amplified by decreasing of λ since a larger amount of workload would be handled by a minority of powerful fogs. Such issue can be directly translated into the increment of time slots needed for the fog nodes in POST to reach the suboptimal point. Consequently, the performance of POST gets closer to that of POMT as μ increases and λ decreases.

The performance improvement achieved by the proposed solutions is mainly a result from two main mechanisms: (i) the adaptive task offloading and (ii) fog resource aware allocation. With the employment of these two mechanism, the associated TPRA and MaxRU, can divide the tasks into the subtasks flexibly and then map them efficiently to the fog resources.

4.6.4   Further Analysis of Computation Time and Complexity

The PSO algorithm is based on an iteration mechanism to obtain the optimal solution within the determined search space, thus incurring an additional delay to reach the global optimum. Regarding the computational complexity of the algorithm, in each PSO iteration, the position and velocity of all articles are updated, and their fitness is evaluated. The number of particles N and their dimension D determine the number of calculations required to update the position and velocity of particles. The complexity depends on the number of tasks T in each workflow and the number of fog resources in the colony R used for task-resource mapping. Given that $D = T$ in our proposition, the proposed algorithm has an overall complexity of order $O(N*T^2*R)$ per iteration [40]. The disadvantages of particle swarm optimization (PSO) algorithm are that it is easy to fall into local optimum in high-dimensional space and has a low convergence rate in the iterative process. However, in our algorithm, each workflow contains a small number of tasks, which are further assigned to maximally four fog resources. In addition, the linear feature of cost function enables the algorithms to reach the global optimal solution in a certain number of iterations.

4.7   Conclusions

The paper proposes FRATO—a framework for the IoT-fog-cloud system—to provide the IoT computing services with the context-aware minimized delay. The fundamental of FRATO is to obtain a set of efficient offloading strategies including the optimal and suboptimal solutions to map the computing tasks to the fog and cloud resources. In addition, based on these offloading solutions, two distributed resource allocation mechanisms (TPRA and MaxRU) are developed to effectively handle the conflicts of resource usages and then derive the optimized task-resource mappings. The extensive simulation results show that the proposed solutions enable the systems to reduce the service provisioning delay as compared to the related works. Especially, thanks to the adaptive task offloading strategy, the task division and the associated collaborative task offloading techniques are fully exploited to achieve low delay performance in the systems characterized by complicated heterogeneous fog environments.

4.8   Future Works

The proposed general framework promises multiple open directions to address the limitations of current work.

4.8.1   Data Fragmentation

As evaluated in the simulation results, the data division is a key approach contributing in reducing the delay in the complicated heterogeneous fog environment. However, the diversity of input data structure in practical application requires alternative division solutions for improving or optimizing the system performance. For instance, as the data dependency constraints among the subtasks are taken into account in the associated workflow model, the collaborative task offloading mechanism must be adapted to such a change accordingly. In addition, the data can be divided according to different features, such as by size explicitly. In this way, an optimization can be formulated to find the optimal number of data subsets and associated sizes of data subset for optimizing the system performance.

4.8.2   Distribution of Fog Networks

The distribution of heterogeneous fogs also affects the performance of algorithms. This current work assumed a uniform distribution of fogs in the operating region; thus, workload can be balanced. However, the task imbalance can be a significant issue when the fogs are placed in a non-uniform manner. Therefore, the offloading solutions must be redesigned to deal with such change. In addition, the mobility of fog nodes and/or the end user, which strongly impacts on the fog resource status, must be taken into account in designing the algorithms.

4.8.3 Advance of Optimization Algorithms

We would like to implement different optimization strategies such as mix-integer linear programming (MILP) and compare their performance with PSO. In addition, the algorithms are advanced to reduce the convergence time, thus accelerating the offloading decisions. In this way, we intend to evaluate the performance of systems in providing delay-sensitive services, which are bounded by the predefined deadlines.

4.8.4 Comprehensive Performance Analysis

Finally, the other potential studies include a comprehensive evaluation of system performance in terms of energy consumption, bandwidth utilization, and overall cost to use the fog and cloud services.

References

1. Zanella A, Bui N, Castellani A, Vangelista L, Zorzi M (2014) Internet of things for smart cities. IEEE Internet Things J 1(1):22–32
2. Saleem Y, Crespi N, Rehmani MH, Copeland R (2019) Internet of things-aided smart grid: technologies, architectures, applications, prototypes, and future research directions. IEEE Access 7:62962–63003
3. Chekired DA, Khoukhi L, Mouftah HT (2018) Industrial IoT data scheduling based on hierarchical fog computing: a key for enabling smart factory. IEEE Trans Industr Inform 14(10):4590–4602
4. Jin J, Gubbi J, Marusic S, Palaniswami M (2014) An information framework for creating a smart city through internet of things. IEEE Internet Things J 1(2):112–121
5. Tran-Dang H, Kim D (2018) An information framework for internet of things services in physical internet. IEEE Access 6:43967–43977
6. Botta A, de Donato W, Persico V, Pescape A (2016) Integration of cloud computing and internet of things: a survey. Futur Gener Comput Syst 56:684–700
7. Bonomi F, Milito R, Zhu J, Addepalli S (2012) Fog computing and its role in the internet of things. In: Proceedings of the first edition of the MCC workshop on Mobile cloud computing – MCC '12. ACM Press
8. Dastjerdi AV, Buyya R (2016) Fog computing: helping the internet of things realize its potential. Computer 49(8):112–116

9. Sarkar S, Chatterjee S, Misra S (2018) Assessment of the suitability of fog computing in the context of Internet of things. IEEE Trans Cloud Comput 6(1):46–59

10. Aazam M, Zeadally S, Harras KA (2018) Offloading in fog computing for IoT: review, enabling technologies, and research opportunities. Futur Gener Comput Syst 87:278–289

11. Mattson T, Sanders B, Massingill B (2004) Patterns for parallel programming, 1st edn. Addison-Wesley Professional, Boston

12. Jiang Y-S, Chen W-M (2014) Task scheduling in grid computing environments. In: Advances in intelligent systems and computing. Springer, Cham, pp 23–32

13. Cassar G, Barnaghi P, Wang W, De S, Moessner K (2013) Composition of services in pervasive environments: a divide and conquer approach. In: 2013 IEEE symposium on computers and communications (ISCC), pp 226–232

14. Elgazar A, Harras K, Aazam M, Mtibaa A (2018) Towards intelligent edge storage management: determining and predicting mobile file popularity. In: 2018 6th IEEE international conference on mobile cloud computing, services, and engineering (MobileCloud), pp 23–28

15. Meurisch C, Gedeon J, Nguyen TAB, Kaup F, Muhlhauser M (2017) Decision support for computational offloading by probing unknown services. In: 2017 26th international conference on computer communication and networks (ICCCN), pp 1–9

16. Skarlat O, Nardelli M, Schulte S, Dustdar S (2017) Towards QoS-aware fog service placement. In: 2017 IEEE 1st international conference on fog and edge computing (ICFEC), pp 89–96

17. Skarlat O, Nardelli M, Schulte S, Borkowski M, Leitner P (2017) Optimized IoT service placement in the fog. Service Orient Comput Appl 11(4):427–443

18. Xia Y, Etchevers X, Letondeur L, Coupaye T, Desprez F (2018) Combining hardware nodes and software components ordering-based heuristics for optimizing the placement of distributed IoT applications in the fog. In: Proceedings of the 33rd annual ACM symposium on applied computing, ser. SAC '18. ACM, New York, pp 751–760

19. Zhang G, Shen F, Liu Z, Yang Y, Wang K, Zhou M (2019) FEMTO: fair and energy-minimized task offloading for fog-enabled IoT networks. IEEE Internet Things J 6(3):4388–4400

20. Chen X, Jiao L, Li W, Fu X (2016) Efficient multi-user computation offloading for mobile-edge cloud computing. IEEE/ACM Trans Netw 24(5):2795–2808

21. Xian C, Lu Y-H, Li Z (2007) Adaptive computation offloading for energy conservation on battery-powered systems. In: 2007 international conference on parallel and distributed systems, pp 1–8

22. Huang D, Wang P, Niyato D (2012) A dynamic offloading algorithm for mobile computing. IEEE Trans Wirel Commun 11(6):1991–1995

23. Liu L, Chang Z, Guo X, Mao S, Ristaniemi T (2018) Multiobjective optimization for computation offloading in fog computing. IEEE Internet Things J 5(1):283–294

24. Yao J, Ansari N (2019) Fog resource provisioning in reliability-aware IoT networks. IEEE Internet Things J 6(5):8262–8269

25. Yousefpour A, Ishigaki G, Gour R, Jue JP (2018) On reducing IoT service delay via fog offloading. IEEE Internet Things J 5(2):998–1010

26. Yousefpour A, Patil A, Ishigaki G, Kim I, Wang X, Cankaya HC, Zhang Q, Xie W, Jue JP (2019) FOGPLAN: a lightweight QoS-aware dynamic fog service provisioning framework. IEEE Internet Things J 6(3):5080–5096

27. Mukherjee M, Guo M, Lloret J, Iqbal R, Zhang Q (2020) Deadline-aware fair scheduling for offloaded tasks in fog computing with inter-fog dependency. IEEE Commun Lett 24(2): 307–311

28. Mukherjee M, Kumar S, Mavromoustakis CX, Mastorakis G, Matam R, Kumar V, Zhang Q (2020) Latency-driven parallel task data offloading in fog computing networks for industrial applications. IEEE Trans Industr Inform 16(9):6050–6058

29. Liu J, Zhang Q (2019) Code-partitioning offloading schemes in mobile edge computing for augmented reality. IEEE Access 7:11222–11236

30. Du J, Zhao L, Feng J, Chu X (2018) Computation offloading and resource allocation in mixed fog/cloud computing systems with min-max fairness guarantee. IEEE Trans Commun 66(4): 1594–1608
31. Mukherjee M, Kumar S, Zhang Q, Matam R, Mavromoustakis CX, Lv Y, Mastorakis G (2019) Task data offloading and resource allocation in fog computing with multi-task delay guarantee. IEEE Access 7:152911–152918
32. Yang Y, Liu Z, Yang X, Wang K, Hong X, Ge X (2019) POMT: paired offloading of multiple tasks in heterogeneous fog networks. IEEE Internet Things J 6(5):8658–8669
33. Liu Z, Yang Y, Wang K, Shao Z, Zhang J (2020) POST: parallel offloading of splittable tasks in heterogeneous fog networks. IEEE Internet Things J 7(4):3170–3183
34. Pang A, Chung W, Chiu T, Zhang J (2017) Latency-driven cooperative task computing in multi-user fog-radio access networks. In: 2017 IEEE 37th international conference on distributed computing systems (ICDCS), pp 615–624
35. Al-khafajiy M, Baker T, Al-Libawy H, Maamar Z, Aloqaily M, Jararweh Y (2019) Improving fog computing performance via fog-2-fog collaboration. Futur Gener Comput Syst 100:266–280
36. Masri W, Ridhawi IA, Mostafa N, Pourghomi P (2017) Minimizing delay in IoT systems through collaborative fog-to-fog (f2f) communication. In: 2017 ninth international conference on ubiquitous and future networks (ICUFN), pp 1005–1010
37. Xiao Y, Krunz M (2017) QoE and power efficiency tradeoff for fog computing networks with fog node cooperation. In: IEEE INFOCOM 2017 – IEEE conference on computer communications, pp 1–9
38. Zhang W, Wen Y, Wu DO (2015) Collaborative task execution in mobile cloud computing under a stochastic wireless channel. IEEE Trans Wirel Commun 14(1):81–93
39. Liu Z, Yang X, Yang Y, Wang K, Mao G (2019) DATS: dispersive stable task scheduling in heterogeneous fog networks. IEEE Internet Things J 6(2):3423–3436
40. Rodriguez MA, Buyya R (2014) Deadline based resource provisioning and scheduling algorithm for scientific workflows on clouds. IEEE Trans Cloud Comput 2(2):222–235
41. Kennedy J, Eberhart R (1995) Particle swarm optimization. In: Proceedings of ICNN'95 – international conference on neural networks, vol 4, pp 1942–1948
42. Qureshi A (2010) Power-demand routing in massive geo-distributed systems. PhD dissertation

Chapter 5
Dynamic Collaborative Task Offloading in Fog Computing Systems

Fog computing systems have been widely integrated in IoT-based applications to improve quality of services (QoS), such as low response service delays. This improvement is enabled by task offloading schemes, which perform task computation near the task generation sources (i.e., IoT devices) on behalf of remote cloud servers. However, reducing delay remains challenging for offloading strategies owing to the resource limitations of fog devices. In addition, a high rate of task requests combined with heavy tasks (i.e., large task size) may cause a high imbalance of the workload distribution among the heterogeneous fog devices, which severely impacts the offloading performance in terms of delay. To address this issue, this chapter proposes a dynamic cooperative task offloading approach called DCTO, which is based on the resource states of fog devices, to dynamically derive the task offloading policy. Accordingly, a task can be executed by either a single fog or multiple fog devices through the parallel computation of subtasks to reduce the task execution delay. Through extensive simulation analysis, the proposed approaches showed potential advantages in reducing the average delay significantly in systems with a high rate of service requests and heterogeneous fog environment compared with the existing solutions. In addition, the proposed scheme can be implemented online owing to its low computational complexity compared with the algorithms proposed in related works.

5.1 Introduction

The Internet of Things (IoT) has become an integral element for realizing smart systems, including smart cities [1], smart grids [2], smart factories [3], smart logistics, and supply chains [4, 5]. The fundamental aspect of IoT is to connect all devices through the Internet protocol to exchange high volume data and process them to create smart services and applications [6, 7]. Owing to limited computation resources, network, storage, and energy, IoT devices are inadequate for executing

© The Author(s), under exclusive license to Springer Nature Switzerland AG 2023
H. Tran-Dang, D.-S. Kim, *Cooperative and Distributed Intelligent Computation in Fog Computing*, https://doi.org/10.1007/978-3-031-33920-2_5

computational tasks, especially tasks with huge volumes and complex data structures. Cloud computing is an essential solution to this problem because it provides powerful resources to fulfill tasks efficiently [8, 9]. However, cloud computing-based solutions do not always meet the expected quality of service (QoS) for delay-sensitive applications because of the long physical distance between the IoT devices and the remote cloud servers, scarce spectrum resources, and intermittent network connectivity.

This has led to the emergence of fog computing, which extends the cloud computing resources (i.e., computing, storage, and networking) closer to the data generation sources (i.e., IoT devices), thereby allowing for the prescribed QoS requirements of services and applications to be met by enabling the fog computing devices (e.g., switches, gateways, and hubs) to process and offload most tasks on behalf of the cloud servers in a distributed manner [10, 11]. Consequently, fog computing systems (FCSs) consisting of connected fog computing devices have become essential in IoT-based systems to support uninterrupted services and applications with low response delay along the things-to-cloud continuum [12].

To realize this benefit of fog computing, FCSs require efficient resource allocation strategies to perform task offloading [13]. However, there are many factors that challenge the delay-reduction objective of offloading algorithms. First, an FCS consists of heterogeneous computing devices with different storage capacity, computation, and networking characteristics. In addition, some fog devices support the processing of only one data type such as image, text, video, or audio [14]. In addition, applications such as artificial intelligence (AI) and machine learning (ML) algorithms require the computation of complex tasks, which typically include multiple types of input data. Second, task size also has a significant impact on offloading performance in the FCS. For example, some fog devices are unable to process the entire data of heavy tasks owing to a lack of storage and/or computational capacity. Consequently, more tasks are likely to be queued in more powerful resource fogs, causing long waiting times in the queues. Third, the request rate directly impacts the queuing state of the fogs. Therefore, without an efficient resource allocation policy, a high rate of task requests may lead to a high workload imbalance among the fog devices, as the fog nodes with powerful computing resources may receive more task requests. As a result, the requirements of latency-sensitive applications can be violated because of the excessive waiting time of long task queues.

These typical issues necessitate the development of a dynamic approach based on the fog resource states to make the best context-aware offloading decisions. One possible solution to overcome these issues is to divide the tasks into subtasks, which can then be executed in parallel by the different limited-resource fog nodes to reduce the overall processing delay. In addition, as parallel computation is enabled for the task execution, the task division may also have the potential to balance the workload in heterogeneous fog devices because fog devices with limited available resource can process subtasks instead of the entire task. Practically, this advantageous feature of the divide and conquer concept has been widely adopted and adopted in parallel computing [15], grid computing [16], and service-providing systems [17]. However, a few existing works used the technique in the context of fog computing, to explore and exploit the potential advantages of parallel computation, thereby improving the performance of the FCS in terms of task execution delay.

In these regards, this chapter proposes a dynamic collaborative task offloading (DCTO) scheme that can make the offloading decision dynamically and efficiently based on the available resources of fog computing devices. Summarily, this chapter provides five key contributions as follows:

- We investigate the model of fog computing that can be applied to in some practical IoT systems to provide specific services and applications.
- Based on the properties of service requests (i.e., computation tasks) and the resource states of fog nodes, full and partial offloading models are dynamically applied to utilize the available resources of fog computing devices efficiently.
- An optimal scheduling to schedule the data communication and data execution of subtasks is derived for each single fog node that significantly contributed to achieving the objective of delay reduction.
- A dynamic collaborative task offloading (DCTO) scheme is achieved as an optimal solution of an optimization problem that incorporates the dynamic task offloading and optimal scheduling of data communication and data execution of subtasks.
- Extensive simulations and comparative analysis are conducted to demonstrate and evaluate the performance of DCTO.

5.2 Related Works

A number of offloading algorithms for minimizing task execution delay have been proposed in literature. However, only a few of them analyze the impact of multiple factors simultaneously on the performance of offloading policies such as the task request rate, dynamic task division, and queuing states of fog devices.

In most task offloading solutions, offloading multiple tasks of fog nodes (FNs) to multiple neighbor FNs (i.e., helper nodes (HNs)) is modeled as a multitask multi-helper (MTMH) problem, which aims to allocate the fog computing resources for processing tasks to minimize the average delay of task execution. This problem can be formulated in the form of multi-objective optimization to examine the tradeoff of performance in terms of energy consumption, delay, and execution cost [18–20]. Likewise, in [21], a paired offloading strategy of multiple tasks (POMT) in heterogeneous fog networks was modeled as a strategic game between the FNs and HNs to decide which tasks are offloaded by which HNs to minimize the average task execution delay. Game theory has been applied and developed to obtain the Nash equilibrium (NE) point for the POMT, at which the FCS can achieve near-optimal performance in terms of average delay. The work [22] assessed the role of the fog layer in reducing the service response delay in IoT-fog-cloud systems. An intensive analytical model was derived to examine the impact of communication delays between fog devices, queuing delay, and task sizes on the service response delay. In particular, fog-to-fog communication channels with good conditions were exploited in the proposed task offloading mechanisms to contribute to the overall delay reduction. According to the analytic model, all tasks should be processed by both the fog and cloud to reduce the delay and adaptively balance the workload at the computing fog nodes. However, fog resources were not fully used in these works because the majority of heavy tasks need to be processed by the cloud servers. In addition, none of the aforementioned task offloading approaches consider the division of heavy tasks, which can further reduce the delay through the parallel processing of subtasks while increasing the utilization ratio of fog nodes and reducing the cost of cloud usage.

Regarding task division, most existing works only considered dividing each task into two subtasks. For example, according to the FEMTO model in [23], each task is divided into two subtasks with different data sizes, which are then processed by the IoT node and offloaded to the fog entity. An optimization problem is associated with minimizing the energy consumption of task offloading while achieving a fair workload among the fog nodes and satisfying the deadline constraints of tasks. Similarly, in the task offloading methods introduced in [24, 25], each fog divides the tasks into only two parts, which are processed locally by itself and one HN in parallel. Dividing a task into multiple subtasks was first applied in [26] to exploit the parallel computation of subtasks, thereby reducing the task execution delay. Based on the MTMH problem, a game theory-based algorithm called POST was developed to find the optimal matching pair of subtasks and fog nodes to achieve the delay minimization objective. Accordingly, the number of subtasks for each task was dynamically optimized depending on the number of idle HNs in each time slot and the resource contention update of fogs having tasks in queues. In particular, POST can reach the generalized NE (GNE) fixed-point, thus achieving near-optimal performance in terms of average task execution delay. However, there is a lack of investigation regarding the impact of the queuing status of fog nodes, scheduling of subtasks, and task arrival rate on system performance.

The work [27] introduced an online algorithm for task offloading in the IoT-fog cloud systems, which applies parallel communication and computation at multiple computing nodes (i.e., fog and cloud servers) to minimize latency. Considering the scenarios with varying task arrival rates, the queuing delays of fog nodes are analyzed to optimize the number of tasks offloaded to other computing nodes to achieve the objective. However, the task transmission and computation at the computing nodes are performed according to the first come and first serve (FCFS) scheduling policy rather than the optimal task scheduling policy. In addition, task division is not considered to balance the workload of heterogeneous fog computing nodes. Recently, a recursive computation offloading algorithm (RCO) was developed in [28] to jointly perform task offloading and task scheduling for Fog-Radio Access Networks (Fog-RANs). Considering the execution of tasks residing in a mobile device (MD), the tasks can be offloaded by edge or cloud tiers. The optimization of task scheduling is associated with the RCO to contribute to achieving the delay reduction objective. However, queuing delay and task division have not yet been investigated thoroughly.

5.3 System Model and Problem Formulation

5.3.1 System Model

This chapter considered an FCS, as illustrated in Fig. 5.1, which comprises $N + 1$ fog devices denoted as $F_0, F_1, \ldots,$ and F_N. F_0 serves as a fog controller (e.g., gateway) that can process and distribute tasks to its neighbors, while the other fogs are helper nodes (HNs), which can connect to F_0 directly and have available computation resources to process the tasks assigned and scheduled by F_0. In addition, the FCS can be connected to a cloud for further purposes such as computation, storage, and caching. However, this study aimed to investigate the performance of the FCS when all the tasks are processed only by fog devices without the need for cloud servers. In this context, F_0 involves two main tasks: data transmission (i.e., transmitting the input data of tasks to the intended offloadees) and data processing. The main role of HNs is to process the tasks in queues according to a first-come-first-serve (FCFS) policy.

This FCS model can be deployed in many practical IoT systems, such as smart cities, smart factories, and smart warehouse management systems. Generally, these systems include multiple domains for providing IoT services and applications, and

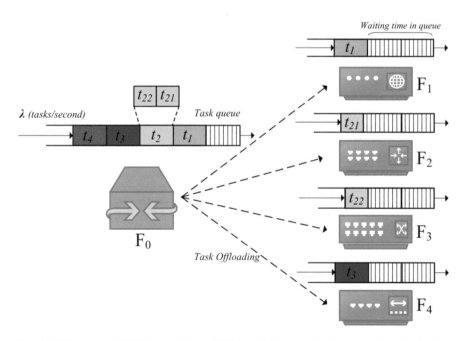

Fig. 5.1 The proposed DCTO model for the FCS, in which some tasks (e.g., task t_2) can be divided into multiple subtasks (e.g., t_{21}, and t_{22}) to reduce the overall task execution delay through parallel computing

Table 5.1 Resource table of neighbors of fog node F_0

| Fog nodes | Specifications and resource status of fog nodes | | | |
	Residual memory M (MB)	Frequency f (GHz)	Processing capability γ (cycles/bit)	Expected waiting time W (seconds)
F_1	128	5	500	1.20
F_2	256	10	600	2.55
F_3	256	15	750	0.68
F_4	512	10	1000	4.22
F_5	1024	20	1200	3.56

each FCS is designed to serve a specific set of services in a single domain such as smart parking services and smart inventory monitoring in the warehouses.

To make an efficient offloading policy, F_0 is based on a table of neighbor resources that contains updated information about the available resources of HNs. We assumed that fog devices of the FCS use a common protocol to communicate and update their resource status periodically [29]. We also assumed that during the offloading decision, the resource states of the HNs are unchanged.

Table 5.1 shows an example of neighbor resource table stored by F_0, which records the resource states of neighbors with respect to the memory capacity of queue buffer (M), CPU frequency (f), CPU processing density (γ), and expected waiting time in the queue (W).

5.3.2 Computational Task Model

Computation tasks arriving at the queue of F_0 follow an exponential distribution with an average rate of λ tasks per second (tasks/s). At a given time, there is a set $T = \{t_1, t_2, \ldots, t_K\}$, including K computational tasks, which reside in the queue of F_0. A single task t_i can be processed by either F_0 or F_k ($k = 1, \ldots, N$). In addition, a task t_i with a size a_i can be divided into $m = N + 1$ subtasks (i.e., t_{ik}, $k = 0, \ldots, N$), which can be processed in parallel by different fog nodes. As illustrated in Fig. 7.1, two subtasks, t_{21} and t_{22}, divided from t_2 can be computed simultaneously by F_2 and F_3, respectively. When $m = 1$, the entire task is processed by a single fog. We define a_{ik} as the data size of subtask t_{ik}; thus, we have

$$\sum_{k=0}^{N} a_{ik} = a_i, \forall t_i \in T. \tag{5.1}$$

For each subtask t_{ik}, we define a vector $\alpha_{ik} = \left(\alpha_{ik}^o, \ldots, \alpha_{ik}^n, \ldots, \alpha_{ik}^N\right)$ to indicate which node is allocated to process t_{ik}. Basically, $\alpha_{ik}^n = 1$ if t_{ik} is computed by F_n, and $\alpha_{ik}^n = 0$, otherwise. Hence, we have

$$\sum_{k=0}^{N} \alpha_{ik}^n = 1, \forall i = 1, \ldots, K \& \forall n = 0, \ldots, N. \tag{5.2}$$

Table 5.2 Summary of key notations

Notation	Description
t_i	Task i
a_i	Size of task i (bits)
t_{ik}	Subtask t_{ik} devided from t_i
a_{ik}	Size of subtask t_{ik} (bits)
T_i^a	Arrival time of t_i at F_0
T_i^t	Start time to transmit t_i to an offloadee by F_0
T_i^p	Start time to process t_i by an offloadee
T_i^f	Finish time of processing t_i by offloadee
D_i, D_{ik}	Total delays for executing t_i and t_k
W_i	Expected waiting time in que of F_i
M_i	Memory capacity of queu buffer of F_i
λ	Arrival rate of tasks at F_0 queue (tasks/s)
F_i	Fog node i
r_{ik}	Data transmission rate from F_i to F_k
f_i	CPU frequency of F_i (cycles)
γ_i	CPU processing density of F_i (cycles/bit)

5.3.3 Problem Formulation

This study paper aimed to develop an online approach for the fog controller F_0 to offload each individual task whenever it arrives at the queue of F_0 so that the execution delay of the task is minimized. Based on the resource table, the algorithm also considers dividing the task dynamically, thereby exploiting the parallel computation of subtasks to achieve the delay reduction objective. In addition, because data transmission and data processing are not performed simultaneously by F_0, the algorithm requires an efficient scheduling mechanism for subtasks. The next section formulates an optimization problem that combines task offloading and subtask scheduling to minimize the execution delay of an individual task. For the sake of clarity, the key notations used in this paper are summarized in Table 5.2.

5.4 Optimization Problem for Minimization of Task Execution Delay

The overall delay for executing task t_i (D_i) is the interval from the arrival time of task (T_i^a) at the queue of F_0 until the end of the processing time (T_i^f) at an offloadee. As illustrated in Fig. 5.2, $D_i = T_i^f - T_i^a$.

Suppose that there is no data dependency between the subtasks of t_i; therefore, the subtasks can be computed in parallel by different HNs. In addition, the results of processing the subtasks need not be aggregated; thus, $D_i = \max\{D_{ik}\}, k = 0, \ldots, N$. Notably, $D_{ik} = T_{ik}^f - T_i^a$. In this sense, besides subtask offloading (i.e., which fog node processes which subtask), subtask scheduling (i.e., which subtask is transmitted or processed first) has a significant impact on the total task execution delay.

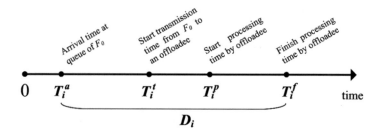

Fig. 5.2 Timeline to calculate the task execution delay

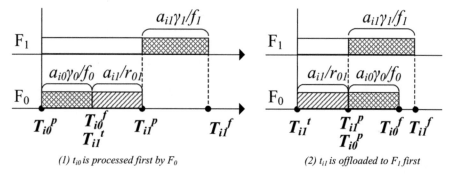

(1) t_{i0} is processed first by F_0   *(2) t_{i1} is offloaded to F_1 first*

Fig. 5.3 T_{ij}^p depends on the relationship between Wn and transmission delay (a_{ij}/r_{0n})

The priority of tasks is not considered during processing; thus, they will be processed according to the FCFS policy in the queue of F_0. In addition, to minimize the execution delay of individual tasks, scheduling is employed for the subtasks of a task. Because data transmission and data processing are not performed simultaneously by F_0, an optimal schedule is required to minimize the delay. Lemma 5.1 specifies an efficient schedule for exploiting the parallel computation of subtasks to reduce the delay.

Lemma 5.1 *When the subtasks of a task are processed by both F_0 and HNs, data transmission is performed before data computation to obtain the benefit of parallel computation.*

Proof Suppose that task t_i is divided into two subtasks, t_{i0} and t_{i1}, which are processed by F_0 and F_1, respectively. We consider the first scenario, as illustrated in Fig. 5.3, in which the queue of F_1 is empty at the time of the offloading decision (i.e., $W_1 = 0$).

We consider case 1, in which t_{i0} is processed first by F_0. The total delay to execute t_{i0} is:

$$D_{i0} = \frac{a_{i0}\gamma_0}{f_0}. \tag{5.3}$$

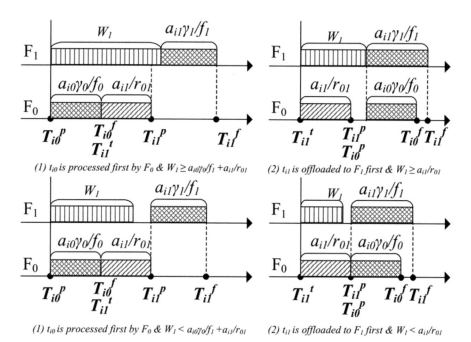

Fig. 5.4 T_{ij}^p depends on the relationship between W_n and transmission delay (a_{ij}/r_{0n})

Because data processing and data transmission are not handled simultaneously by F_0, the total delay to execute t_{i1} including D_{i0}, as the waiting time is calculated by $D_{i1} = D_{i0} + \frac{a_{i1}}{r_{01}} + \frac{a_{i1}\gamma_1}{f_1}$. Because $D_i = \max\{D_{i0}, D_{i1}\}$, $D_i = \frac{a_{i0}\gamma_0}{f_0} + \frac{a_{i1}}{r_{01}} + \frac{a_{i1}\gamma_1}{f_1}$, definitely.

When t_{i1} is processed first in Case 2, the total delay to execute the subtasks is calculated as follows:

$$D_{i1}^* = \frac{a_{i1}}{r_{01}} + \frac{a_{i1}\gamma_1}{f_1}. \tag{5.4}$$

$$D_{i0}^* = \frac{a_{i1}}{r_{01}} + \frac{a_{i0}\gamma_0}{f_0}. \tag{5.5}$$

The total delay to finish t_1 in Case 2 is $D_i^* = \max\{D_{i0}^*, D_{i1}^*\}$. Obviously, $D_i^* < D_i$; the lemma is proved in this case.

We now examine the second scenario where the queue of F_1 is not empty (i.e., $W_1 > 0$), as shown in Fig. 5.4.

In case 1, $D_{i0} = \frac{a_{i0}\gamma_0}{f_0}$ because t_{i0} is executed first by F_0. Moreover, the delay to finish t_{i1} is achieved by:

$$D_{i1} = \begin{cases} W_1 + \dfrac{a_{i1}\gamma_1}{f_1}, & \text{if } W_1 \geq D_{i1} + \dfrac{a_{i1}}{r_{01}}, \\[2mm] D_{i0} + \dfrac{a_{i1}}{r_{01}} + \dfrac{a_{i1}\gamma_1}{f_1}, & \text{otherwise.} \end{cases} \tag{5.6}$$

Obviously, D_i is minimized when $W_1 < D_{i1} + \frac{a_{i1}}{r_{01}}$; thus $D_i = \frac{a_{i0}\gamma_0}{f_0} + \frac{a_{i1}}{r_{01}} + \frac{a_{i1}\gamma_1}{f1}$.

In Case 2 of the second scenario (i.e., t_{i1} is transmitted first to F_1), the delay to finish t_{i0} is $D_{i0}^* = \frac{a_{i0}\gamma_0}{f_0} + \frac{a_{i1}}{r_{01}}$. The execution delay of t_{i1} is as follows:

$$
\begin{cases}
D_{i1}^* = \dfrac{a_{i1}}{r_{01}} + \dfrac{a_{i1}\gamma_1}{f_1}, & \text{if } W_1 < \dfrac{a_{i1}}{r_{01}}, \\[2mm]
\overline{D_{i1}^*} = W_1 + \dfrac{a_{i1}\gamma_1}{f_1}, & \text{if } W_1 \geq \dfrac{a_{i1}}{r_{01}}.
\end{cases}
\tag{5.7}
$$

Recall that the delay to finish t_i is obtained by $D_i^* = \max\{D_{i0}^*, D_{i1}^*\}$, or $D_i^* = \max\{D_{i0}^*, \overline{D_{i1}^*}\}$. Therefore, if $D_i^* = D_{i0}^*$ or $D_i^* = D_{i1}^*$, then $D_i^* < D_i$. This means that Case 2 is beneficial for delay reduction compared with Case 1. If $D_i^* = \overline{D_{i1}^*}$, we also have $D_i^* < D_i$ because the condition $W_1 < \frac{a_{i0}\gamma_0}{f_0} + \frac{a_{i1}}{r_{01}}$ still holds (see Eq. 5.6).

Consequently, DCTO has the potential to reduce the delay only if all subtasks scheduled to be offloaded to HNs are transmitted first from F_0. The lemma is proofed definitely.

Based on the lemma, we define o_{ij}^k to represent the scheduling order between subtask t_{ik} and t_{jk} for wireless transmission. In particular, if t_{ik} is scheduled on a wireless link before t_{jk}, we have $o_{ij}^k = 1$; otherwise, $o_{ij}^k = 0$. Because t_{ik} is transmitted either before or after t_{jk}, we have:

$$
o_{ij}^k + o_{ji}^k = 1, \forall i,j = 0, \ldots, N \& i \neq j.
\tag{5.8}
$$

We define T_{ij}^t as the start time for transmitting t_{ij}. There is no overlap between the wireless transmission times of the two subtasks t_{ij} and t_{ik}; therefore, their start transmission times must satisfy the following:

$$
T_{ij}^t - \sum_{(n=0)}^{N} o_{ik}^n \left(T_{ik}^t + \frac{a_{ik}}{r_{0n}} \right) \geq -L o_{jk}^i,
\tag{5.9}
$$

where L is a large possible constant and $r_{00} = \infty$ indicates that t_{ik} is processed by F_0. Notably, the propagation delay is neglected because it is much smaller than the transmission delay (a_{ik}/r_{0n}).

Additionally, the start processing time T_{ij}^p of t_{ij} must not be smaller than the arrival time at an offloadee as well as the finish time of the last task in the queue of the offloadee (see Fig. 5.5). Therefore,

$$
T_{ij}^p \geq T_{ij}^t + \sum_{n=1}^{N} o_{ij}^n \left(\theta_n W_n + (1 - \theta_n) \frac{a_{ij}}{r_{0n}} \right), \forall j = 0, \ldots, N,
\tag{5.10}
$$

where

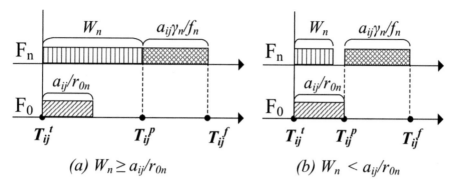

Fig. 5.5 T_{ij}^p depends on the relationship between W_n and transmission delay (a_{ij}/r_{0n})

$$\theta_n = \begin{cases} 1, & \text{if } W_n \geq \dfrac{a_{ij}}{r_{0n}}, \\ 0, & \text{otherwise.} \end{cases} \tag{5.11}$$

Because all the tasks in the queue of F_n $(n = 1, \ldots, N)$ are transmitted only from F_0, the expected waiting time in the queue of F_n can be achieved by:

$$W_n = \gamma_n \sum_i \frac{a_i}{f_n}, \tag{5.12}$$

where $\sum_i a_i$ is the total data size of tasks resided in the queue of F_n.

In addition, the buffer sizes of queues of fog devices are limited, thus

$$W_n \frac{f_n}{\gamma_n} + \sum_{k=0}^{N} \alpha_{ik}^n a_{ik} \leq M_n, n = 1, \ldots, N. \tag{5.13}$$

The end time T_{ij}^f to finish t_{ij} is calculated as follows:

$$T_{ij}^f = T_{ij}^p + \sum_{n=0}^{N} \alpha_{ik}^n \frac{a_{ij}\gamma_n}{f_n} \leq M_n. \tag{5.14}$$

Recall that $D_{ij} = T_{ij}^f - T_i^a$, therefore $D_i = \max_j\{D_{ij} | j = 0, \ldots, N\} = \max_j \left\{ T_{ij}^f \right\} - T_{ij}^a$. The optimization problem P is modeled as follows to minimize D_i:

$$\textbf{P} : \text{Min } D_i$$

$$S.t.(5.1), (5.2), (5.8), (5.10), (5.13), (5.9)$$

The problem P can be solved by linear programming (LP), thus requiring a low computation complexity as compared to the algorithms in the related works. The solutions to the problem P indicate dynamic approaches that specify which tasks and how many subtasks should be divided, which subtask is processed by which fog devices and also the transmission and processing order of subtasks. In the next section, many simulation scenarios are conducted to examine the performance of proposed offloading schemes under the impact of many factors.

5.5　Simulation and Performance Evaluation

5.5.1　Simulation Environment Setup

The event-driven framework supported SimPy library in Python is used to conduct the simulation scenarios, which investigate the performance of DCTO as well as the comparative study with the related algorithms. Table 5.3 summarizes the important parameters and values for the simulation scenario, where $U(x, y)$ indicates the uniform distribution on interval $[x, y]$.

All the simulation results are averaged over 100 simulation rounds, and each round lasts 100 s according to the clock of CPU. We compare the proposed DCTO approach with RCO and POST. Recall that RCO considers to schedule and offload multiple tasks at each time of decision-making, and task division is not employed. In addition, the queuing states of fog devices and task request rate are not taken into account in the RCO algorithm. Meanwhile, POST uses the game theory to find the GNE point for mapping task/subtasks to the fog devices [26]. The impacts of task request rate, task scheduling, and queuing states are not also considered and investigated in POST.

Table 5.3 Parameters for simulation

Parameters	Values
N	{4,5,6,7}
a_i	U(5,10) MB
λ	{0.5, 1.0, 1.5, 2.0, 2.5} tasks/second
M	Randomly in {128, 256, 512, 1024} MB
γ	U(500,1200) (cycles/bit)
f	U(5,20) GHz
r_{oi}	U(100, 150) Mb/s

5.5.2 *Evaluation and Analysis*

We conduct the first simulation scenario, in which all the queues of fog nodes are empty initially. Figure 5.6 depicts the average delay achieved by POST, RCO, and DCTO when λ and N are varied.

DCTO always outperforms RCO and POST because it can dynamically adjust the task offloading decision according to the states of available fog resources. When the queues are empty at the beginning of simulation, there would be no benefits to reduce the delay through task division at the low task arrival rate (i.e., $\lambda = \{0.5, 1\}$). Therefore, DCTO and RCO can obtain similar performance and be better than POST due to the optimal scheduling of tasks. When the task rate increases, the delay is no longer impacted by the queuing states of fog devices. The task division and the associated parallel computation of subtasks are beneficial to cope with the situation. Notably, as the number of HNs increases ($N = 5$), DCTO is able to exploit efficiently the available resource of fogs to perform the parallel computation, thus enabling a gradual delay increase even when the task arrival rate increases.

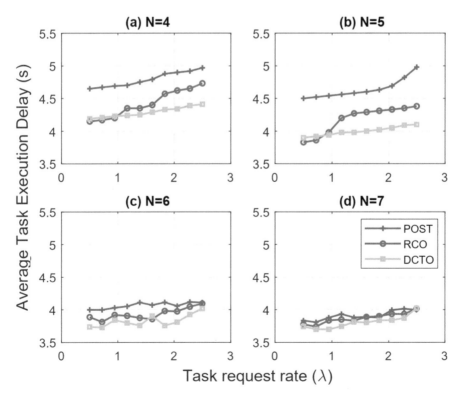

Fig. 5.6 The average execution delay offered by the comparative offloading schemes as a function of λ and N

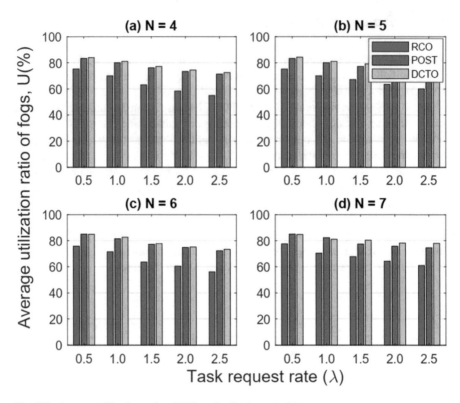

Fig. 5.7 Average utilization ratio of HNs under the impact of λ

Figure 5.7 supports such a claim through the average utilization ratio (U) of HNs. As shown in this figure, the task division employed in the POST and DCTO schemes can increase the utilization ratio of fog computing devices since the limited resource fogs can process the subtasks. As the rate of request is low, the task division mechanism is not significantly beneficial. Although both DCTO and POST use the task division and parallel commutation of subtasks to improve the fog resource utilization, the benefit of delay reduction is not the same. This is because DCTO includes the optimal subtask scheduling based on the resource states of HN to minimize the delay. In addition, POST takes more running time for iteration to reach the near-optimal task-resource mapping.

In the simulation scenario 2, we analyze the impact of queuing state (i.e., waiting time in queue) on the average delay. Initially, all the queues of fog nodes have a number p of tasks, and p is randomly selected from a set $\{1, 2, 3, 4\}$. In addition, the size of task is randomly selected from a set $\{3, 4, 5\}$ (MB). Notably, the expected waiting times (W) in the queues of HNs can be derived as Eq. 5.12. Figure 5.8 shows the average execution task delay obtained by DCTO, RCO, and POST. Besides the improved performance of DCTO as compared to RCO and POST, the simulation result shows that parallel computation and scheduling employed simultaneously in DCTO can decrease the impact of queuing states of fogs effectively. Although the

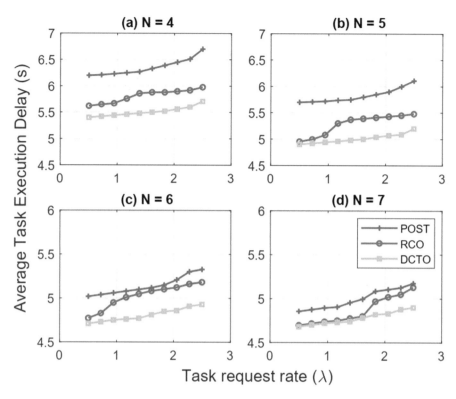

Fig. 5.8 The average task execution delay under the impact of λ, N, and waiting times in the queues of fog nodes

task division and parallel subtask computation are used in POST, the performance efficiency is maximized. That is because POST only tries to obtain the optimal mapping between tasks and subtasks with the available fog resources through time slots. This mechanism is negatively influenced by waiting times in the queues of fog devices. In other words, POST without the usage of scheduling and resource allocation is unable to exploit the fog resources maximally since some fogs with queued tasks are not allocated to perform the task offloading. Meanwhile, DCTO divides the tasks adaptively aiming to schedule and allocate the fog resources for offloading the subtasks effectively. RCO also is unable to maximize the fog resources since the task division is not employed. For example, some fogs with less available computation and storage resources may not be allocated to process single tasks in the RCO algorithms. Meanwhile, they absolutely process subtasks as specified in DCTO if scheduled efficiently.

To examine the impact of task size, we conduct the third simulation scenario, in which all the tasks have the same sizes (i.e., $a_i = a$). Two types of tasks are considered including medium tasks ($a = 5$ MB) and heavy tasks ($a = 10$ MB).

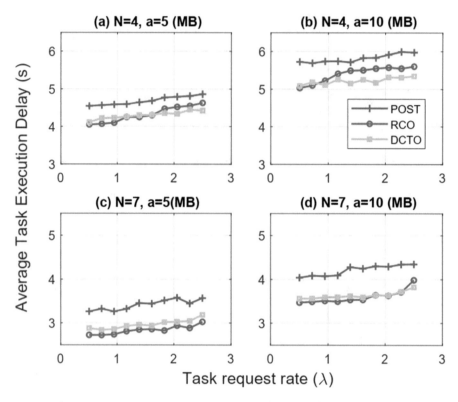

Fig. 5.9 The average task execution delay under the impact of task sizes and number of HNs

Simulation results as shown in Fig. 5.9 indicate that when all the tasks are medium ($a = 5$ MB), the performance of DCTO is not significantly better than RCO since the division of medium size tasks is not beneficial. In addition, DCTO is just to minimize the execution delay of each single task, while RCO can schedule multiple tasks, just achieving a better average task reduction when the task arrival rate is low. However, as the task arrival rate is high, there exist longer queuing delays in some powerful fog devices; thus, the task division employed in DCTO is essential to balance the workload as well as reduce the delay through parallel computation. As a result, the performance of DCTO is slightly improved. As expected, the heavy tasks (i.e., $a = 10$ MB) have significant impacts on the fog computing environment since some fogs with limited resources individually are unable to process the whole data of single task. Therefore, the system performance is affected negatively by workload imbalance of heterogeneous fog devices. Although optimal resource allocation is employed in RCO, the delay is higher than DCTO, which exploits task division and parallel computation to decrease the task execution delay effectively.

5.6 Conclusions and Future Works

This chapter proposes DCTO, a dynamic collaborative task offloading approach for FCS to reduce the delay of task execution. DCTO is used by the fog controller of FCS to derive the offloading solution dynamically based on the state of available resources of HNs. Accordingly, by applying task division technique and the associated parallel computation, DCTO allows a task to be processed by multiple fog computing devices to further reduce the overall task execution delay. The optimal scheduling of subtask transmission and subtask processing is also integrated in the DCTO policy to contribute to the delay reduction objective. The intensive simulation results show that DCTO is an effective offloading solution to achieve reduced execution delay for fog computing environment, in which the resources of fog computing devices are heterogeneous and complicated. Especially, DCTO outperforms the existing related offloading schemes in the scenarios that the rate of task requests is high and task sizes are large.

Future works consider to offload multiple tasks for each time of offloading decision-making. In this case, the scheduling model is required to be redesigned to jointly schedule the order of tasks and also subtasks of different tasks.

References

1. Zanella A, Bui N, Castellani A, Vangelista L, Zorzi M (2014) Internet of things for smart cities. IEEE Internet Things J 1(1):22–32
2. Saleem Y, Crespi N, Rehmani MH, Copeland R (2019) Internet of things-aided smart grid: technologies, architectures, applications, prototypes, and future research directions. IEEE Access 7:62962–63003
3. Chekired DA, Khoukhi L, Mouftah HT (2018) Industrial iot data scheduling based on hierarchical fog computing: a key for enabling smart factory. IEEE Trans Industr Inform 14(10): 4590–4602
4. Tran-Dang H, Krommenacker N, Charpentier P, Kim D-S (2022) The internet of things for logistics: perspectives, application review, and challenges. IETE Tech Rev 39:1–29
5. Tran-Dang H, Krommenacker N, Charpentier P, Kim D (2020) Toward the internet of things for physical internet: perspectives and challenges. IEEE Internet Things J 7(6):4711–4736
6. Jin J, Gubbi J, Marusic S, Palaniswami M (2014) An information framework for creating a smart city through internet of things. IEEE Internet Things J 1(2):112–121
7. Tran-Dang H, Kim D (2018) An information framework for internet of things services in physical internet. IEEE Access 6:43967–43977
8. Rimal BP, Choi E, Lumb I (2009) A taxonomy and survey of cloud computing systems. In: 2009 fifth international joint conference on INC, IMS and IDC, pp 44–51
9. Botta A, de Donato W, Persico V, Pescape A (2016) Integration of cloud computing and internet of things: a survey. Futur Gener Comput Syst 56:684–700
10. Bonomi F, Milito R, Zhu J, Addepalli S (2012) Fog computing and its role in the internet of things. In: Proceedings of the first edition of the MCC workshop on Mobile cloud computing – MCC 2012. ACM Press
11. Sarkar S, Chatterjee S, Misra S (2018) Assessment of the suitability of fog computing in the context of internet of things. IEEE Trans Cloud Comput 6(1):46–59

12. Dastjerdi AV, Buyya R (2016) Fog computing: helping the internet of things realize its potential. Computer 49(8):112–116
13. Aazam M, Zeadally S, Harras KA (2018) Offloading in fog computing for IoT: review, enabling technologies, and research opportunities. Futur Gener Comput Syst 87:278–289
14. Tran-Dang H, Kim D-S (2021) Frato: fog resource based adaptive task offloading for delay-minimizing iot service provisioning. IEEE Trans Parallel Distrib Syst 32(10):2491–2508
15. Mattson T, Sanders B, Massingill B (2004) Patterns for parallel programming, 1st edn. Addison-Wesley Professional
16. Jiang Y-S, Chen W-M (2014) Task scheduling in grid computing environments. In: Advances in intelligent systems and computing. Springer International Publishing, pp 23–32
17. Elgazar A, Harras K, Aazam M, Mtibaa A (2018) Towards intelligent edge storage management: determining and predicting mobile file popularity. In: 2018 6th IEEE international conference on mobile cloud computing, services, and engineering (MobileCloud), pp 23–28
18. Liu L, Chang Z, Guo X, Mao S, Ristaniemi T (2018) Multiobjective optimization for computation offloading in fog computing. IEEE Internet Things J 5(1):283–294
19. Yao J, Ansari N (2019) Fog resource provisioning in reliability-aware iot networks. IEEE Internet Things J 6(5):8262–8269
20. Yousefpour A, Patil A, Ishigaki G, Kim I, Wang X, Cankaya HC, Zhang Q, Xie W, Jue JP (2019) Fogplan: a lightweight QoS-aware dynamic fog service provisioning framework. IEEE Internet Things J 6(3):5080–5096
21. Yang Y, Liu Z, Yang X, Wang K, Hong X, Ge X (2019) POMT: paired offloading of multiple tasks in heterogeneous fog networks. IEEE Internet Things J 6(5):8658–8669
22. Yousefpour A, Ishigaki G, Gour R, Jue JP (2018) On reducing iot service delay via fog offloading. IEEE Internet Things J 5(2):998–1010
23. Zhang G, Shen F, Liu Z, Yang Y, Wang K, Zhou M (2019) Femto: fair and energy-minimized task offloading for fog-enabled IoT networks. IEEE Internet Things J 6(3):4388–4400
24. Liu Z, Yang X, Yang Y, Wang K, Mao G (2019) DATS: dispersive stable task scheduling in heterogeneous fog networks. IEEE Internet Things J 6(2):3423–3436
25. Mukherjee M, Kumar S, Mavromoustakis CX, Mastorakis G, Matam R, Kumar V, Zhang Q (2020) Latency-driven parallel task data offloading in fog computing networks for industrial applications. IEEE Trans Industr Inform 16(9):6050–6058
26. Liu Z, Yang Y, Wang K, Shao Z, Zhang J (2020) Post: parallel offloading of splittable tasks in heterogeneous fog networks. IEEE Internet Things J 7(4):3170–3183
27. Lee G, Saad W, Bennis M (2019) An online optimization framework for distributed fog network formation with minimal latency. IEEE Trans Wirel Commun 18(4):2244–2258
28. Guo K, Sheng M, Quek TQS, Qiu Z (2020) Task offloading and scheduling in fog ran: a parallel communication and computation perspective. IEEE Wireless Commun Lett 9(2):215–218
29. Al-khafajiy M, Baker T, Al-Libawy H, Maamar Z, Aloqaily M, Jararweh Y (2019) Improving fog computing performance via fog-2-fog collaboration. Futur Gener Comput Syst 100:266–280

Chapter 6
Fundamentals of Matching Theory

'

Matching theory has been considered and applied in practical systems to handle the rational and selfish problems of agents, offering mutational benefits for them over time. This chapter presents the fundamental concepts of matching theory, describing the classified models, their structures, and algorithmic aspects. The conventional applications of using matching theory are also reviewed and discussed.

6.1 Introduction

So far, the mathematical optimization models have been mostly used to provide the optimal solutions for resource allocation and combinatorial problems of systems and organization. To formulate these kinds of models, the general assumption is to achieve global information regarding the states of systems. However, in practice, acquiring all the updated information of the complete systems is challenging due to the dynamic nature. In addition, these solutions require a centralized control to gather the global system information, thus incurring a significant overhead and computation complexity of algorithms. This complexity is further amplified by the rapid increase of density of systems and when dealing with combination integer programming problems [1] Furthermore, in these systems, the selfishness and rational nature of individual agents expose the coupling resource problems, which are hard to be solved.

The aforementioned limitations of optimization have led to a second group of solutions that apply the noncooperative game theory to avoid the cost-intensive centralized resource management as well as substantially reduce the complexity of algorithms. Game theory has been widely exploited to formulate efficient resource allocation and management models in the complex systems and organizations ranging from economy, politics, and philosophy to sociology disciplines [2–4]. However, traditional game theory-based solutions can only deal with simple scenarios. In many complex networks, different types of agents with various characteristics and requirements can interact with each other exposing complex interactions among different sets of agents. Game theory may fail to be used for modeling and designing an efficient solution in these scenarios. In addition, the classical game theoretical algorithms such as best response require some information regarding the actions of other players [5].

Correspondingly, many assumptions are introduced in the game theory-based algorithms to simplify the system models that, in some cases, are impractical. Moreover, most game-theoretic solutions, for example, Nash equilibrium, investigate one-sided stability notions in which equilibrium deviations are evaluated unilaterally per player. Meanwhile, the stability must be achieved by both sides of players of the systems because they have different roles.

Recently, matching theory (MT) [6, 7] has been considered to be a powerful tool, which can alleviate the shortcomings of game theory and optimization-based approaches. Basically, MT can support the examination of the formation of dynamic and mutually beneficial relations among different types of rational and selfish agents in complex systems. In particular, the MT-based algorithms can be implemented in a distributed manner with low computation complexity and have been shown to offer high performance for the overall systems. In particular, it can deal with the high dynamics of systems, selfish, competitive, and distributed nature of systematic elements, limited radio resources, and dynamic nature of different agents.

Matching theory has been widely used to develop programs and platforms to find stable matching in practical applications, such as stable marriage, stable roommate problem, college admission problem, kidney exchange [8], carpooling [9], and dynamic ride-sharing [10, 11]. In particular, the national resident matching program (NRMP) creates huge platforms to support deriving matching solutions for practical applications such as labor market, resident-hospital problem, and doctor-hospital problems in the United States.

6.2   Basic Concepts and Terminologies

Although most of matching models in the literature deal with two sets of agents, there are other matching models involving only one set (i.e., stable roommate problem [12]) and three sets of agents [13].

The inherent presence of selfishness and rational of agents prevents the systems to derive global optimal solutions of combinatorial problems. The objective of matching games is to achieve stability instead of optimality, at which there is no incentive incurred to devise the currently matched pairs of agents. Alternatively, a matching is to stably match agents in two sets based on their individual, objectives, and exchanged information. Each agent builds a ranking of other agents in the other side individually using a preference relation, thus creating its own preference list (PL). Depending on the characteristics of agents, PLs can be in three forms: complete, ties, and incomplete PL with ties. Basically, a preference can be calculated based on an objective utility function that quantifies the QoS achieved by a certain matching between two agents of two sides. Based on the created PLs, agents can implement distributed algorithms as described following to derive the matching outcome.

6.3 Classification

The matching models developed and applied in the different contexts can be classified in many ways. For example, the study [14] considers canonical, matching with externalities, matching with dynamics model for solving the resource allocation problems in the wireless communication networks. Regarding the number of agent sets involved in the matching game, the game can be played by one, two, and three sets of players. The typical matching model for one set of agent is roommate matching problem [12, 15]. Meanwhile, the matching models involving three sets of agents such as in the works [13, 16] are rarely studied. The most used and studied matching models in the practice emphasize on the two disjoint sets of agents, which can expose three typical models as follows based on the capacity/quota allowed to match for each agent. Figure 6.1 illustrates three stable matching models including one-to-one (OTO), many-to-one (MTO), and many-to-many (MTM) models.

In the following, we present and discuss the concepts and key properties of these three matching models.

6.3.1 One-to-One (OTO) Matching

The most prominent model of OTO matching is the marriage model. In this model, there are two distinct sets of agents represented by $X = \{x_1, x_2, \ldots, x_n\}$ and $Y = \{y_1, y_2, \ldots, y_n\}$, respectively. Each agent has a complete PL over the agents on the other

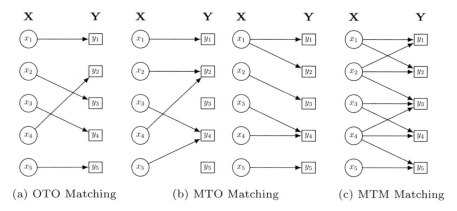

(a) OTO Matching   (b) MTO Matching   (c) MTM Matching

Fig. 6.1 Three major types of stable matching models

side. Assume that an arbitrary agent x in X has a PL denoted as $P(x) = \{y_2, y_4, x, y_1, y_3, \ldots\}$. This means that x prefers agent y_2 to y_4 and prefers remaining single (x) over matching with y_1 or y_3. Denote $y_i >_x y_j$ to express that an agent x prefers agent y_i to y_j in the matching game. In particular, as $y_i \geq_x y_j$, there exists a tie in the PL of agent x. In summary, the OTO matching model is defined as follows:

Definition 6.1
The outcome of the OTO matching model is a matching function $M : X \cup Y \rightarrow X \cup Y$ such that the three following constraints are satisfied:

- For any $x \in X$, $M(x) \in Y \cup \{x\}$
- For any $y \in Y$, $M(y) \in X \cup \{y\}$
- For any $x \in X$ and $y \in Y$, $x = M(y)$ if and only if $y = M(x)$

In the one-to-one matching model, each agent x can only be matched with one agent y, and x remains unmatched if $M(x) = x$. The objective of matching is to reach a stable status for all pairs.

Definition 6.2
A matching M is pairwise stable if there is no block pair (x, y).

Definition 6.3
(x, y) is a block pair for a matching M if the three following conditions are satisfied:

- $M(x) \neq y$
- $y >_x M(x)$
- $x >_y M(y)$

6.3.2   Many-to-One (MTO) Matching

In the MTO matching modes, each agent of one side can be matched with multiple agents of the other side, but the reverse is not valid. In particular, each agent y has a positive quota q_y to represent the maximum number of agents in the set X it can be matched with. Similar to the OTO matching, $P(y) = \{x_1, x_2, y, x_4, x_5\}$ represents the PL of agent y, which illustrates that the agent y prefers x_1 to x_5 and prefers keeping the position unfilled over other agents like x_4 and x_5. Generally, the MTO matching can be defined as follows:

Definition 6.4
The outcome of the MTO matching model is a matching function $M : X \cup Y \rightarrow X \cup Y$ such that the three following constraints are satisfied:

- $|M(x)| = 1$ for every $x \in X$, and $M(x) = x$ *if x is unmatched*
- $|M(y)| = q_y$ for every $y \in Y$; if the number of agents in $M(y)$ is k *and* $k < q_y$, *then* $M(y)$ *will have* q_y-k *copies of y*
- $M(y) = x$ if and only if *x is an element of M(y)*

With this definition, $M(x) = y$ means that agent x is matched with agent y, and $M(y) = \{x_1, x_2, y, y\}$ indicates that the agent y with the quota $q_y = 4$ has been matched with two agent x_1 and x_2 and has two unfilled matching positions. The objective of MTO matching is to obtain the stable matching, which is defied in the same way as OTO matching.

6.3.3 Many-to-Many (MTM) Matching

In the models of MTM matching, the number of matchings for the agents on both sides is not restricted to one. Denote q_x and q_y as the respective quotas for agents $x \in X$ and $y \in Y$. Generally, the MTM matching is defined as follows:

Definition 6.5
The outcome of the MTM matching model is a matching function $M : X \cup Y \rightarrow X \cup Y$ such that the three following constraints are satisfied:

- $|M(x)| = q_x$ for every $x \in X$; if the number of agents in $M(x)$ is k *and* $k < q_x$, *then* $M(x)$ *will have* q_x-k *copies of* x
- $|M(y)| = q_y$ for every $y \in Y$; if the number of agents in $M(y)$ is m *and* $m < q_y$, *then* $M(y)$ *will have* q_y-m *copies of* y
- $M(y) = x$ if and only *if x is an element of* $M(y)$

The objective of MTM matching is to obtain stable matching, which is defined in the same way as OTO and MTO matching.

6.3.4 Variants of Matching Models

Depending on the specific structure and properties of systems and agents, additional features can be integrated into the above three matching models, resulting in wide variants of matching models [17].

Matching with Externaties

Externalities refer to factors causing change of preference relations when a couple of agents are matched. Therefore, the preferences of any agent depend not only on the properties and characteristics of itself but also on the information of the entire matchings.

Matching with Transfer

When the agents have any transactions during matching process, the model is called transfer matching. The transaction between two agents of two sets can impact on the utility functions, just sequentially changing the preference relations. There are many kinds of transactions and transfer considered in the relevant literature including real money, fictitious money, credit, and services.

Matching with Incentive

The nature of selfishness and rationality of agents can prevent them from participating in the matching processes because they just want to maximize their own utilities without taking into account the other ones and the overall system performance. Therefore, there is a need for incentive integration to encourage the agents to join in the matching procedure.

Matching with Groups

In many scenarios of MTO and MTM matching problems, certain groups of agents prefer to match with individual agents of the opposite side [18, 19]. For example, some pairs of students ("couples") would like to be assigned to universities that are geographically close together. Some couples of doctors would like to be assigned to same hospital in NRMP and labor markets.

Matching with Variants of PLs

There are various types of preference relations among agents as described in the following, which result in different models of matchings.

A. *Complete and Incomplete PLs*: When all agents of one side are present in the list of all agents of the other side, the PLs are complete. On the contrary, incomplete PLs are used to indicate that some agents have no chance to pair with each other. For example, in the network, some nodes that are out of their communication range are unable to communicate, just no pairing established between them.

B. *PLs with Ties*: When the PL of an agent has multiple elements (i.e., agents of opposite side) with the same preference value, the PL is called PL with a tie. In this case, the outcome of matching is of among three stability that are weak stability, strong stability, and super-stability.

6.4   Matching Algorithms

The basic algorithm, known as deferred acceptance (DA), was introduced first in [20] to find the one-to-one stable matching for the marriage problem. This algorithm can reach the convergence in the polynomial time for the one-to-one matching problems and very fast for the many-to-one matching models. Fundamentally, DA is an iterative method over the players of sets, in which one side proposes and the other side decides to reject or accept the proposal based on PLs. With this approach, DA is completely distributed since the play is just based on the local information for deriving the decisions. Algorithm 6.1 shows the key procedures to implement the DA algorithm to achieve the outcome for the one-to-one matching problem. The DA algorithm is used and developed to support other matching problems based on the application scenarios.

Algorithm 6.1: The Classical DA Algorithm for One-to-One Matching Problem

---

   Input: $\mathcal{P}(x)$, $\mathcal{P}(y)$
    // Preference lists of x and y
   Output: $\mathcal{M}$
1 **begin**
2 | Initialize: $\mathcal{M}(x) = x$ & $\mathcal{M}(y) = y$, $\forall x \in \mathcal{X}$, $\forall y \in \mathcal{Y}$
         // All agents x and y are unmatched
3 | **while** $\exists x \, (\mathcal{M}(x) = x)$ **do**
4 | $\mathcal{M}(x) \leftarrow y \, (y = \mathcal{P}(y)[0])$
             // Proposing the first $y \in \mathcal{P}(y)$ to be matched with x
5 | **if** $\mathcal{M}(y) = y$ **then**
6 | $\lfloor$ $\mathcal{M}(x) = y$ // Match y with x
7 | **else**
8 | $\mathcal{M}(y) = x'$ // y is already matched with x'
9 | **if** $x \succ_y x'$ **then**
10 | $\mathcal{M}(x) = y$ // Match x with y
11 | $\mathcal{M}(x') = x'$ // x' becomes unmatched
12 | **else**
13 | $\mathcal{M}(x) = x$ // x is still unmatched
14 | $\mathcal{M}(y) = x'$ // (x', y) remains matched

The DA algorithm has been widely used to achieve the stable matching for many problems such as marriage, roommate, and college admission in polynomial time. The classical marriage problem involves two sets of men and women with the equal number of player in each set. The DA algorithm is used to achieve the stable matching. Indeed, there are many stable matchings depending on the proposing side. However, the DA algorithm based on the proposal mechanism results in biased outcome. That is the optimal matching of one side, which incidentally is also the worst stable matching for the other side of the market.

The inequitable treatment of the participants on different sides of the market persists in most known matching mechanisms. This has motivated the need for the design of fair stable matching mechanisms, which do not overtly favor one side of the market over the other. Considerable efforts have been devoted to finding "fair" stable matchings that satisfy some more equitable or egalitarian criterion of optimality such as minimization of the sum of the ranks of matched agents and regret minimization of matched agents [21]. The studies [15, 22] introduced the efficient algorithms for the stable roommate and stable marriage problems that maximize the satisfactory level of matched players. The fundamental behind the algorithms is the unique properties of stability that integrate the rotation concept and graph-theoretic methods to build the stable matching. The algorithms can ensure to achieve the stable matching in $O(n^4)$ time, where n is number of players in each side.

In some research works, the probabilistic distribution is integrated to study the fairness in the matchings [23] that examine three typical probabilistic stable matching mechanisms: employment by lotto [24], the random order mechanism [25, 26], and the equitable random order mechanism [27]. The analysis shows that the three randomized mechanism results in different matching outcomes.

Recently, deep learning (DL) is used to approximate the stable matching [28]. The proposal and procedure algorithms mentioned above can achieve the stability but strategy-proofness (SP). DL can be developed to examine the tradeoff between these two criteria given the ordinal preference inputs of agents.

6.5   Conclusions

This chapter presented the fundamentals of matching theory (MT) covering the conceptual definition, mathematical models, matching model classification, and classical algorithmic solution. The major primary applications of MT have been briefly received that include the practical market (marriage markets, advertisement markets, and kidney exchange market), economy, job assignments, college admission, and National Resident Matching Program (NRMP). More focus is devoted to presenting the algorithms to achieve stable matchings. Apart from the DA algorithm known as proposal algorithm, there have been many mechanisms developed to find stable matchings that satisfy some optimal criteria.

References

1. Guo K, Sheng M, Quek TQS, Qiu Z (2020) Task offloading and scheduling in fog ran: a parallel communication and computation perspective. IEEE Wireless Commun Lett 9(2):215–218
2. Dasilva LA, Bogucka H, Mackenzie AB (2018) Game theory in wireless networks. IEEE Commun Mag 49(8):110–111
3. Debbah M (2008) Mobile flexible networks: the challenges ahead. In: 2008 international conference on advanced technologies for communications, pp 3–7
4. Hossain E, Niyato D, Han Z (2019) Dynamic spectrum access and management in cognitive radio networks. Cambridge University Press
5. Durand S, Gaujal B (2016) Complexity and optimality of the best response algorithm in random potential games. In: Symposium on algorithmic game theory (SAGT), pp 40–51

6. Roth AE (2007) Deferred acceptance algorithms: history, theory, practice, and open questions. National Bureau of Economic Research, Working Paper 13225
7. Roth AE, Sotomayor MAO (2013) Two-sided matching: a study in game-theoretic modeling and analysis, Ser. Econometric society monographs. Cambridge University Press
8. Park K, Moon JI, Kim SI, Kim YS (1999) Exchange donor program in kidney transplantation. Transplantation 67(2):336–338
9. Ostrovsky M, Schwarz M (2019) Carpooling and the economics of self-driving cars. In: Proceedings of the 2019 ACM conference on economics and computation, Ser. EC'19. Association for Computing Machinery, New York, pp 581–582
10. Ozkan E, Ward AR (2020) Dynamic matching for real-time ride sharing. Stoch Syst 10(1): 29–70
11. Schreieck M, Safetli H, Siddiqui SA, Pflugler C, Wiesche M, Krcmar H (2016) A matching algorithm for dynamic ridesharing. Transp Res Procedia 19:272–285
12. Gusfield D (1988) The structure of the stable roommate problem: efficient representation and enumeration of all stable assignments. SIAM J Comput 17(4):742–769
13. Eriksson K, Sjostrand J, Strimling P (2006) Three-dimensional stable matching with cyclic preferences. Math Soc Sci 52(1):77–87
14. Gu Y, Saad W, Bennis M, Debbah M, Han Z (2014) Matching theory for future wireless networks: fundamentals and applications. IEEE Commun Mag 53(5):52–59
15. Irving RW (1985) An efficient algorithm for the stable roommates problem. J Algorithms 6(4): 577–595
16. Lam C-K, Plaxton CG (2019) On the existence of three-dimensional stable matchings with cyclic preferences. Theory Comput Syst 66(3):679–695
17. Iwama K, Miyazaki S (2008) A survey of the stable marriage problem and its variants. In: International conference on informatics education and research for knowledge-circulating society (ICKS 2008), pp 131–136
18. Klaus B, Klijn F (2005) Stable matchings and preferences of couples. J Econ Theory 121(1): 75–106
19. Aldershof B, Carducci OM (1996) Stable matchings with couples. Discret Appl Math 68(1–2): 203–207
20. Gale D, Shapley LS (1996) College admissions and the stability of marriage. Am Math Mon 69(1):9–15
21. Johnson R (1989) The stable marriage problem: structure and algorithms (Gusfield D, Irving R, eds), vol 24, no 2. MIT Press, Cambridge, MA, pp 129–130
22. Irving RW, Leather P, Gusfield D (1987) An efficient algorithm for the "optimal" stable marriage. J ACM 34(3):532–543
23. Klaus B, Klijn F (2006) Procedurally fair and stable matching. Economic Theory 27(2): 431–447
24. Aldershof B (1999) Refined inequalities for stable marriage. Constraints 4(3):281–292
25. Ma J (1996) On randomized matching mechanisms. Economic Theory 8(2):377–381
26. Roth AE, Vate JHV (1990) Random paths to stability in two-sided matching. Econometrica 58: 1475–1480
27. Romero-Medina A (2005) Equitable selection in bilateral matching markets. Theor Decis 58(3): 305–324
28. Ravindranath SS, Feng Z, Li S, Ma J, Kominers SD, Parkes DC (2021) Deep learning for two-sided matching. ArXiv abs/2107.03427

Chapter 7
Matching Theory for Distributed Computation in IoT-Fog-Cloud Systems

This chapter provides a state-of-the-art review regarding matching theory-based distributed computation offloading frameworks for IoT-fog-cloud (IFC) systems. In this review, the key solution concepts and algorithmic implementations proposed in the literature are highlighted and discussed thoroughly. Given the powerful tool of matching theory, its full capability is still unexplored and unexploited in the literature. We thereby discover and discuss existing challenges and corresponding solutions that the matching theory can be applied to resolve them. Furthermore, new problems and open issues for application scenarios of modern IFC systems are also investigated.

7.1 Introduction

Practically, the Internet of Things (IoT) has become an integral element for realizing smart practical systems such as smart cities [1], smart factories [2], smart logistics, and supply chain [3, 4]. The fundamental aspect of IoT-based systems is to connect all devices through the Internet protocol to exchange high volume data and process them to create smart services and applications. Owing to limited computation resources, network, storage, and energy, IoT devices are inadequate for executing all computational tasks, especially tasks with huge volumes and complex data structures. Cloud computing is an essential solution to this problem because it provides powerful resources to fulfill tasks efficiently [5, 6]. However, cloud computing-based solutions do not always meet the expected quality of service (QoS) and quality of experience (QoE) requirements for some classes of IoT applications, especially latency-sensitive ones because of the long physical distance between the IoT devices and the remote cloud servers, scarce spectrum resources, and intermittent network connectivity.

This has led to an integration of fog computing in the middle between the IoT and cloud layer to process and offload most tasks on behalf of the cloud servers, thereby allowing for the QoS and QoE requirements to be met [7, 8]. Besides providing cloud-like services to EUs, fog computing potentially improves the performance of fog-based systems such as reduction of service delay [9] and energy saving [10]. Recently, the advance of networking generation (i.e., 5G and beyond) leads to an increasing demand for ubiquitous computing and pervasive service access by a numerous number of Internet-connected mobile devices and end users (EUs). Motivated by the necessity of network architecture enhancement, a paradigm of fog radio access networks (F-RANs) has emerged as a promising evolution architecture for 5G networks [11, 12], which along with cloud radio access networks (C-RANs) [13] provide the pervasive computing services. Therefore, F-RANs provide great flexibility to satisfy QoS requirements of various 5G-based services and applications.

To further realize the above benefits of computing paradigms, the IFC systems require efficient resource allocation and management strategies to perform computational offloading operations [14]. However, there are many factors that challenge the design and development of effective offloading strategies such as the heterogeneity of computing devices and various types of computational tasks with different requirements [15]. There are a large number of centralized optimization techniques and algorithms proposed in the literature to provide optimal solutions to the aforementioned resource allocation problems [16]. However, these solutions require a centralized control to gather the global system information, thus incurring a significant overhead and computation complexity of algorithms. This complexity is further amplified by the rapid increase in density and heterogeneity of IFC computing systems [17].

The aforementioned limitations of optimization have led to a second group of solutions that apply the noncooperative game theory to avoid the cost-intensive centralized resource management as well as substantially reduce the complexity of algorithms [18, 19]. Despite their potentials, such approaches pose several limitations. First, classical game theoretical algorithms such as best response require some information regarding actions of other players [20]. Correspondingly, many assumptions are introduced in the game theory-based algorithms to simplify the system models that, in some cases, are impractical. Second, most game-theoretic solutions, for example, Nash equilibrium, investigate one-sided stability notions in which equilibrium deviations are evaluated unilaterally per player. In addition, in the IFC systems, the stability must be achieved by both sides of players including the resource providers and resource requesters.

Ultimately, managing resource allocation effectively in such a complex environment of IFC systems leads to a fundamental shift from the traditional centralized mechanism toward distributed approaches. Recently, matching theory has emerged as a promising technique for resource allocation problems in many applications, which can alleviate the shortcomings of game theory and optimization-based approaches. Alternatively, while the optimization and game theory-based solutions are efficient in some limited scenarios, the matching-based approaches have potential advantages owing to the distributed and low computational complexity algorithm. However, to reap the benefits of matching theory for task offloading and resource allocation in fog environment, there is a need of advanced frameworks to handle their intrinsic properties such as heterogeneity of fog computing devices as well as the novel QoS demands of future generation systems. This directly exposes new challenges and associated open issues.

In these regards, this chapter provides three important contributions as follows.

- A model of IFC systems and related concepts such as architecture, computation tasks, computation offloading models, and a generic optimization form of task offloading problems are escribed to highlight the intrinsic properties of fog-based computing systems.
- An intensive literature review is conducted to discuss and investigate the proposed matching-based distributed computation offloading frameworks.
- Existing challenges and open issues are explored and discussed to provide the future directions of researches and development regarding the usage of matching theory in the new problems and applications.

7.2 System and Offloading Problem Description

7.2.1 System Model

A general IFC system with three-tier architecture is illustrated in Fig. 7.1. The system consists of three layers: IoT, fog, and cloud, which are connected by LAN and WAN to provide various services for IoT-connected users such as computing, caching, storage, and networking services.

The IoT layer is recorded by a set $I = \{d_1, d_2, \ldots, d_{|I|}\}$ of IoT nodes, which generate computation tasks recorded in a set $T = \{T_1, T_2, \ldots, T_{|T|}\}$. Similarly, $F = \{F_1, F_2, \ldots, F_{|F|}\}$ and $C = \{C_1, C_2, \ldots, C_{|C|}\}$ represent the sets of fog nodes (FNs), and cloud servers, respectively. In practical applications, FNs are grouped into clusters, and each provides a set of specific IoT applications for the end users (EUs). Generally, FNs in each domain are deployed in a distributed manner. In some scenarios, there is a presence of centralized fog controllers such as fog service providers (FSPs) to manage the fog resources in the domains as well as security-related issues. In many scenarios, the cloudlets [21] and micro data centers (mDCs) [22, 23] are added to the fog domains to enhance the computing capability as mini-servers.

7.2.2 Computational Tasks

Each computing task T_k can be described with a tuple $T_k = \langle A_k, O_k, B_k, D_k \rangle$, where A_k and O_k represent the input and output data size (bits) of task, B_k is the computational resource demands to execute the task, and D_k is the deadline to process T_k. The input

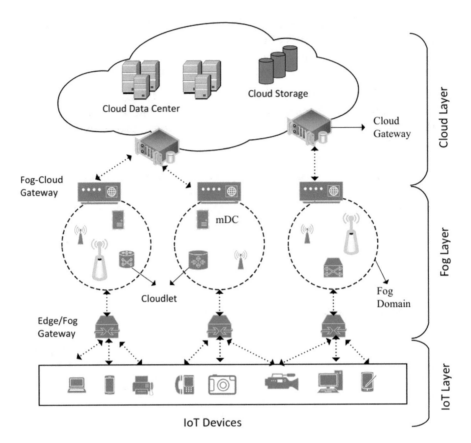

Fig. 7.1 The typical architecture of IFC systems

data sizes of tasks can be ranged from kilobytes to terabytes depending on specific applications [24]. Based on this feature, the tasks can be classified into light, medium, and heavy tasks [9, 25].

Task divisibility is also investigated in offloading cases. As a task is indivisible, its entire data is definitely processed by a single computing device (e.g., FN, cloud, or even a powerful IoT node). In many scenarios, a single task can be divided into multiple subtasks based on data size and data type. Such task division is employed to get benefit from parallel computing since the subtasks can be processed by different devices simultaneously [26, 27]. Regarding the resources needed for computation offloading operations, some of the existing works just only consider B_k as the number of central processing units (CPU cycles) [28]. In another scenario, GPU and memory requirements are considered during resource allocation for executing heavy and complex tasks such as the AI and ML ones [29].

7.2.3 Computational Offloading Model

Depending on application scenarios, appropriate offloading models are formed to support the systems to achieve their ultimate objectives such as minimization of total energy consumption, minimization of offloading delay, maximization of resource utilization, and fairness and balance of workload. Besides the system objectives, designing an offloading model depends on multiple factors including the system architecture, the task properties to derive efficient algorithms that determine offloading locations, times to offload, and how a task is offloaded (how data of task is handled). In the following paragraphs, we summarize and discuss these relevant aspects to highlight the key features of offloading models in the literature.

Regarding the offloading locations, there are two major classes of offloading models including intra-layer and inter-layer offloading. The former refers to models allowing offloading operations to take place within a layer, whereas the latter involves multiple layers. In the IoT layer, the emergence of device-to-device (D2D) communication in 5G networks makes the computational offloading between IoT devices ubiquitous in future IFC systems. Similarly, tasks can be offloaded within the fog layer and cloud layer, mainly to balance the workload as well as improve the resource utilization of FNs and cloud servers [30].

In most of the application scenarios, the offloading processes involve multiple layers. For example, as per [9], a task generated by an IoT device can be processed by itself locally or offload to a FN or the cloud finally depending on, for example, the task characteristics. In addition, as the tasks can be divisible, one part of the task can be processed by IoT node and the other by the fog or cloud. Finally, there exist several application scenarios, in which the upper layers require the lower layers to execute the task. These uncommon offloading models include cloud offloading to fog/IoT and end user devices, fog offloading to the IoT, and end user devices for specific purposes of applications [14].

The determination of times to offload tasks is an important aspect in the offloading models. Generally, offloading is needed when task nodes (TNs) are unable to process their tasks locally, or processing them may not satisfy the QoS requirements. Although the modern IoT devices can process some types of tasks locally, the majority of tasks (e.g., complex and heavy tasks and sporadic tasks emergency cases) generated in the IoT layer are offloaded to the upper layers. However, the task offloading incurs additional costs, such as communication delay and energy consumption. Therefore, the offloading model requires the inclusion of mechanism to monitor the system performance, traffic flow rates, and network conditions that can support to make the offloading decisions appropriately. For example, the FOGPLAN framework in [31] can provide dynamic offloading strategies to adapt to the dynamic change of QoS requirements. Network reliability is also a concern in the fog networks because it directly impacts on the communication delay of offloading processes [32].

The offloading models also specify how the input data of tasks is offloaded and processed. Generally, a full offloading method is applied for a task when its whole data is indivisible and must be offloaded by a single helper node (HN, a neighbor IoT, fog, and cloud node with available resource). Conversely, as a divisibility of task is enabled, a partial offloading scheme can be used to offload a fractional part of task to HNs, while the other part of task is processed locally by TN. In most studies, a task is assumed to be decomposed into two subtasks; thus, there needs only one HN to offload the subtask. As the subtasks are totally independent, the task division is an effective technique employed in the offloading models to cope with the heterogeneity of computing device resources and simultaneously improve the performance of computing operations such as energy consumption minimization [33] and execution delay reduction [18]. Dividing a task into multiple (more than two) subtasks is also considered in [26] to exploit the parallel computation of subtasks at different FNs to get more advantages in terms of delay reduction, energy saving, resource utilization, and workload balancing. The independence of subtasks enabling the parallel processing of subtasks is obviously key to achieving these advantages. However, in practice, some or all subtasks of a task can be data dependent. Thus, completing the task requires a subtask scheduling plan to respect to the subtask processing order. An investigation is presented in [34] that considers three models of task processing, in which the subtasks can be executed in sequential, parallel, and mixed processing order.

7.2.4 Optimization Problems of Computational Offloading

Denote $\pi = \{\pi_i, \pi_j, \pi_k, \ldots\}$ as the set of objective functions, established by individual computing nodes (i.e., IoT nodes, FNs, or clouds) and by the system for the computational offloading performance at a given time. Some of the systematic objective functions include total consumption energy, average task execution delay, total payment cost of resource usage, fairness and workload balancing index, and outage probability. The other objective functions of individual computing nodes are formulated to indicate their inherent selfishness and rational of HNs to maximize their own benefits and revenues. Summarily, the generic optimization problem in the IFC systems can be expressed in the following form:

$$P: \text{Min}\ (\pi_i)\, \&/\text{Max}\ (\pi_j)\, \&/\text{Max}\ (\pi_k)\, \&/\ldots$$

$$\text{Subject to: A set of Constraints}$$

Depending on the application scenarios, problem P can be in the form of single or multi-objective model. Regardless of the ultimate objectives of problems, the constraints involve resource competition, resource limitations, and task scheduling. Concretely, a HN can receive multiple requests for task offloading. However, a certain number of requests are accepted to be processed owing to the limitation of resources such as limited buffer capacity and low residual energy. Furthermore, scheduling the tasks in HNs is considered to respect to the QoS requirements. From the global point of view, the problem becomes a combinatorial problem, which is proven to be NP-hard due to the natural presence of coupling resource problems [35]. Therefore, achieving a globally optimized solution is infeasible, especially in large-scale systems. In addition, there is an extensive cost of overhead to collect global information. These issues urge the need to design distributed algorithms to support the computational offloading processes efficiently.

7.3 Proposed Matching-Based Models for Distributed Computation

This section reviews matching-based models for distributed computation offloading proposed in the literature according to the three types of matching models (i.e., one-to-one, one-to-many, and many-to-many) as described in Chap. 6.

7.3.1 One-to-One (OTO) Matching-Based Models

A task assignment problem is formulated in [36] to describe the computation offloading in vehicular fog networks (VFNs). In these networks, vehicles with available computing resources can act as vehicle FNs to offload tasks of user equipment (UEs) to avoid the overload of base station (BS) during the peak time, thereby improving QoS or QoE (e.g., delay). Given that sharing resources for offloading is conditioned in the VFNs, a contract-based incentive mechanism is proposed by BS to promote FNs to offload tasks. In addition, different contract items (i.e., reward) are given to FNs depending on their available resources and offloading performance. When a FN is able to offload only a task, the task assignment problem is treated as an OTO matching game. A preference function G encapsulating the delay performance and resource pricing is used by UEs to rank the vehicles. Concretely, as a task generated by UE U_n is offloaded by a vehicle V_m, $G_{n,m}$ is defined by:

$$G_{n,m} = \frac{1}{D_{n,m}} - P_m,$$

Where $D_{n,m}$ is the total delay of offloading and P_m is the price for using the resource of V_m. P_m is zero initially and will increase according to the price-rising rule proposed in the price-based stable matching algorithm. The simulation-based evaluation and analysis show that the proposed resource allocation and task assignment scheme can achieve suboptimal performance in terms of social welfare and offloading delay.

A one-sided one-to-one matching is applied in [37] to develop a distributed algorithm for task offloading in vehicular fog computing (VFC) environment, where a task generated by user vehicle (UV) is offloaded only by either a neighbor vehicle (i.e., vehicle fog server (VFS)) or by the remote edge server. Upper confidence bounds (UCBs) for online learning in the studied scenario are adopted to cope with the information uncertainty owing to time-varying states of vehicle-to-vehicle (V2V) communication channels, available resources, and volatility of VFSs. The role of UCB is to estimate the future state based on historical observations while considering the uncertainty of these data known as confidence bound (CB). Furthermore, to capture the volatility of VFSs, additional factors including occurrence awareness and matching conflict awareness are embedded in CB to increase the estimation accuracy. Consequently, the authors propose a preference function used by a UV i to rank a certain VFS j at a time slot t, which is defined as:

$$U_{i,j,t} = \frac{1}{D_{i,j,t-1}} + CB - H_j,$$

where $D_{i,j,t}$ is the historical offloading delay at time slot t- and H_j is the price for using the resource of VFS j. The simulation analysis demonstrates that the proposed approach can efficiently alleviate the severe impacts of volatility and resource conflict. More importantly, it enables the system to obtain close-to-optimal delay performance compared to the case of global information availability.

An integration of the Stackelberg game and matching game is used in [38] to solve the task allocation problem in three-tier fog networks for patient health monitoring applications. Periodic tasks (i.e., patient health data analysis) and sporadic tasks (e.g., emergency case) are sent and requested from home agents (HA) to the cloud node (CN). In turn, CN assigns FNs to execute these tasks such that the task deadlines are met. Transfer is considered in this game for the interaction of HAs, CN, and FNs. With this configuration, the objective of system is to maximize resource utilization while minimizing the outages. From the game perspective, the objective is to maximize the utilities of three players. To achieve these objectives simultaneously, the author divides the problem into three sub-problems. Accordingly, a pricing model is proposed to optimize the price of per resource unit, thus maximizing the utility of CN. Hence, HAs are based on the prices and the deadline constraint of task to derive the required resources such that it maximizes the utilities of HAs. Finally, CN allocates FNs to HAs efficiently to maximize the utility of FN and maximize the resource utilization and minimize the outages. While the first two sub-problems are solved by the Stackelberg game, the last is addressed using the one-to-one matching-based algorithm.

7.3.2 Many-to-One (MTO) Matching-Based Models

The study [39] considers a problem of pairing the IoT nodes for sharing their available resources that are then modeled as a roommate matching game. Based on the state of resources, each device can determine its quota, indicating the number of IoT devices it can pair to share the resources. A utility function accounting for energy consumption and resource pricing cost is established and used to produce PLs of nodes. The Irvings matching algorithm [40] is applied and refined to endure a stable pairing between IoT devices. The simulation results are provided to show that the proposed pairing scheme gains more benefits in terms of energy consumption reduction and resource utilization improvement as compared to the pairing model between IoT node and access points (APs).

The work [41] models the task offloading problem as a many-to-one matching game between a set F of FNs and a set of IoT nodes generating a corresponding set T of computation tasks. Recall that there is a limited number q of tasks offloaded by a certain FN due to the limitation of resource (i.e., computing and buffer storage). The agents of sets construct their PLs based on utility functions, which account for the communication cost, waiting time in queues, and the execution delay of task. Accordingly, the utility of a task $t \in T$ is calculated as follows:

$$U_t^f = \frac{1}{D_{tf}^c + W_{tf}},$$

Where D_{tf}^c is the communication delay cost required to transmit the task t from the IoT device to the fog node f and W_{tf} is the expected waiting time in the queue of fog node f before the task is being processed. On the other side, the agent f of computing resource can obtain the utility according to the following equation:

$$U_f^t = \frac{1}{D_{tf}^c + W_{tf} + D_{tf}^{ex}},$$

where D_{tf}^{ex} is the execution delay to complete the task t by fog node f.

The association of waiting time into the utility function leads to the presence of externalities of matching problem, in which the preference lists of agents can change after a pair is matched. Therefore, the DA-based algorithm requires a cost of overhead resulted from the exchange of control packets among FNs to adjust the decision-making (i.e., acceptance or rejection of proposals) over iterations. With this approach, the outcome of matching game is to achieve a two-sided exchange-stable (2ES) matching, which handles the externality efficiently. The simulation results show that the proposed algorithm outperforms greedy and random offloading solutions in terms of worst total completion time, mean waiting time per task, mean total time per tasks, and fairness.

The work [42] studies dynamic task offloading combining partial and full offloading in the fog-cloud networks to minimize the total energy consumption. At a certain time of offloading decision-making, the system has two sets of agents: the set T of TNs and the set H of helpers including HNs and cloud, which are involving in a many-to-one matching game. Each helper $H_i \in H$ constructs its PL based on a service efficiency (SE) indicating the channel quality (i.e., transmitting data rate) from TNs to it, whereas energy efficiency (EE) is used by TNs to rank the agents of helper set. In mathematical form, $EE(k, i) = R_{k,i}/P_{k,i}$, where $R_{k,i}$ is the CPU computation capability and $P_{k,i}$ is the computation power when a task T_i is offloaded by a helper H_i. The work then proposes SMETO algorithm based on the DA procedure and the constructed PLs to achieve the one-to-many stable matching between T and H. Evaluated by the simulation analysis, the outcome of matching shows its benefit in reducing significantly the offloading consumption energy compared to the random approach.

A task offloading framework known as METO is presented in [43] aiming to reduce the total energy consumption and overall full offloading delay in the IoT-fog network. In this network model, each IoT device generates a single task, and the resource of each fog node (FN) is represented by a number q of virtual resource units (VRU), and each is able to process only a single task. This offloading model is equivalent to a form of one-to-many matching problem between the IoT device set I and the FN set F, in which q_i is the quota of agent $F_i \in F$. As considering jointly multiple criteria (i.e., energy consumption minimization and delay minimization) for the offloading decision-making, METO employed a hybrid CRITIC and TOPSIS-based technique to produce the preferences of both sets. Criteria importance through inter-criteria correlation (CRITIC) is used to evaluate the criteria and determine the weights of resource allocation strategies, whereas technique for order of preference by similarity to ideal solution (TOPSIS) uses these weights for ranking the agents of opposite sets. With this approach, the produced PLs are strict, complete, and transitive, therefore ensuring to obtain stable matching. Using the simulation-based comparative analysis, METO shows its advantage in reducing the total consumption energy as well as the overall delay compared to the baseline algorithms including ME [41], SMETO [42], and a random resource allocation policy.

Similar to METO, a one-to-many matching model between the task set T and the FN set F is used in [44] to seek for an efficient task offloading algorithm in the IoT-fog systems. However, the system considers the presence of fog service providers (SPs), each of which manages the resources of fog nodes in its domain. Consequently, the task offloading problems are transformed into a student project allocation (SPA) game [45], in which IoT devices (or tasks), FNs, and SPs correspond to students, projects, and lectures, respectively. The work further presents a DA-based distributed task offloading algorithm called SPATO to tackle the selfishness and rational of individual agents. In particular, PLs of agents are constructed using the analytical hierarchy process (AHP) [46] that accounts for multiple criteria of system-wise objectives to obtain the rankings. The simulation results indicate that the proposed algorithms enable the network to achieve a reduced offloading delay and energy consumption as well as minimum outage compared to the random offloading plan and SMETO [42].

In the same consideration of task offloading problem as studied in [44], an efficient offloading algorithm called LETO is proposed in [47], aiming at balancing the workload of FNs. A one-to-many matching model between a task set T and a FN set F with minimum and maximum quotas is formulated to access the impact of resource capability of FNs on the workload distribution strategy. In addition, with respect to the deadlines of tasks, the PLs of TNs and FNs are constructed based on the expected offloading delay and the deadlines, respectively. Basically, $f_i >_{t_k} f_j$ if $D_{k,i} < D_{k,j}$, where $\{f_i, f_j\} \in F$, $t_k \in T$, and $D_{k,i}$ is the total offloading delay if t_k is processed by f_i. On the other side, $t_i >_{f_k} t_j$ if $d_i < d_j$, where d_i is the deadline of t_i. The work then introduces a multi-stage deferred acceptance algorithm (MSDA) to achieve fair and pareto optimal matching. Based on the simulation analysis, LETO is able to balance the workload of FNs efficiently while minimizing the outages.

The work [25] introduces a DATS algorithm for offloading dispersive tasks in fog and cloud networks. Given the presence of TNs and helpers (i.e., coalition of FNs and cloud) in the network, the tasks can be processed by either partial or full offloading mode dynamically. DATS incorporates two algorithms to minimize the task offloading delay, which are progressive computing resource competition (PCRM) and synchronized task scheduling (STS). PCRM is a one-to-many matching-based algorithm to yield an efficient resource allocation strategy between task set T and resource set H of helpers. A new index called processing efficiency (PE) is defined to support the production of PLs for the helpers. PE encapsulates communication and computation delay to examine the delay-oriented performance of resource allocation strategy. Recall that PE is calculated, as follows, for a fog node FN m and the cloud k when they execute a task T_n:

$$PE(n,m) = \frac{1}{r_{n,m}} + \frac{\eta_n}{f_m} + \frac{\mu_n}{r_{m,n}},$$

Where $r_{n,m}$ is data rate from TN n to FN m, η_n is processing density of T_n, f_m is CPU frequency of FN m, and μ_n is output-input ratio of T_n.

$$PE(n,k) = \frac{1}{r_n^t} + \frac{\eta_n}{f_k} + \frac{\mu_n}{r_n^r},$$

Where r_n^t and r_n^r are transmitting and receiving data rate from TN n to the cloud. TNs rank the agents of helpers based on the QoS that helpers can provide. Alternatively, a TN prefers to match with a helper that minimizes the offloading delay. Second, STS algorithm is proposed to optimize the subtask assignment and scheduling for each task given the matching obtained by PCRM. The extensive simulation analysis is conducted to evaluate the performance of DATS under the impact of many factors including task size, quota of helpers, and network bandwidth. Summarily, DATS can significantly reduce the task offloading delay compared to random and greedy offloading policies.

Another one-to-many matching game is modeled in [48] for assigning the fog resources to serve the requests sent from the end users (EUs) in the IoT networks.

Considering the minimum and maximum quotas of FNs (i.e., the minimum and maximum number of EUs that a fog can serve), a multistage differed acceptance (MSDA) algorithm is developed to adjust the resource allocation strategies to reach stable matching. EUs are based on QoS metrics (i.e., response latency) provided by FNs to derive PLs, whereas FNs take into account the fog load distribution to rank EUs. The outcome of matching allows an efficient assignment, which minimizes the delay experienced by users while balancing the load of FNs.

A problem of allocation of FSPs to IoT devices is studied in [49]. Taking into account the heterogeneity of system, the IoT devices are assumed to have different services requested periodically. Likewise, FSPs vary in terms of services that they can provide. This configuration is equivalent to a many-to-one matching model, where some FSPs can serve multiple IoT devices. In particular, incomplete PLs with ties are produced by the agents of both sides. A truthful and pareto optimal mechanism is employed to achieve the stability of matching. Through the achieved matching, the SPs can allow short or long access to IoT devices efficiently to use the non-money services respecting to deadlines of tasks. In addition, compared to the random allocation strategy, the proposed approach enables to achieve the maximized best allocation, in which the maximum number of IoT devices are served by the best FSPs in their PLs.

Considering the provision of content and services in the fog-based system, the works [50, 51] employ the one-to-many matching model to formulate the resource allocation problem. The requests sent from EUs are handled by FNs or cloud server depending on type of requests (i.e., content retrieval or computing). In the form of two-sided matching game, EUs and FNs construct their PLs based on the service response latency and consumed energy, respectively. Based on simulation analysis, the proposed algorithm demonstrates its benefit when improving the cache hit ratio, reducing energy consumption, and service response delay.

Similar to [48], the work [52] introduced a FoGMatch framework to perform task scheduling in the IoT-Fog network. A one-to-many matching game between the IoT set and FN set is applied to model and study the resource allocation problem in the fog stratum. Link quality (i.e., data rate) and required resource for computing are two measurements used by the IoT nodes and FNs, respectively, to rank the agents in their opposite sets. In other words, an IoT node i ranks a FN j the best if the data rate from TN i to FN j is the highest and FN has the maximum available resource. On the other side, a FN prefers to serve a task if executing it consumes the largest amount of available resource. Compared to Min-Min and Max-Min scheduling approaches, FoGMatch shows its advantage in improving the makespan of IoT service execution and resource utilization of FNs.

The work [53] focuses on minimizing the total energy consumption during computation offloading processes for cache-enabled F-RANs. In the considered system, all task requests are sent from UEs to the centralized cloud through FAPs. Then, the cloud is responsible for deciding simultaneously EU-FAP association and task offloading strategies (i.e., which tasks are processed by FAPs and cloud) to achieve the systematic objective. Recall that the objective is constrained by the resource limitation of FAPs (i.e., computing and storage) and deadlines of tasks. By modeling the UE-FAP association problem as a one-to-many matching game, a greedy algorithm based on the DA procedure is designed. PLs of agents of both sides are constructed based on energy consumption. Hence, a swap matching condition is introduced as a constraint to evaluate the stability of matching. Through evaluating the algorithm by simulation approaches, the results show that consumed energy of network can be reduced significantly through efficient and stable EU-FAP association, thus enabling the green F-RANs.

A one-to-many matching game is established to model the association problem of fog network, in which each IoT node (user) can be associated with only a cloudlet while a cloudlet can have multiple IoT nodes matched with it [54]. However, there is a limited number of IoT nodes connecting to a cloudlet to respect its maximal workload. In addition, the presence of wireless interference between IoT nodes located in proximity regions when connecting wirelessly to the cloudlets indicate external effect in the matching game. This externality makes PLs of agents change whenever a pair of IoT nodes and cloudlet is matched. The work introduces a concept called swap matching to handle externalities and then achieve the stable matching outcome. The extensive simulation is provided to show the benefits of proposed algorithms that include latency minimization and throughput enhancement compared to the random association approach.

The work [55] concerns the joint optimization problem of radio and computational resource allocation in the IoT-Fog computing systems to optimize the system performance in terms of service delay, user satisfaction, and system cost. Sucha problem involves three entities including the set of IoT EUs, FNs, and CSPs (which manage the resources of FNs). From the matching perspective, the mutual interaction of these sets can be modeled in a SPA problem since they correspond to students, projects, and lectures, respectively. To handle the external effect, a procedure called user-oriented cooperation (UOC) is developed. Fundamentally, UOC is a strategy to remove possible blocking pairs in the matching given the presence of externality by swap operations, which evaluate the change of utility values of agents. As a swap is applied for any two current pairs and the corresponding utility values are changeable, the two pairs are considered as blocking ones. In this way, the proposed algorithm can achieve stable matching with an additional cost of computation complexity resulted in from the swap operations. Regarding the performance, the simulation results show that the proposed framework enables the system to achieve low service latency as well as minimized outages.

A two-sided matching model is proposed [56] for data stream processing. Applying the micro-services to server the DAG-based stream processing applications, the matching is configured to allocate the micro-services to fog and cloud computing resource. Regarding the preference relation construction, the micro-service ranks the resources based on their processing time. In addition, the resources rank the miroservice according to their residual bandwidth. The stable matching achieved by the DA algorithm offers mutual benefits for two sides (i.e., micro-service side and resource side). The simulation results demonstrate that the proposed matching mechanism can help the system to reduce significant processing time of stream while lowering the total stream traffic traversed through the fog-fog and fog-cloud paths.

7.3.3   Many-to-Many (MTM) Matching-Based Models

The work [57] integrates the Stackelberg game and matching game to study the computing resource allocation problem in three-tier IoT fog networks. The considered network consists of multiple clusters, and each includes a set of FNs and is managed by a centralized data service operator (DSO). These FNs are responsible to provide resources to serve the services requested by data service subscribers (DSSs) such as mobile phones and IoT devices such that QoS in terms of service delay is satisfied. The work first models the interaction of DSOs and DSSs as a Stackelberg game, in which DSOs are leaders and DSSs are followers. Based on the resource price announced by the leaders, the followers can optimize the resource amount measured by the number of CRBs required to achieve the desired QoS. When the optimal resources demanded by DSSs are determined, the framework is to come to resource allocation problems. Given the determined CRBs and the available resources of FNs, the many-to-many matching game is applied to model the interaction of DSOs and FNs. Finally, for each cluster of FNs owned by a DSO, the resource allocation is investigated to assign appropriate CRBs of FNs to serve the requests of DSSs. This problem is modeled as a many-to-many matching game, which aims at maximizing the utility values of FNs and DSSs. The performance of framework is evaluated by simulation scenarios, which further show that the proposed approach is able to maximize the utility of all entities (i.e., DSOs, DSSs, and FNs) while satisfying the QoS demanded by DSSs.

The work [58] studies the problem of placement of virtual functions (VFs) on FNs such that they can serve IoT applications with maximal QoS (i.e., minimized worst application time and outage probability). A many-to-many matching game is applied to model the placement problem of a set of VF types (V) on a set of FNs (F). Concretely, an FN can contain multiple types of VFs depending on the available resource of FN represented by computing resource blocks (CRBs), and each VF type can appear in different FNs. The work then introduces two utility functions for the agents of both sets to support the creation of PLs. On the side of the VF set, the utility function $U_z(f)$ of a VF $z \in V$ is formulated as follows when placed on a FN f. The objective of MTM matching is to obtain stable matching, which is defined in the same way as OTO and MTO matching.

$$U_z(f) = r_f - r_z,$$

where r_f is the available CRBs on FN f and r_z is the number of CRBs required to load the VF z on the FN f. Based on this function, the order for any two FN f and f' in the PL of VF z is as follows: $f >_z f' \leftrightarrow U_z(f) < U_z(f')$. In the other side, the utility function $U_z(f)$ of FN f takes into account the occurrence probability of VF z that appears in the FN set. Accordingly, $U_f(z)$ is calculated by:

$$U_f(z) = h_z \left(1 - \sum_{f \in F} \frac{\tau_{f,z}}{n} \right),$$

where h_z is the occurrence frequency of VF z in the IoT application set A, $\tau_{f,z} = 1$ if v_z is placed on FN f; otherwise $\tau_{f,z} = 0$, and n is the total number of types of VFs in the network. Based on this utility function, the preference relation of two certain VF z and z' ranked by FN f as follows: $z >_f z' \leftrightarrow U_f(z) < U_f(z')$. In other words, FNs prefer to allocate VFs such that they have higher values of occurrence frequency in the set A of applications [58]. With this PL construction, the work applies the DA procedure to produce the distributed VF placement algorithm named blind matching game (BMG). Additional analysis is provided to show that the proposed algorithm can lead to a stability convergence, at which the outcome of matching game is in the form of strictly two-sided exchange-stability (S2ES). In addition, BMG can achieve a suboptimal performance in terms of minimization of the work application completion time and the outages.

A recent study as per [59] investigates the data offloading problem in the fog network, in which FNs are responsible for receiving and then processing the data periodically transmitted by the subscribed IoT devices. Given the heterogeneity of FN resource, FNs can be classified into two sets: S of surplus FNs (SFNs) and D of deficit FNs (DFNs). As these definitions, SFNs have available resources for data processing, while DFNs are characterized by the lack of resource for handling the requests of their subscribers. In addition, each FN is managed and owned by a unique FSP, thus leading to the nature of selfish and rational, indicating that it tends to maximize its own profit without considering system-wise performance maximization. The objective focused in the paper is to design an efficient offloading policy such that it can maximize the monetization of FNs subject to the required QoS. To achieve the objective, a matching-based algorithm is proposed that models the interaction of SFNs and DFNs as a many-to-many matching game without quotas. In this game, the agents of both sets produce their PLs based on their own utility functions. For each pair of FNs ($f_s \in S, f_d \in D$), their utility functions are formulated as follows if they match:

$$U_{f_s}(f_d) = K_d . x_d,$$

where K_d is the maximum data packets that can be offloaded to f_s from f_d and x_d is normalized payoff received by f_s when processing a data packet offloaded from f_d. Therefore, $U_{f_s}(f_d)$ refers to the total profit received by f_s when offloading the data packets from f_d. Meanwhile, f_d is interested in the maximum number of packets that can offload to f_s. In other words, the utility function of f_d is $U_{f_d}(f_s) = K_d$. For any two DFNs f_d and $f_{d'}$, their preference relation determined based on the utility function values is represented as follows: $f_d >_{f_s} f'_d \leftrightarrow U_{f_s}(f_d) < U_{f_s}(f_{d'})$. This preference relation is similar for two SFNs f_s and $f_{s'}$. Based on these PLs, the proposed DA-based algorithm is designed to seek for a stable matching. The analysis is provided to prove its stability convergence, thus ensuring the feasibility and efficiency of algorithm. The primary simulation results show that the proposed algorithm is able to maximize the monetization while satisfying the demanded QoS of the subscriber users (i.e., total latency of data packer processing).

7.4 Remaining Challenges and Open Research Issues

The review as discussed in the previous section exposes the potential of matching theory in solving the computational offloading problems in a distributed manner. Many models and algorithms have been introduced to apply to different computing scenarios. However, there still exist several challenges appeared in new context of IFC systems. This section explores and investigates such issues. The associated research directions also are included to discuss the full potential of matching theory to address the issues.

7.4.1 Matching with Dynamics

In many application scenarios, the matching model should consider the dynamic of environment such as the mobility of fog devices and time-varying tasks. In these contexts, the preferences of agents might change accordingly at each time scheduling interval. Consequently, the time dimension must be accounted for in designing the matching solution.

7.4.2 Matching with Groups

In many scenarios, a group of players of a set prefers to match with a single agent of the other set. For example, a group of tasks with the same type should be processed by fog devices supporting to process this type specially. That will lead to a task placement problem. A similar issue might also appear in federated fog-based systems, where many domains (clusters) of fog networks are connected and a group of IoT nodes in a certain domain prefers to be processed by the fog networks of other domains.

7.4.3 Matching with Externality

The nature of resource competition in the computing environment potentially leads to externalities in the matching problem, which are not investigated widely in the existing literature. The interference is only a factor making the continuous change of

PLs of agent [60] in the fog and edge computing environment. For example, in the many-to-one matching model, the scheduling of tasks at a single fog can be served as an external impact on the consistency of PLs. To the best of our knowledge, there has been no research works in the literature considering this kind of externalities in modeling the matching problems and designing the matching-based algorithms.

The presence of sporadic tasks is added as an external source since it can make the task scheduling plan change. In some scenarios, it can be addressed by offloading these tasks to the cloud. However, as the clouded-based solution is inappropriate, FNs are considered to be alternatives to process the offloaded tasks. This situation may result in a change of PLs of some agents since the scheduled tasks must be postponed.

There are additional sources acting as externalities in many contexts of computing systems. Common ones include the system fault and network unreliability, which directly impact on the task offloading operations. Equivalently, PLs are immediately changed in these contexts because, for example, some HNs in the PLs are inaccessible. Therefore, it requires matching models that take into account these situations to enable the system to reconfigure responsively.

7.4.4 Security and Privacy of Data and End Users

The heterogeneity and distributed nature of fog computing environment poses potential risks regarding security and privacy of data and EUs. Therefore, the choice of offloading locations is not only to achieve improved performance but also to guarantee reliability, security, and privacy criteria. This aspect has been not considered during constructing PLs in the reviewed studies that, in other hand, open future directions.

7.4.5 New Offloading Application Scenarios

All the reviewed works consider that the computation tasks can be totally processed in either a parallel or serial manner. In many practical applications, the computation tasks are more complicated, such as Directed Arched Graph (DAG) tasks, which require a complex framework for scheduling since there exist parallel and serial computation processes [61]. Typical DAG tasks are related to the modern AI and ML applications such as real-time video processing [62] and automation in the industrial internet [63]. The presence of scheduling complexity can be considered as an external effect impacting directly on the consistence of PLs of agents.

7.4.6   Application of AI and ML-Based Techniques

AI and ML tools provide efficient techniques to analyze and predict the states of system accurately. Reinforcement learning is such kind of techniques [64, 65], which can help to build PLs efficiently through online learning mechanism (i.e., exploitation and exploration). Thus, using these in the context of computational offloading enables the system to make dynamic and efficient offloading decisions. In addition, deep learning (DL) can be used to approximate and examine the matching outcomes [66].

7.5   Conclusions

The matching theory has been widely applied to offer distributed algorithms in scenarios, where the optimal solutions are infeasible or feasible with incurring expensive expenditure and high computation complexity by the centralized global optimization approaches. The intrinsic feature of architecture of the IFC systems characterized by a geographic distribution of computing devices over large-scale exposes the suitability of matching-based distributed algorithms for perform the computation offloading and resource allocation-related problem. This chapter surveys the literature regarding the matching theory-based solutions for distributed computing offloading in the IFC systems. Based on a brief description of matching theory, related concepts and matching models are identified and differences among them are presented. These different models are used to critically review the application scenarios and algorithms proposed in the existing literature in the area of computational offloading. The remaining challenges and corresponding open issues are discussed thoroughly to motivate research directions.

References

1. Zanella A, Bui N, Castellani A, Vangelista L, Zorzi M (2014) Internet of things for smart cities. IEEE Internet Things J 1(1):22–32
2. Chekired DA, Khoukhi L, Mouftah HT (2018) Industrial iot data scheduling based on hierarchical fog computing: a key for enabling smart factory. IEEE Trans Industr Inform 14(10): 4590–4602
3. Tran-Dang H, Krommenacker N, Charpentier P, Kim D-S (2022) The internet of things for logistics: perspectives, application review, and challenges. IETE Tech Rev 2022:1–29
4. Tran-Dang H, Krommenacker N, Charpentier P, Kim D (2020) Toward the internet of things for physical internet: perspectives and challenges. IEEE Internet Things J 7(6):4711–4736
5. Rimal BP, Choi E, Lumb I (2009) A taxonomy and survey of cloud computing systems. In: 2009 fifth international joint conference on INC, IMS and IDC, pp 44–51
6. Botta A, de Donato W, Persico V, Pescape A (2016) Integration of cloud computing and internet of things: a survey. Futur Gener Comput Syst 56:684–700

7. Bonomi F, Milito R, Zhu J, Addepalli S (2012) Fog computing and its role in the internet of things. In: Proceedings of the first edition of the MCC workshop on mobile cloud computing – MCC 2012. ACM Press

8. Sarkar S, Chatterjee S, Misra S (2018) Assessment of the suitability of fog computing in the context of internet of things. IEEE Trans Cloud Comput 6(1):46–59

9. Yousefpour A, Ishigaki G, Gour R, Jue JP (2018) On reducing iot service delay via fog offloading. IEEE Internet Things J 5(2):998–1010

10. Sarkar S, Misra S (2016) Theoretical modelling of fog computing: a green computing paradigm to support iot applications. IET Netw 5(2):23–29

11. Ku Y-J, Lin D-Y, Lee C-F, Hsieh P-J, Wei H-Y, Chou C-T, Pang A-C (2017) 5g radio access network design with the fog paradigm: confluence of communications and computing. IEEE Commun Mag 55(4):46–52

12. Peng M, Yan S, Zhang K, Wang C (2022) Fog-computing-based radio access networks: issues and challenges. IEEE Netw 30(4):46–53

13. Quek TQS, Peng M, Simeone O, Yu W (2017) Cloud radio access networks: principles, technologies, and applications. Cambridge University Press

14. Aazam M, Zeadally S, Harras KA (2018) Offloading in fog computing for IoT: review, enabling technologies, and research opportunities. Futur Gener Comput Syst 87:278–289

15. Abdulkareem KH, Mohammed MA, Gunasekaran SS, Al-Mhiqani MN, Mutlag AA, Mostafa SA, Ali NS, Ibrahim DA (2019) A review of fog computing and machine learning: concepts, applications, challenges, and open issues. IEEE Access 7:153123–153140

16. Liu L, Chang Z, Guo X, Mao S, Ristaniemi T (2018) Multiobjective optimization for computation offloading in fog computing. IEEE Internet Things J 5(1):283–294

17. Lee G, Saad W, Bennis M (2019) An online optimization framework for distributed fog network formation with minimal latency. IEEE Trans Wirel Commun 18(4):2244–2258

18. Liu Z, Yang Y, Wang K, Shao Z, Zhang J (2020) Post: parallel offloading of splittable tasks in heterogeneous fog networks. IEEE Internet Things J 7(4):3170–3183

19. Yang Y, Liu Z, Yang X, Wang K, Hong X, Ge X (2019) Pomt: paired offloading of multiple tasks in heterogeneous fog networks. IEEE Internet Things J 6(5):8658–8669

20. Durand S, Gaujal B (2016) Complexity and optimality of the best response algorithm in random potential games. In: Symposium on algorithmic game theory (SAGT) 2016, pp 40–51. [Online]. Available https://hal.archives-ouvertes.fr/hal-01404643

21. Satyanarayanan M, Bahl P, Caceres R, Davies N (2009) The case for vm-based cloudlets in mobile computing. IEEE Pervasive Comput 8(4):14–23

22. Bahl V (2015) Emergence of micro datacenter (cloudlets/edges) for mobile computing. In: Microsoft devices & networking summit 2015, vol 5

23. Bilal K, Khalid O, Erbad A, Khan SU (2018) Potentials, trends, and prospects in edge technologies: fog, cloudlet, mobile edge, and micro data centers. Comput Netw 130:94–120

24. Ahmed A, Arkian H, Battulga D, Fahs AJ, Farhadi M, Giouroukis D, Gougeon A, Gutierrez FO, Pierre G, Souza PR Jr et al (2019) Fog computing applications: taxonomy and requirements. arXiv preprint arXiv:190711621

25. Liu Z, Yang X, Yang Y, Wang K, Mao G (2019) Dats: dispersive stable task scheduling in heterogeneous fog networks. IEEE Internet Things J 6(2):3423–3436

26. Tran-Dang H, Kim D-S (2021) Impact of task splitting on the delay performance of task offloading in the IoT-enabled fog systems. In: 2021 IEEE international conference on information and communication technology convergence (ICTC)

27. Tran-Dang H, Kim D-S (2021) Frato: fog resource based adaptive task offloading for delay-minimizing iot service provisioning. IEEE Trans Parallel Distrib Syst 32(10):2491–2508

28. Guo K, Sheng M, Quek TQS, Qiu Z (2020) Task offloading and scheduling in fog ran: a parallel communication and computation perspective. IEEE Wireless Commun Lett 9(2):215–218

29. Bian S, Huang X, Shao Z, Yang Y (2019) Neural task scheduling with reinforcement learning for fog computing systems. In: 2019 IEEE global communications conference (GLOBECOM), pp 1–6

30. Contreras-Castillo J, Zeadally S, Guerrero-Ibanez JA (2017) Internet of vehicles: architecture, protocols, and security. IEEE Internet Things J 5(5):3701–3709
31. Yousefpour A, Patil A, Ishigaki G, Kim I, Wang X, Cankaya HC, Zhang Q, Xie W, Jue JP (2019) Fogplan: a lightweight qos-aware dynamic fog service provisioning framework. IEEE Internet Things J 6(3):5080–5096
32. Yao J, Ansari N (2019) Fog resource provisioning in reliability-aware iot networks. IEEE Internet Things J 6(5):8262–8269
33. Zhang G, Shen F, Liu Z, Yang Y, Wang K, Zhou M (2019) Femto: fair and energy-minimized task offloading for fog-enabled iot networks. IEEE Internet Things J 6(3):4388–4400
34. Al-khafajiy M, Baker T, Al-Libawy H, Maamar Z, Aloqaily M, Jararweh Y (2019) Improving fog computing performance via fog-2-fog collaboration. Futur Gener Comput Syst 100:266–280
35. Wang T, Liang Y, Jia W, Arif M, Liu A, Xie M (2019) Coupling resource management based on fog computing in smart city systems. J Netw Comput Appl 135:11–19
36. Zhou Z, Liu P, Feng J, Zhang Y, Mumtaz S, Rodriguez J (2019) Computation resource allocation and task assignment optimization in vehicular fog computing: a contract-matching approach. IEEE Trans Veh Technol 68(4):3113–3125
37. Liao H, Zhou Z, Zhao X, Ai B, Mumtaz S (2019) Task offloading for vehicular fog computing under information uncertainty: a matching-learning approach. In: 2019 15th international wireless communications mobile computing conference (IWCMC), pp 2001–2006
38. Joshi N, Srivastava S (2019) Task allocation in three tier fog iot architecture for patient monitoring system using stackelberg game and matching algorithm. In: 2019 IEEE international conference on advanced networks and telecommunications systems (ANTS), pp 1–6
39. Abedin SF, Alam MGR, Tran NH, Hong CS (2015) A fog based system model for cooperative iot node pairing using matching theory. In: 2015 17th Asia-Pacific network operations and management symposium (APNOMS), pp 309–314
40. Irving RW (1985) An efficient algorithm for the "stable roommates" problem. J Algorithm 6(4):577–595
41. Chiti F, Fantacci R, Picano B (2018) A matching theory framework for tasks offloading in fog computing for iot systems. IEEE Internet Things J 5(6):5089–5096
42. Zu Y, Shen F, Yan F, Shen L, Qin F, Yang R (2019) Smeto: stable matching for energy-minimized task offloading in cloud-fog networks. In: 2019 IEEE 90th vehicular technology conference (VTC2019-Fall), pp 1–5
43. Swain C, Sahoo MN, Satpathy A, Muhammad K, Bakshi S, Rodrigues JJPC, de Albuquerque VHC (2020) Meto: matching-theory-based efficient task offloading in iot-fog interconnection networks. IEEE Internet Things J 8(16):12705–12715
44. Swain C, Sahoo MN, Satpathy A (2021) Spato: a student project allocation based task offloading in iot-fog systems. In: ICC 2021 – IEEE international conference on communications, pp 1–6
45. Abraham DJ, Irving RW, Manlove DF (2007) Two algorithms for the student-project allocation problem. J Discrete Algorithms 5(1):73–90
46. Satpathy A, Sahoo MN, Behera L, Swain C, Mishra A (2020) Vmatch: a matching theory based vdc reconfiguration strategy. In: 2020 IEEE 13th international conference on cloud computing (CLOUD), pp 133–140
47. Swain C, Sahoo MN, Satpathy A (2021) Leto: an efficient load balanced strategy for task offloading in iot-fog systems. In: 2021 IEEE international conference on web services (ICWS), pp 459–464
48. Abouaomar A, Kobbane A, Cherkaoui S (2018) Matching-game for user-fog assignment. In: 2018 IEEE global communications conference (GLOBECOM), pp 1–6
49. Bandyopadhyay A, Singh VK, Mukhopadhyay S, Rai U, Xhafa F, Krause P (2020) Matching IoT devices to the fog service providers: a mechanism design perspective. Sensors 20(23):6761

50. Assila B, Kobbane A, El Koutbi M (2018) A many-to-one matching game approach to achieve low-latency exploiting fogs and caching. In: 2018 9th IFIP international conference on new technologies, mobility and security (NTMS), pp 1–2

51. Assila B, Kobbane A, Walid A, El Koutbi M (2018) Achieving low-energy consumption in fog computing environment: a matching game approach. In: 2018 19th IEEE Mediterranean electrotechnical conference (MELECON), pp 213–218

52. Arisdakessian S, Wahab OA, Mourad A, Otrok H, Kara N (2020) Fogmatch: an intelligent multi-criteria iot-fog scheduling approach using game theory. IEEE/ACM Trans Networking 28(4):1779–1789

53. Wang C, Sun Y, Ren Y (2020) Distributed user association for computation offloading in green fog radio access networks. In: 2020 IEEE information communication technologies conference (ICTC), pp 75–80

54. Ali M, Riaz N, Ashraf MI, Qaisar S, Naeem M (2018) Joint cloudlet selection and latency minimization in fog networks. IEEE Trans Industr Inform 14(9):4055–4063

55. Gu Y, Chang Z, Pan M, Song L, Han Z (2018) Joint radio and computational resource allocation in iot fog computing. IEEE Trans Veh Technol 67(8):7475–7484

56. Mehran N, Kimovski D, Prodan R (2021) A two-sided matching model for data stream processing in the cloud and fog continuum. In: 2021 IEEE/ACM 21st international symposium on cluster, cloud and internet computing (CCGrid), pp 514–524

57. Zhang H, Xiao Y, Bu S, Niyato D, Yu FR, Han Z (2017) Computing resource allocation in three-tier iot fog networks: a joint optimization approach combining stackelberg game and matching. IEEE Internet Things J 4(5):1204–1215

58. Chiti F, Fantacci R, Paganelli F, Picano B (2019) Virtual functions placement with time constraints in fog computing: a matching theory perspective. IEEE Trans Netw Serv Manag 16(3):980–989

59. Srinivasa Desikan KE, Kotagi VJ, Murthy CSR (2021) A novel matching theory-based data offloading framework for a fog network with selfish and rational nodes. IEEE Netw Lett 3(4): 172–176

60. Gu B, Zhou Z, Mumtaz S, Frascolla V, Kashif Bashir A (2018) Context-aware task offloading for multi-access edge computing: matching with externalities. In: 2018 IEEE global communications conference (GLOBECOM), pp 1–6

61. Fu X, Tang B, Guo F, Kang L (2021) Priority and dependency-based dag tasks offloading in fog/edge collaborative environment. In: 2021 IEEE 24th international conference on computer supported cooperative work in design (CSCWD), pp 440–445

62. Zhang X, Pal A, Debroy S (2021) Effect: energy-efficient fog computing framework for real-time video processing. In: 2021 IEEE/ACM 21st international symposium on cluster, cloud and internet computing (CCGrid), pp 493–503

63. Yang L, Zhong C, Yang Q, Zou W, Fathalla A (2020) Task offloading for directed acyclic graph applications based on edge computing in industrial internet. Inf Sci 540:51–68

64. Tran-Dang H, Bhardwaj S, Rahim T, Musaddiq A, Kim D-S (2022) Reinforcement learning based resource management for fog computing environment: literature review, challenges, and open issues. J Commun Netw 24:1–16

65. Misra S, Rachuri SP, Deb PK, Mukherjee A (2020) Multiarmed-bandit-based decentralized computation offloading in fog-enabled IoT. IEEE Internet Things J 8(12):10010–10017

66. Ravindranath SS, Feng Z, Li S, Ma J, Kominers SD, Parkes DC (2021) Deep learning for two-sided matching. arXiv preprint arXiv:2107.03427. [Online]. Available https://arxiv.org/abs/2107.03427

Chapter 8
Distributed Computation Offloading Framework for Fog Computing Networks

Fog computing networks have been widely integrated in IoT-based systems to improve the quality of services (QoS) such as low response service delay through efficient offloading algorithms. However, designing an efficient offloading solution is still facing many challenges including the complicated heterogeneity of fog computing devices and complex computation tasks. In addition, the need for a scalable and distributed algorithm with low computational complexity can be unachievable by global optimization approaches with centralized information management in dense fog networks. In these regards, this chapter proposes a distributed computation offloading framework abbreviated as DISCO for offloading the splittable tasks using matching theory. Through the extensive simulation analysis, the proposed approaches show potential advantages in reducing the average delay significantly in the systems compared to some related works.

8.1 Introduction

Practically, the Internet of Things (IoT) has become an integral element for realizing smart practical systems such as smart cities [1], smart factories [2], smart logistics, and supply chain [3, 4]. The fundamental aspect of IoT-based systems is to connect all devices through the Internet protocol to exchange high volume data and process them to create smart services and applications. Owing to limited computation resources, network, storage, and energy, IoT devices are inadequate for executing all computational tasks, especially tasks with huge volumes and complex data structures. Cloud computing is an essential solution to this problem because it provides powerful resources to fulfill tasks efficiently [5, 6]. However, cloud computing-based solutions do not always meet the expected quality of service (QoS) and quality of experience (QoE) requirements for some classes of IoT applications, especially latency-sensitive ones because of the long physical distance

© The Author(s), under exclusive license to Springer Nature Switzerland AG 2023
H. Tran-Dang, D.-S. Kim, *Cooperative and Distributed Intelligent Computation in Fog Computing*, https://doi.org/10.1007/978-3-031-33920-2_8

between the IoT devices and the remote cloud servers, scarce spectrum resources, and intermittent network connectivity.

These contexts have to integrate fog computing between the IoT and cloud layer to process and offload most tasks on behalf of the cloud servers, thereby allowing systems to satisfy the QoS and QoE requirements [7, 8]. Besides providing cloud-like services to EUs, fog computing potentially improves the performance of fog-based systems such as reduction of service delay [9] and energy saving [10]. Recently, the advance of networking generation (i.e., 5G and beyond) leads to an increasing demand for ubiquitous computing and pervasive service access by a numerous number of Internet-connected mobile devices and end users (EUs). Motivated by the necessity of network architecture enhancement, a paradigm of fog radio access networks (F-RANs) has emerged as a promising evolution architecture for 5G networks [11, 12], which along with cloud radio access networks (C-RANs) [13] provide the pervasive computing services. Therefore, F-RANs provide great flexibility to satisfy QoS requirements of various 5G-based services and applications.

However, to realize these benefits of fog computing networks (FCNs), there require efficient resource allocation strategies to perform task offloading operations [14]. Indeed, there are many factors that challenge the design and development of effective offloading strategies such as the heterogeneity of computing devices and various types of computational tasks with different requirements [15] such as many applications related to artificial intelligence (AI), machine learning (ML), and augmented reality (AR). There are a large number of centralized optimization techniques and algorithms proposed in the literature to provide optimal solutions to the aforementioned resource allocation problems [16]. Typically, offloading multiple tasks of fog nodes (FNs) to multiple neighbor FNs (i.e., helper nodes (HNs)) is modeled as a multitask multi-helper (MTMH) problem, which deals with the allocation of fog computing resources for processing tasks to achieve single or multiple objectives [16–18]. However, these solutions require a centralized control to gather the global system information, thus incurring a significant overhead and computation complexity of algorithms. This complexity is further amplified by the rapid increase of density and heterogeneity of FCNs [19] when dealing with combination integer programming problems [20].

The aforementioned limitations of optimization have led to a second class of game theory-based offloading solutions that can avoid the cost-intensive centralized resource management and substantially reduce the complexity of algorithms. For example, a paired offloading strategy of multiple tasks (POMT) in heterogeneous fog networks in [21] is modeled as a strategic game between the FNs and HNs for deciding which tasks are offloaded by which HNs to minimize the average task execution delay. The game theory is applied and developed to obtain the Nash Equilibrium point (NE) for the POMT, at which the fog network can reach the near-optimal performance in terms of average delay. A similar model is proposed in POST [22], however, which considers the division of tasks into subtasks for parallel computation. Despite their potential, these approaches pose several limitations. First, classical game theoretical algorithms such as best response require some information regarding actions of other players [23]. Correspondingly, many assumptions are introduced in the game theory-based algorithms to simplify the system models that, in some cases, are impractical. Second, most game-theoretic solutions, for example, Nash equilibrium, investigate one-sided stability notions in which equilibrium deviations are evaluated unilaterally per player. In addition, the stability must be concerned by both sides of players (i.e., resource providers and resource requesters) in the context of fog computing environment.

Ultimately, managing resource allocation effectively in such a complex environment of IFC systems leads to a fundamental shift from the traditional centralized mechanism toward distributed approaches. Recently, matching theory has emerged as a promising technique for solving resource allocation problems in many applications such as wireless communication networks [24] because it can alleviate the shortcomings of game theory and optimization-based approaches. Alternatively, while the optimization and game theory-based solutions are efficient in some limited scenarios, the matching-based approaches have potential advantages owing to the distributed and low computational complexity algorithm. However, to reap the benefits of matching theory for task offloading and resource allocation in the FCNs, there is a need of advanced frameworks to handle their intrinsic properties, such as heterogeneity of fog computing devices and the complex structure of computation tasks.

In these regards, this chapter proposes a distributed computation offloading algorithm called DISCO to minimize the overall task execution delay in the FCNs. Summarily, this chapter provides four key contributions as follows:

- We generalized the model of fog computing networks and model the task offloading problem in the fog network as a many-to-one matching game.
- Unlike the models of related works, we construct the preference profiles of task set and HN set according to groups.
- Based on the PLs, we design a distributed algorithm based on DA algorithm to produce stable matching.
- An intensive simulation analysis is conducted to evaluate the performance of proposed algorithms.

The remainder of this chapter is organized as follows. Section 8.2 highlights the primary concept of many-to-one matching model and reviews the related works. Section 8.3 presents the system model relating to the architecture of heterogeneous fog network and computational tasks. Section 8.4 describes the design of distributed computation offloading (DISCO) approach. Section 8.5 provides the simulation results and comparative analysis to highlight the performance of the proposed algorithm. Section 8.6 concludes the paper and discusses potential directions for extending the proposed model.

8.2   Preliminary and Related Works

8.2.1   Preliminary of Many-to-One (M2O) Matching Model

Although most of matching models in the literature deal with two sets of agents, there are other matching models involving only one set (i.e., stable roommate problem [25]) and three sets of agents [26]. In the scope of the paper, we consider a M2O matching model of two distinct sets of agents, in which each agent of one side can be matched with multiple agents of the other side, but the reverse is not valid. We denote these two sets as $X = \{x_1, x_2, \ldots, x_n\}$ and $Y = \{y_1, y_2, \ldots, y_k\}$. Figure 8.1 shows an example of M2O matching.

Generally, a M2O matching can be defined as follow:

Definition 8.1
The outcome of MTO matching model is a matching function $M : X \cup Y \rightarrow X \cup Y$ such that the three following constraints are satisfied:

- $|M(x)| = 1$ for every $x \in X$, and $M(x) = x$ if x is unmatched
- $|M(y)| = q_y$ for every $y \in Y$; if the number of agents in $M(y)$ is k and $k < q_y$, then M (y) will have q_y-k copies of y
- $M(y) = x$ if and only if x is an element of M(y)

Recall that each agent y has a positive quota q_y to represent the maximum number of agents in the set X, where it can be matched with. With this definition, $M(x) = y$ means that agent x is matched with agent y, and $M(y) = \{x_1, x_2, y, y\}$ indicates that the agent y with the quota $q_y = 4$ has been matched with two agents x_1 and x_2 and has two unfilled matching positions.

The objective of matching games is to achieve stability instead of optimality, at which there is no incentive incurred to devise the current matched pairs of agents. A stable matching is defied in the following Definition 8.2.

Definition 8.2
A matching M is pairwise stable if there is no blocking pair (x, y).

Alternatively, a matching is to stably match agents in two sets based on their individual, objectives, and exchanged information. Each agent builds a ranking of

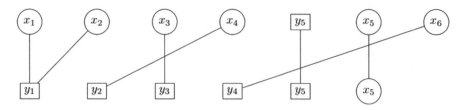

Fig. 8.1 An example of a M2O matching established between two sets X and Y in which $M(y_1) = \{x_1, x_2\}$, $M(y_2) = \{x_4\}$, $M(y_3) = \{x_3\}$, $M(y_4) = \{x_6\}$, x_5 and y_5 are unmatched agents (i.e., $M(y_5) = \{y_5\}$, $M(x_5) = \{x_5\}$)

other agents in the other side individually using a preference relation and then creating its own preference list (PL). Basically, a preference can be calculated based on an objective utility function that quantifies the QoS achieved by a certain matching between two agents of two sides. Defining $P(x)$ and $P(y)$ as preference lists of agent $x \in X$ and $y \in Y$, respectively. Basically, $P(x) = \{y_1, y_2, x, y_4, y_5, \ldots\}$ illustrates that agent x prefers y_1 to y_2 (denoted as $y_1 >_x y_2$) and prefers keeping the position unfilled over other agents like y_4 and y_5. A blocking pair is defined as follows:

Definition 8.3

(x, y) is a blocking pair for a matching M if the three following conditions are satisfied:

- $M(x) \neq y$
- $y >_x M(x)$
- $x >_y M(y)$

Based on the created PLs, agents can implement distributed algorithms called deferred acceptance algorithm (DAA) to derive the matching outcome. Deferred acceptance (DA) algorithm known as the Gale-Shapley algorithm [27] is the classical algorithm to find the stable matching in marriage problem, which can be used to find the matching in M2O matching model. The DA algorithm is an iterative procedure, in which each player in one set makes proposals to the other set, whose players, in turn, decide to accept or reject these proposals, respecting their quota and PLs. Basically, an acceptance decision is made when the proposing agent has a higher rank order of PL than the current matched agent. With this procedure, the algorithm admits many distributed implementations, which do not require the players to know each other's preferences. In addition, the DA algorithm ensures to achieve the stable matching outcome in a polynomial time.

8.2.2   Related Works

This section highlights the key related works that proposed the many-to-one matching-based offloading solutions to minimize the task execution delay in the fog networks. The key concerns focus on modeling the two sets of agents, formulation to construct the preference profiles, and stability analysis of distributed matching algorithms. We also examine the models that consider the offloading of splittable tasks.

Scheduling for Parallel Offloading and Communication

When the computation tasks are splittable, the parallel processing of multiple subtasks is exploited to reduce the overall task execution. In addition, scheduling for subtask offloading and transmission is taken into account at individual node to get the benefits of parallel computation. However, these aspects have not been deeply investigated in the literature.

Regarding the task division, most of the existing works only consider dividing each task into two subtasks to reduce the delay and balance the workload among FNs through parallel computation of subtasks. For example, according to the FEMTO model in the work [28], each task is divided into two subtasks with different data sizes, which are then processed by the IoT node and offloaded to the fog entity. Similarly, in the task offloading methods introduced in [29, 30], each FN divides the tasks into only two parts, which are processed by itself locally and one HN in parallel. Dividing a task into multiple subtasks is first applied in POST algorithm presented in [22]. POST is based on the game theory concept to find the optimal matching pair of subtasks and FNs to achieve the delay minimization objective. Accordingly, the number of subtasks for each task is dynamically optimized depending on the number of idle HNs and tasks in queues in each time slot. The evaluation analysis shows that POST is able to reach the generalized NE (GNE) fixed-point, thus achieving near-optimal performance in terms of average task execution delay. However, it lacks an investigation regarding scheduling of subtask offloading and transmission at individual FN.

The work [19] introduces an online algorithm for task offloading in the IoT-fog-cloud systems, which applies parallel communication and computation at multiple computing nodes (i.e., fog and cloud servers) to minimize the latency. Considering the scenarios with varying task arrival rates, the queuing delays of fog nodes are analyzed to optimize the number of tasks offloaded to other computing nodes to achieve the objective. However, the task transmission and computation at the computing nodes are performed according to the first coming and first scheduling (FCFS) policy rather than the optimal task scheduling policy. In addition, the task division is not considered to balance the workload of heterogeneous fog computing nodes. Recently, a recursive computation offloading algorithm (RCO) is developed in [20] to jointly perform task offloading and task scheduling for F-RANs. Considering the execution of tasks resided in the mobile device (MD), the tasks can be offloaded by the edge or cloud tiers. The optimization of task scheduling is associated in RCO to contribute to achieve the delay reduction objective. However, the task division and subtask offloading are not investigated.

M2O Models for Computation Offloading

The work [31] models the task offloading problem as an M2O matching game between a set F of FNs and a set of IoT nodes generating a corresponding set T of computation tasks. Recall that there is a limited number q of tasks offloaded by a certain FN due to the limitation of resources (i.e. computing, buffer storage). The agents of sets construct their PLs based on utility functions, which account for the communication cost, waiting time in queues, and the execution delay of task. The DA algorithm is applied to achieve a two-sided exchange-stable (2ES) matching between two sets. The simulation results show that the proposed algorithm outperforms greedy and random offloading solutions in terms of worst total completion time, mean waiting time per task, mean total time per tasks, and fairness.

A task offloading framework known as METO is presented in [32] aiming to reduce the total energy consumption and overall full offloading delay in the IoT-fog network. In this network model, each IoT device generates a single task, and the resource of each FN is represented by a number q_i of virtual resource units (VRU), and each is able to process only a single task. This offloading model is equivalent to a form of M2O matching problem between the IoT device set I and the FN set F, in which q_i is the quota of agent $F_i \in F$. As considering jointly multiple criteria (i.e., energy consumption minimization and delay minimization) for the offloading decision-making, METO employed a hybrid CRITIC and TOPSIS-based technique to produce the preferences of both sets. With this approach, the produced PLs are strict, complete, and transitive, therefore ensuring to obtain the stable matching. Using the simulation-based comparative analysis, METO shows its advantage in reducing the total consumption energy as well as the overall delay compared to the baseline algorithms including ME [31], SMETO [33], and a random resource allocation policy.

Similar to METO, a one-to-many matching model between the task set T and the FN set F is used in [34] to seek for an efficient task offloading algorithm in the IoT-fog systems. However, the system considers the presence of fog service providers (SPs), each of which manages the resources of fog nodes in its domain. Consequently, the task offloading problems are transformed into a student project allocation (SPA) game [35], in which IoT devices (or tasks), FNs, and SPs correspond to students, projects, and lectures, respectively. The work further presents a DA-based distributed task offloading algorithm called SPATO to tackle the selfishness and rational of individual agents. In particular, PLs of agents are constructed using the analytical hierarchy process (AHP) [36] that accounts for multiple criteria of system-wise objectives to obtain the rankings. The simulation results indicate that the proposed algorithms enable the network to achieve a reduced offloading delay and energy consumption as well as minimum outage compared to the random offloading plan and SMETO [33].

The work [29] introduces a DATS algorithm for offloading dispersive tasks in the fog and cloud networks. In these networks, the tasks can be processed by either partial or full offloading mode dynamically. DATS incorporates two algorithms to minimize the task offloading delay, which are progressive computing resource competition (PCRM) and synchronized task scheduling (STS). PCRM is an M2O matching-based algorithm to yield an efficient resource allocation strategy between task set T and resource set H of helpers. A new index called processing efficiency (PE) is defined to support the production of PLs for the helpers. PE encapsulates communication and computation delay to examine the delay-oriented performance of resource allocation strategy. TNs rank the agents of helpers based on the QoS that helpers can provide. Alternatively, a TN prefers to match with a helper that minimizes the offloading delay. Second, STS algorithm is proposed to optimize the subtask assignment and scheduling for each task given the matching obtained by

PCRM. The extensive simulation analysis is conducted to evaluate the performance of DATS under the impact of many factors including task size, quota of helpers, and network bandwidth. Summarily, DATS can significantly reduce the task offloading delay compared to random and greedy offloading policies.

An M2O game is established to model the association problem of fog network, in which each IoT node (user) can be associated with only a cloudlet while a cloudlet can have multiple IoT nodes matched with it [37]. However, there are a limited number of IoT nodes connecting to a cloudlet to respect its maximal workload. In addition, the presence of wireless interference between IoT nodes located in proximity regions when connecting wirelessly to the cloudlets indicates external effect in the matching game. This externality makes PLs of agents change whenever a pair of IoT node and cloudlet is matched. The work introduces a concept called swap matching to handle externalities and then achieve a stable matching outcome. The extensive simulation is provided to show the benefits of proposed algorithms that include latency minimization and throughput enhancement compared to the random association approach.

The work [38] concerns the joint optimization problem of radio and computational resource allocation in the IoT-Fog computing systems to optimize the system performance in terms of service delay, user satisfaction, and system cost. Such problem involves three entities including the set of IoT EUs, FNs, and CSPs (which manage the resources of FNs). From the matching perspective, the mutual interaction of these sets can be modeled in a SPA problem since they correspond to students, projects, and lectures, respectively. To handle the external effect, a procedure called user-oriented cooperation (OUC) is developed. Fundamentally, OUC is a strategy to remove possible blocking pairs in the matching given the presence of externality by swap operations, which evaluate the change of utility values of agents. As a swap is applied for any two current pairs and the corresponding utility values are changeable, the two pairs are considered as blocking ones. In this way, the proposed algorithm can achieve stable matching with an additional cost of computation complexity resulted from the swap operations. Regarding the performance, the simulation results show that the proposed framework enables the system to achieve low service latency as well as minimized outages.

8.3   System Model

8.3.1   Fog Computing Networks

This paper considers an FCN with flat architecture (i.e., no centralized fog controller) as illustrated in Fig. 8.2, which includes a set F of N FNs ($F = \{F_1, \ldots, F_N\}$) and a cloud data center C providing M virtual machines (VMs).

FNs can connect together through wired and wireless links for sharing resources. A cloud server can be reached by any FN for providing the cloud services such as computation, storage, and caching. The FNs operate in a distributed manner to

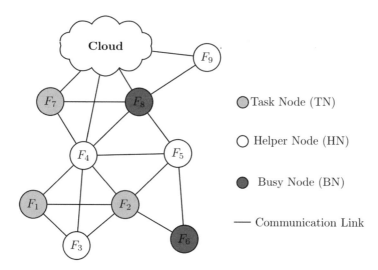

Fig. 8.2 An illustrative model of FCN includes three TNs (F_1, F_2, F_7), two BNs (F_6, F_8), and four HNs (F_3, F_4, F_5, F_9), which can connect to the cloud to request the cloud services

process and offload tasks. At an arbitrary scheduling time slot, an FN can be in one of three modes: (i) a task node (TN) that has tasks in its queue, (ii) busy node (BN) that is busy processing tasks, and (iii) helper node (HN) that has available resource to offloading tasks. The state of nodes can change over scheduling times. For example, a BN at a time slot τ will become an HN in the next time slot ($\tau + 1$) if there is no task residing in its queue. Notably, the cloud always serves as an HN because it has a set of virtual machines.

To design an efficient offloading policy, TNs are based on a table of neighbor resources that contains updated information about the available resources of neighbor HNs. We define H_i as the set of HNs neighboring to a TN F_i; thus, $H_i = \{F_p, F_k \dots C\}$. We assume that the fog devices use a common protocol to communicate and update their resource status periodically [39]. The computing capability of a FN is represented through CPU frequency (f (cycles/s)) and CPU processing density (γ (cycles/bit)).

8.3.2 Computation Offloading Model

Computation tasks from the end user devices such as IoT sensors and smartphones arriving at the queues of FNs follow an exponential distribution with average rate λ tasks per second (tasks/s). Figure 8.3 shows the overview of task offloading model in the FCN.

At a certain time slot τ, the FCN has a set $T = \{t_1, t_2, \dots, t_K\}$ including K computational tasks required to be processed. A single task t_i currently resided

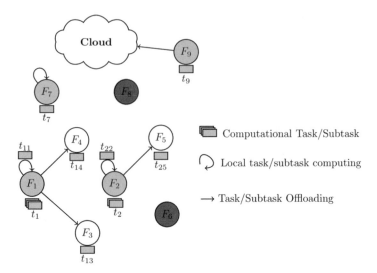

Fig. 8.3 The offloading model for the FCN includes full and partial offloading

in the queue of TN F_i can be processed locally by F_i or fully offloaded by an HN F_k ($F_k \in H_i$). In addition, a task t_i with a size a_i can be divided into $m = |H_i| + 1$ subtasks, which are denoted as t_{ik} ($k = 0, \ldots, N$). These subtasks then can be processed in parallel by multiple HNs. As illustrated in Fig. 8.3, two subtasks t_{14} and t_{13} divided from t_1 can be computed simultaneously by F_4 and F_3, respectively, while t_{10} is computed locally. We define a_{ik} as the data size of subtask t_{ik}; thus, we have:

$$\sum_{k=0}^{N} a_{ik} = a_i, \forall t_i \in T. \tag{8.1}$$

In addition, when $a_{ik} = 0$, the HN F_k is not assigned to offload t_i.

8.4 Problem Formulation

The overall delay for executing a task t_i (D_i) is an interval from the arrival time of task (T_i^a) at the queue of F_i until finish processing time (T_i^f) at other fog node (F_i or some HNs). As illustrated in Fig. 8.4, $D_i = T_i^f - T_i^a$.

When the partial offloading policies are applied for executing t_i, we define D_{ik} as the delay to process the subtask t_{ik}. Suppose that there is no data dependency between subtasks of t_i, therefore the subtasks can be computed in parallel by different HNs. In addition, no aggregation of subtask processing results is required; thus, $D_i = \max\{D_{ik}\}$, $k = 1, \ldots, N$. Notably, $D_{ik} = T_{ik}^f - T_i^a$. In this sense, besides

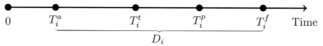

T_i^a : Arrival time of task t_i at a TN F_i

T_i^t : Transmission time of task t_i to an arbitray HN F_k

T_i^p : Processing time of task t_i at F_k

T_i^f : Finish time of task t_i at F_k

Fig. 8.4 Timeline to calculate the delay to execute an arbitrary task T_i

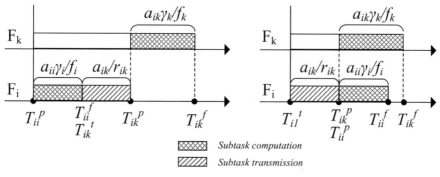

Fig. 8.5 Two scheduling cases of data communication and computation at a TN

subtask offloading policies (i.e., which FN processes which subtask), subtask scheduling (i.e., which subtask is transmitted or processed first) has a significant impact on the total task execution delay. Because the data transmission and data processing are not performed simultaneously by FNs, offloading and transmission scheduling must be taken into account to minimize the delay.

The following Proposition 8.1 supports to derive an efficient data computation and communication schedule at a TN to reduce the task execution delay.

Proposition 8.1

When subtasks of a task T_i are processed both by F_i locally and offloaded by HNs, the subtask transmission to the HNs is performed before performing the subtask computation locally at F_i to get the benefit of parallel computation.

Proof

Suppose that a task t_i is divided into two subtasks t_{ii} and t_{ik}, which are processed locally by F_i and offloaded by F_k, respectively. We consider the first case as illustrated in Fig. 8.5(1), in which t_{ii} is processed first by F_i.

The total delay to execute t_{ii} is:

$$D_{ii} = \frac{a_{ii}\gamma_i}{f_i}. \tag{8.2}$$

Because data processing and data transmission are not performed simultaneously by F_i, the total delay to execute t_{ik} including D_{ii} as waiting time is calculated by:

$$D_{ik} = D_{ii} + \frac{a_{ik}}{r_{ik}} + \frac{a_{ik}\gamma_k}{f_k} \tag{8.3}$$

where r_{ik} is the data rate on the channel between F_i and F_k. It can be derived from:

$$r_{ik} = B \log_2 \left(1 + \frac{GP_i^t}{BN_0} \right) \tag{8.4}$$

where B is the bandwidth of channel, G is the channel gain, P_i^t is the transmission power of F_i, and N_0 is the noise power spectral density. The channel gain can be obtained given the path loss PL of the channel, which can be calculated as follows:

$$PL = 10 \log \left(d^{km} \right) + 20 \log \left(B^{kHz} \right) + 32.45 \text{ (dB)} \tag{8.5}$$

Notably, the propagation delay is neglected since it is much smaller than the transmission delay (a_{ik}/r_{ik}). Because $D_i = \max\{D_{ii}, D_{ik}\}$, $D_i = \frac{a_{ii}\gamma_i}{f_i} + \frac{a_{ik}}{r_{ik}} + \frac{a_{ik}\gamma_k}{f_k}$.

When t_{ik} is transmitted to F_k first in case 2 (Fig. 8.5(2)), the total delay to execute the subtasks is calculated as follows:

$$D_{ik}^* = \frac{a_{ik}}{r_{ik}} + \frac{a_{ik}\gamma_k}{f_k} \tag{8.6}$$

$$D_{ii}^* = \frac{a_{ik}}{r_{ik}} + \frac{a_{ii}\gamma_i}{f_i} \tag{8.7}$$

The total delay to finish t_1 in case 2 is $D_i^* = \max\{D_{ii}^*, D_{ik}^*\}$. Obviously, $D_i^* < D_i$; hence, the proposition is proved. In other words, the delay is potentially reduced if all subtasks offloaded by HNs are scheduled to be transmitted first from TNs.

Based on the proved proposition, we define o_{ij}^i to represent the scheduling order between two subtasks t_{ij} and t_{ik} for wireless transmission. Particularly, if t_{ij} is scheduled on wireless link before t_{ik}, we have $o_{ik}^i = 1$; otherwise, $o_{kj}^i = 0$. Since t_{ij} is transmitted either before or after t_{ik}, we have

$$o_{ij}^i + o_{ik}^i = 1, \forall i, j = 0, \ldots, N \& i \neq j \tag{8.8}$$

We define T_{ij}^t as the start time for transmitting t_{ij}. There is no overlap between their wireless transmission times of two subtasks t_{ij} and t_{ik}; therefore, their start transmission times must satisfy:

$$T_{ij}^t - \left(T_{ik}^t + \frac{a_{ik}}{r_{ik}} \right) \geq -Lo_{ik}^i, \forall k,j \in H_i \qquad (8.9)$$

where L is a large possible constant.

Additionally, the start processing time T_{ij}^p of t_{ij} must not be smaller than the arrival time at a HN F_j, therefore:

$$T_{ij}^p \geq T_{ij}^t + \frac{a_{ij}}{r_{ij}}, \forall j \in H_i \qquad (8.10)$$

Finally, the end time T_{ij}^f to finish t_{ij} is calculated as follows:

$$T_{ij}^f = T_{ij}^p + \frac{a_{ij}\gamma_j}{f_j}, \forall j \in H_i \qquad (8.11)$$

Recall that $D_{ij} = T_{ij}^f - T_i^a$, therefore $D_i = \max_j \{ D_{ij} | j \in H_i \cup \{i\} \}$ $= \max_j \left\{ T_{ij}^f \right\} - T_{ij}^a$. We denote $P(t_i|H_i)$ as a problem to minimize the execution delay of t_i given the available computation resource set H_i. The optimization problem P is modeled as follows to minimize D_i:

$$P(t_i|H_i): \min_{a_i, T_i^t, T_i^p, o_i} D_i$$

$$\textbf{s.t.} \quad (10.1), (10.8), (10.9), (10.10).$$

As each fog node selfishly aims to minimize its own task execution delay, the minimization of overall delay of all tasks is infeasible because of coupling resource problem. In addition, achieving the global optimization (i.e., minimizing the sum of total delay of all tasks) faces a critical challenge regarding the computation complexity, especially in dense fog networks. In the next section, we propose a distributed algorithm based on matching theory for allowing the fog nodes to perform task offloading in a distributed manner with low computational complexity.

8.5 Description of DISCO Framework

8.5.1 Overview

Based on the system model, we model the computational offloading problem in the FCNs as an M2O matching game between the set of tasks T and the set of HNs H. Unlike the M2O matching models studied in the related work, this paper considers an M2O matching with group model in which a task t_i prefers a group of HNs, which can collaboratively offload the task t_i with the minimized execution delay.

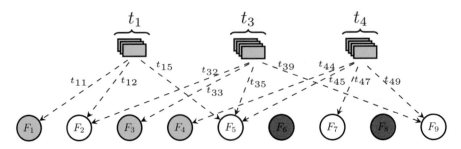

Fig. 8.6 An example of optimal resource allocation solutions for offloading three task t_1, t_3, and t_4: $\overline{H_1^*} = \{F_1, F_2, F_5\}$, $\overline{H_3^*} = \{F_2, F_3, F_5, F_9\}$, $\overline{H_4^*} = \{F_4, F_5, F_7, F_9\}$ obtained from their own optimization problems. Because a HN can only process a task/subtask, the resource contention occurs at F_2, F_5, and F_9

Define $\overline{H_i}$ as a subset of H_i and $\overline{H_i^*}$ is the most preferred subset of HNs to derive the minimal execution delay achieved by solution of problem $P(t_i|H_i)$. Notably, as $\overline{H_i^*} = \{F_i\}$, t_i is processed locally by F_i. Basically, for each task t_i, there is an optimal subset to offer the task offloading solution with minimal delay, thus inherently incurring the coupling resource problem as illustrated in Fig. 8.6.

The DISCO framework includes three algorithms, which are developed to create the PLs of agents (i.e., tasks and HNs), produce a stable matching based on the DA algorithm, and derive an optimal task offloading and scheduling (OSTO) mechanism.

8.5.2   PL Construction

Because not all FNs in the network are connected together, the PLs of agents are not complete. In addition, HNs have preferences over individual tasks, and tasks have preferences over subsets of HNs.

A. PLs of Tasks Faced with a set H_i of HNs, each task t_i can rank all subsets of H_i based on the minimal delay they can offer to offload t_i. However, when $|H_i|$ is large in dense fog networks, this method is inefficient because it incurs high overhead of computation. To overcome this issue, we first determine quotas for task agents as follows.

Definition 8.4
The quota q_i for a task t_i is the number of HN optimized by the problem $P(t_i|H_i)$. Alternatively, $q_i = \overline{H_i^*}$ and $qi \leq |H_i|$.

Consequently, the tasks may have different quotas for matching with agents of HNs that is contrary to the model in [29] considering the same quota for all tasks.

Definition 8.5
When $q_i > 1$, the least preferred agent in the PL of t_i is F_i.

This definition specifies that eventually t_i is computed locally by F_i if there is no optimal solution for offloading t_i by HNs. In addition, t_i can be executed in the full offloading method by a single HN. Therefore, t_i also ranks individual HNs in its PL.

Definition 8.6
A HN F_k is acceptable to a task t_i if and only if $D_i^*(t_i|F_k) < D_i^*(t_i|F_i)$.

This means that delay achieved by full offloading $D_i^*(t_i|F_k)$ is lower than delay achieved by local computing $D_i^*(t_i|F_i)$. Finally, we have an acceptable list of HN agents denoted as L_i that t_i can match with, and $L_i = H_i^* \cup \{F_k, F_j, \ldots\}$, where F_k, F_j are HNs selected according to Definition 8.6 and $F_k, F_j \in H_i$. Each t_i can construct its own PLs from the subsets of L_i. Basically, $P(t_i) = \{\overline{H_i^*}, \overline{H_i^x}, \overline{H_i^y}, \ldots, F_i\}$, where $\overline{H_i^x}$, $\overline{H_i^y}$ are subsets of L_i and $D_i^*(t_i| \overline{H_i^*}) < D_i^*(t_i| \overline{H_i^x}) < D_i^*(t_i| \overline{H_i^y}) < \ldots < D_i^*(t_i|F_i)$.

B. PLs of HNs We adopt the concept of processing efficiency (PE) as presented in [29] to evaluate the capability of HNs in offloading. Recall that PE of an HN F_k with respect to a TN F_i denoted as $\rho(k, i)$ is calculated as follows:

$$\rho(k, i) = \frac{1}{r_{ik}} + \frac{\gamma_k}{f_k}$$

This parameter specifies the efficiency of HN F_k to offload a bit data sent from a TN F_i. Based on PE, each HN can construct its PL over individual tasks. The PL of an HN F_j is in this form, $P(F_k) = \{t_m, t_n, t_p\}$. Basically, for a pair of tasks t_m and t_n, $t_m > F_k t_n$ if $\rho(k, m) < \rho(k, n)$.

8.5.3 Matching Algorithm

Based on the PLs of tasks and HNs, DISCO employs the DA algorithm to find the stable matching as shown in Algorithm 8.1. We implement the task-optimal stable matching algorithm, in which the task proposes and the role of HNs is to reject or accept the proposals based on their PLs.

Algorithm 8.1: M2O Matching Algorithm

Input: $\mathcal{P}(t_i)$, $\mathcal{P}(F_k)$, $\forall\, t_i \in \mathcal{T}$ & $F_k \in \mathcal{H}$
// PLs of all tasks and HNs
Output: $\mathcal{M}$

1 **begin**
2   Step 1: Each task t_i proposes to its most prefered subset of HNs (i.e., $\overline{\mathcal{H}_i^*}$)
3   For every $F_k \in \overline{\mathcal{H}_i^*}$:
4   **if** $t_i == \mathcal{P}_k[0]$ // $\mathcal{P}_k[0]$ is the most prefered agent of F_k in the PL of F_k
5   **then**
6   F_k accepts the proprosal
7   **else**
8   F_k rejects the proprosal
9   t_i removes $\overline{\mathcal{H}_i^*}$
10   Update $\mathcal{P}(t_i)$
11   **while** *There is a rejection from HNs* **do**
12   Each task t_i continues to proposes to its most prefered subset of HNs in the updated PLs including all of HNs
          accepted the previous proposals

8.5.4 Optimal Task Offloading and Communication Scheduling (OTOS) Algorithm

The aforementioned matching algorithm determines a set of HNs, H_i^M used to execute a task t_i. Then, solving the problem $P(t_i|H_i^M)$ yields to the optimal scheduling policy of subtask offloading and communication, which is represented by the optimal vectors α_i, T_i^t, T_i^p, and O_i.

8.5.5 Stability Analysis

Proposition 8.2
The matching produced by Algorithm 8.1 is pairwise stable.

Proof
The procedure to produce the PLs of TNs and HNs shows that each task is always matched with the most preferred subset of HNs such that the delay is minimized. At every step in the algorithm, each task is proposing to its most preferred subset of HNs that does not include any HNs, which have previously rejected the proposal. Considering a task t_i and an HN F_k at any step such that $F_k \in Ch_i(M(t_i) \cup F_k)$, where $M(t_i)$ is the set of HNs that t_i is matched with at this current step, and $Ch_i(H_i)$ is referred to as the most preferred subset of H_i (i.e., $\overline{H_i^*}$). At some different steps of the algorithm, t_i proposes to F_k and, for example, was subsequently rejected, so F_k prefers $M(F_k)$ to t_i, and definitely M is not blocked by the pair (t_i, F_k). Because this pair (t_i, F_k) is arbitrary and M is not blocked by any individual agent, M is stable.

8.6 Simulations and Performance Evaluation

8.6.1 Simulation Environment Setup

The event-driven framework supported SimPy library in Python is used to conduct the simulation scenarios, which investigate the performance of DISCO and the benchmark algorithms. Table 8.1 summarizes the important parameters and values for the simulation scenario, where $U[x,y]$ indicates the uniform distribution on interval $[x, y]$. The scenario includes 100 FNs deployed uniformly in a region of area 200 m × 200 m. The coverage of each FN is 40 m. The cloud provides 50 VMs for offloading tasks.

All the simulation results are averaged over 100 simulation rounds, and each round lasts 1000 s according to the clock of CPU. We compare the proposed DISCO approach with DATS and POST. Recall that DATS considers to schedule and offload multiple tasks at each time of decision-making, but the scheduling for data communication and data computation of subtasks is not employed. Meanwhile, POST uses the game theory to find the GNE point for mapping task/subtasks to the HNs [22].

8.6.2 Evaluation and Analysis

Figure 8.7 depicts the average delay achieved by POST, DATS, and DISCO when β is varied.

When there is a large percentage of HNs in the network (i.e., β is small (0.1, 0.2)), DISCO, DATS, and POST have a similar performance. With this scenario, there are abundant resources to offer the optimal solutions for offloading tasks. When β increases, the performance gap between DISCO, DATS, and POST is larger.

Table 8.1 Parameters for simulation

Parameters	Values
Number of FNs, N	100
Number of VMs provided by cloud, M	50
Take size, a_i	{5, 10, 15}(MB)
Active ratio of TNs, β	{0.1–0.9}
Processing density of FNs, γ	$U[500,1000]$ (cycles/bit)
CPU frequency of FNs, f	{1.0, 1.5, 2.0, 2.5} (GHz)
Processing density of each VM, γ_c	100 (cycles/bit)
CPU frequency of each VM, f_c	10 (GHz)
Transmitting power of FNs, P_t	$U[100,350]$ mw
Transmitting power of GW, P_t	20 w
Noise power spectral density, N_0	−174 dBm/Hz
Bandwidth, B	$U[15–90]$ KHz

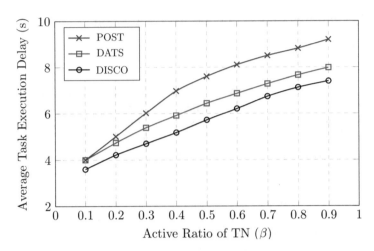

Fig. 8.7 The average task execution delay offered by the comparative offloading schemes

When $\beta = 0.9$, there presents a high workload in the network and a small percentage of available resources (HNs). Therefore, it is likely to have more tasks computed locally by TNs. That leads to a considerable increase of delay for the three algorithms. However, DISCO still outperforms DATS and POST because it can allocate the resources better through stable matching. Concretely, DATS and POST assign the best HNs to tasks in a greedy manner. Meanwhile, DISCO uses the principles of stability in the matching theory to allocate the resource fairly. In addition, the proposed OTOS mechanism embedded in DISCO improves the performance of task offloading compared to random scheduling approaches used in DATS and POST.

To further examine the potential of DISCO, we evaluate the delay reduction ratio (DRR) defined as the total delay reduction compared to the total delay of local computation. Figure 8.8 shows the simulation result regarding the DRR achieved by the three algorithms.

All schemes employed task division and associated task parallel processing, hence reducing the delay considerable compared with the local computing. In particular, DISCO is able to reduce delay substantially compared to DATS and POST owing to OTOS mechanism.

We evaluate the distribution of task execution delay that is shown in Fig. 8.2. For different active ratios of TNs, DISCO offers a uniform distribution of task delays for individual TNs owing to the fair resource allocation and optimal subtask scheduling. Contrarily, the high variance of delays is present in DATS and POST algorithms because of unfairness of HN allocations for offloading tasks. To be specific, there are some tasks in both DATS and POST algorithms, which are offloaded by the coalitions of best HNs. Simultaneously, the other tasks may be suffered by longer delay for execution when offloaded by the remaining low computational HNs. This issue is obvious in the network with the presence of more TNs (e.g., $\beta = 0.8$) as

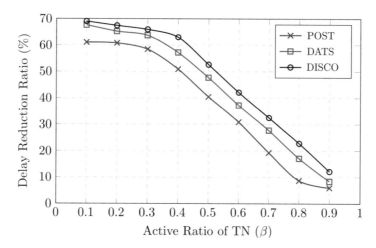

Fig. 8.8 The delay reduction ratio offered by DISCO, DATS, and POST

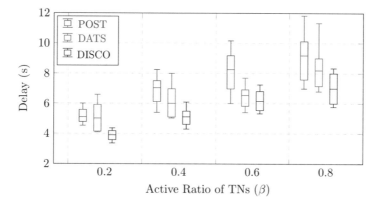

Fig. 8.9 The delay distribution achieved by DISCO, DATS, and POST

shown in Fig. 8.6. The scarcity of HNs leads to the high variance of delay distribution in the DATS and POST algorithms (Fig. 8.9).

Figure 8.5 supports the superior performance of DISCO through the average utilization ratio of HNs. As shown in this figure, the task division employed in the three schemes can increase the utilization ratio of fog computing devices since the limited resource fogs can process the subtasks. However, DISCO is able to use the resource of HNs better than DATS and POST because the proposed matching algorithm allows the tasks to select the subset of HNs fairly. In other words, more percentages of HNs are joined in the collaborative offloading (Fig. 8.10).

In addition, the utilization of fog resources is affected by the convergence of algorithms. Figure 8.11 shows the convergence of the related matching algorithm.

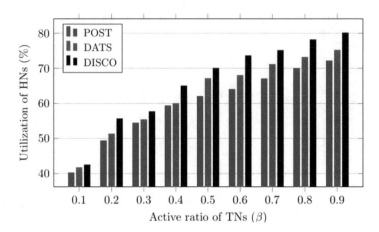

Fig. 8.10 Average utilization ratio of HNs under the impact of β

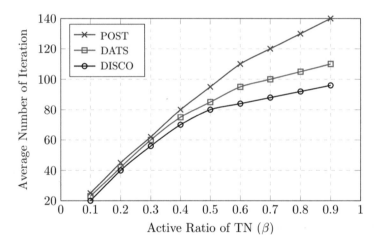

Fig. 8.11 The convergence rate of matching algorithms

DISCO outperform DATS and POST with the minimum iterations for convergence. DATS must iterate over subsets of HNs to determine the quota for each TN.

POST also uses a high number of exchange information to obtain the equilibrium. The different gap is larger when the percentage of TNs in the network increases. Consequently, DISCO with distributed algorithm and low computation complexity offers potential solution for large-scale fog networks. DATS and POST take longer run time to reach the convergence, thus posing an increased delay of subtask processing and offloading. Consequently, a number of BN are slightly increasing for subsequently time scheduling intervals. This leads to increasing the delay of DATS and POST.

8.7 Conclusions

This chapter presented DISCO, a distributed computation offloading framework used for the heterogeneous FCNs to reduce the delay of task execution using matching theory. The intensive simulation results show that DISCO is an effective offloading solution to achieve the reduced execution delay for fog computing environment, in which the fog computing devices are heterogeneous complicated and different kinds of tasks. By applying task division technique and the associated parallel computation, DISCO allows a task to be processed by multiple HNs to significantly reduce the overall task execution delay. The optimal scheduling of subtask transmission and subtask processing is also integrated to contribute to the delay reduction objective. The matching theory-based principals are used to remove the rational and selfishness of individual TNs and simultaneously offer the fair resource allocation.

The model presented in this paper potentially leads to some extension directions. First, a many-to-many matching can be modeled when a HN can process multiple tasks/subtasks. The externality is also considered in this case because the scheduling of tasks in each HN is regarded. Second, two-sided matching is examined in many scenarios as the load balancing and energy consumption criteria are considered in HNs to construct the preference lists.

References

1. Zanella A, Bui N, Castellani A, Vangelista L, Zorzi M (2014) Internet of things for smart cities. IEEE Internet Things J 1(1):22–32
2. Chekired DA, Khoukhi L, Mouftah HT (2018) Industrial iot data scheduling based on hierarchical fog computing: a key for enabling smart factory. IEEE Trans Industr Inform 14(10): 4590–4602
3. Tran-Dang H, Krommenacker N, Charpentier P, Kim D-S (2022) The internet of things for logistics: perspectives, application review, and challenges. IETE Tech Rev 39(1):93–121
4. Tran-Dang H, Krommenacker N, Charpentier P, Kim D (2020) Toward the internet of things for physical internet: perspectives and challenges. IEEE Internet Things J 7(6):4711–4736
5. Rimal BP, Choi E, Lumb I (2009) A taxonomy and survey of cloud computing systems. In: 2009 fifth international joint conference on INC, IMS and IDC, pp 44–51
6. Botta A, de Donato W, Persico V, Pescape A (2016) Integration of cloud computing and internet of things: a survey. Futur Gener Comput Syst 56:684–700
7. Bonomi F, Milito R, Zhu J, Addepalli S (2012) Fog computing and its role in the internet of things. In: Proceedings of the first edition of the MCC workshop on mobile cloud computing – MCC 2012. ACM Press
8. Sarkar S, Chatterjee S, Misra S (2018) Assessment of the suitability of fog computing in the context of internet of things. IEEE Trans Cloud Comput 6(1):46–59
9. Yousefpour A, Ishigaki G, Gour R, Jue JP (2018) On reducing iot service delay via fog offloading. IEEE Internet Things J 5(2):998–1010
10. Sarkar S, Misra S (2016) Theoretical modelling of fog computing: a green computing paradigm to support iot applications. IET Netw 5(2):23–29

11. Ku Y-J, Lin D-Y, Lee C-F, Hsieh P-J, Wei H-Y, Chou C-T, Pang A-C (2017) 5G radio access network design with the fog paradigm: confluence of communications and computing. IEEE Commun Mag 55(4):46–52

12. Peng M, Yan S, Zhang K, Wang C (2016) Fog-computing-based radio access networks: issues and challenges. IEEE Netw 30(4):46–53

13. Peng M, Simeone O, Yu W, Quek T (2017) Cloud radio access networks: principles, technologies, and applications. Cambridge University Press, Cambridge

14. Aazam M, Zeadally S, Harras KA (2018) Offloading in fog computing for IoT: review, enabling technologies, and research opportunities. Futur Gener Comput Syst 87:278–289

15. Abdulkareem KH, Mohammed MA, Gunasekaran SS, Al-Mhiqani MN, Mutlag AA, Mostafa SA, Ali NS, Ibrahim DA (2019) A review of fog computing and machine learning: concepts, applications, challenges, and open issues. IEEE Access 7:153123–153140

16. Liu L, Chang Z, Guo X, Mao S, Ristaniemi T (2018) Multiobjective optimization for computation offloading in fog computing. IEEE Internet Things J 5(1):283–294

17. Yao J, Ansari N (2019) Fog resource provisioning in reliability-aware iot networks. IEEE Internet Things J 6(5):8262–8269

18. Yousefpour A, Patil A, Ishigaki G, Kim I, Wang X, Cankaya HC, Zhang Q, Xie W, Jue JP (2019) Fogplan: a lightweight qos-aware dynamic fog service provisioning framework. IEEE Internet Things J 6(3):5080–5096

19. Lee G, Saad W, Bennis M (2019) An online optimization framework for distributed fog network formation with minimal latency. IEEE Trans Wirel Commun 18(4):2244–2258

20. Guo K, Sheng M, Quek TQS, Qiu Z (2020) Task offloading and scheduling in fog ran: a parallel communication and computation perspective. IEEE Wireless Commun Lett 9(2):215–218

21. Yang Y, Liu Z, Yang X, Wang K, Hong X, Ge X (2019) Pomt: paired offloading of multiple tasks in heterogeneous fog networks. IEEE Internet Things J 6(5):8658–8669

22. Liu Z, Yang Y, Wang K, Shao Z, Zhang J (2020) Post: parallel offloading of splittable tasks in heterogeneous fog networks. IEEE Internet Things J 7(4):3170–3183

23. Durand S, Gaujal B (2016) Complexity and optimality of the best response algorithm in random potential games. In: Symposium on Algorithmic Game Theory (SAGT), pp 40–51. [Online]. Available: https://hal.archives-ouvertes.fr/hal-01404643

24. Jorswieck EA Stable matchings for resource allocation in wireless networks. In: 2011 17th international conference on Digital Signal Processing (DSP), pp 1–8

25. Gusfield D (1988) The structure of the stable roommate problem: efficient representation and enumeration of all stable assignments. SIAM J Comput 17(4):742–769

26. Eriksson K, Sjostrand J, Strimling P (2006) Three-dimensional stable matching with cyclic preferences. Math Soc Sci 52(1):77–87

27. Gale D, Shapley LS (1962) College admissions and the stability of marriage. Am Math Mon 69(1):9–15

28. Zhang G, Shen F, Liu Z, Yang Y, Wang K, Zhou M (2019) Femto: fair and energy-minimized task offloading for fog-enabled iot networks. IEEE Internet Things J 6(3):4388–4400

29. Liu Z, Yang X, Yang Y, Wang K, Mao G (2019) Dats: dispersive stable task scheduling in heterogeneous fog networks. IEEE Internet Things J 6(2):3423–3436

30. Mukherjee M, Kumar S, Mavromoustakis CX, Mastorakis G, Matam R, Kumar V, Zhang Q (2020) Latency-driven parallel task data offloading in fog computing networks for industrial applications. IEEE Trans Industr Inform 16(9):6050–6058

31. Chiti F, Fantacci R, Picano B (2018) A matching theory framework for tasks offloading in fog computing for iot systems. IEEE Internet Things J 5(6):5089–5096

32. Swain C, Sahoo MN, Satpathy A, Muhammad K, Bakshi S, Rodrigues JJPC, de Albuquerque VHC (2020) Meto: matching-theory-based efficient task offloading in iot-fog interconnection networks. IEEE Internet Things J 8(16):12705–12715

33. Zu Y, Shen F, Yan F, Shen L, Qin F, Yang R Smeto: stable matching for energy-minimized task offloading in cloud-fog networks. In: 2019 IEEE 90th Vehicular Technology Conference (VTC2019-Fall), pp 1–5

34. Swain C, Sahoo MN, Satpathy A Spato: a student project allocation based task offloading in iot-fog systems. In: ICC 2021 – IEEE international conference on communications, pp 1–6

35. Abraham DJ, Irving RW, Manlove DF (2007) Two algorithms for the student-project allocation problem. J Discrete Algorithms 5(1):73–90

36. Satpathy A, Sahoo MN, Behera L, Swain C, Mishra A Vmatch: a matching theory based vdc reconfiguration strategy. In: 2020 IEEE 13th International Conference on Cloud Computing (CLOUD), pp 133–140

37. Ali M, Riaz N, Ashraf MI, Qaisar S, Naeem M (2018) Joint cloudlet selection and latency minimization in fog networks. IEEE Trans Industr Inform 14(9):4055–4063

38. Gu Y, Chang Z, Pan M, Song L, Han Z (2018) Joint radio and computational resource allocation in iot fog computing. IEEE Trans Veh Technol 67(8):7475–7484

39. Al-khafajiy M, Baker T, Al-Libawy H, Maamar Z, Aloqaily M, Jararweh Y (2019) Improving fog computing performance via fog-2-fog collaboration. Futur Gener Comput Syst 100:266–280

Chapter 9
Reinforcement Learning-Based Resource Allocation in Fog Networks

In IoT-based systems, fog computing allows the fog nodes to offload and process tasks requested from IoT-enabled devices in a distributed manner instead of the centralized cloud servers to reduce the response delay. However, achieving such a benefit is still challenging in systems with high rate of requests, which implies long queues of tasks in the fog nodes, thus exposing probably an inefficiency in terms of latency to offload the tasks. In addition, a complicated heterogeneous degree in the fog environment introduces an additional issue that many of single fogs cannot process heavy tasks due to lack of available resources or limited computing capabilities. Reinforcement learning is a rising component of machine learning, which provides intelligent decision-making for agents to response effectively to the dynamics of environment. This vision implies a great potential of application of RL in the concept of fog computing regarding resource allocation for task offloading and execution to achieve improved performance. This chapter presents an overview of RL applications to solve resource allocation-related problems in the fog computing environment. The open issues and challenges are explored and discussed for further study.

9.1 Introduction

The Internet of Things (IoT) paradigm has been recognized as a key driving force to realize the smart concept in various domains, such as smart cities [1], smart grids [2], and smart factories [3] since it enables the interconnection and interoperability of IoT-enabled physical and virtual entities to create smart services and informed decision-making for monitoring, control, and management purposes [4, 5]. The underlying principle of realization involves a set of activities that include collecting, processing, analyzing, and getting insights from IoT data perceived by the IoT devices. Traditionally, the cloud computing platform plays an essential role in the realization process since it provides rich and powerful resources (i.e., storage,

© The Author(s), under exclusive license to Springer Nature Switzerland AG 2023
H. Tran-Dang, D.-S. Kim, *Cooperative and Distributed Intelligent Computation in Fog Computing*, https://doi.org/10.1007/978-3-031-33920-2_9

computation, networking) to handle an enormous amount of IoT data (big data) efficiently [6]. However, the data traffic has increased exponentially due to the increase of IoT-enabled devices and growth of customized applications, thus leading to congested networks consequently. Some of the leading IoT applications have put higher demand on resource-constrained devices. Additionally, more stringent quality of service (QoS) requirements of IoT service provisioning such as (ultra)low delay expose crucial limitations of the cloud-based solutions because the delivery of data from the IoT devices to the centralized cloud computing servers seriously affects the performance in processing and analyzing data and results in network congestion issues and excessive delay as an ultimate consequence. This fact context leads to a strong push of fog computing integration into the IoT-cloud systems since it puts computing, storage, communication, and control closer to the IoT devices to meet the prescribed QoS requirements [7, 8]. Technically, the fog computing platform that is placed between the physical IoT devices and the cloud servers can handle a majority of service requests on behalf of the cloud servers to improve the system performance in terms of service delay, workload balancing, and resource utilization [9].

The mutual benefits gained from the combination of fog and cloud enable the resulting IoT-fog-cloud systems to provide uninterrupted IoT services with various QoS requirements for the end users along the things-to-cloud continuum. However, employing fog computing raises another concern regarding decisions on whether the tasks should be processed in the fog or in the cloud. There are many factors impacting on the offloading decision policies such as offloading criteria and application scenarios [9]. Basically, in most existing offloading techniques, the tasks are probably offloaded to the best surrogate nodes, which have the most ample resources (e.g., large storage capacity, high speed processing) and reliable communication network conditions in terms of delay, bandwidth between them and their neighbors, the IoT devices, and even the cloud servers. However, such fog offloading solutions face significant challenges regarding the workload distribution among the complicated heterogeneous fog devices characterized by different computation resources and capabilities. The challenge is further amplified by increasing the rates of service requests, which probably make the task queues of resource-rich fog nodes longer. As a result, the requirements of latency-sensitive applications can be violated because of excessive waiting time of long queue. Furthermore, the reliance on remote cloud servers to accomplish the tasks may not help in improving the situation due to high communication delay or networking-related disturbance.

Executing the tasks in the fog computing tier requires an efficient resource allocation and management to satisfy the QoS requirements. However, the objective is facing many critical challenges due to the complex heterogeneity and limitations of fog resources, locality restrictions, and dynamic nature of resource demands. Most of heuristics existing algorithms are proposed as efficient resource allocation solutions for distributing and executing the tasks in some certain computing scenarios [10, 11]. In other words, they lack a generic framework to study the resource allocation issues in the practical computing context, which encompasses multiple criteria to derive the efficient algorithms such as heterogeneity, QoS management, scalability, mobility, federation, and interoperability [12].

Reinforcement learning (RL) has been increasingly studied and applied to effectively solve resource allocation–related issues in many uncertain computing environments [13]. In principle, RL-based algorithms employ the learning processes to learn the dynamic and changing environment to enrich the experiences, thus deriving the best decisions in the long-term operations [14–16]. For example, a RL-based task scheduling algorithm has been developed and deployed in cloud computing scenarios to reduce the average task execution delay and task congestion level [17]. Many RL-powered algorithms have been proposed to improve computing performance, such as saving energy consumption in data centers [18–20]. Recently, the collaboration between deep learning and RL can further enhance the capabilities of resulting deep RL (DeepRL) approaches, which achieves outstanding performance in complex control fields and strongly shows its superiority of decision-making in complex and uncertain environment [21, 22]. For example, such a DeepRL algorithm is developed to optimize the task scheduling in the data center [23]. The resource allocation problem is also tackled by using a DeepRL algorithm to achieve optimal job-virtual machine scheduling in the cloud [24]. The dynamic task scheduling problems are effectively addressed by RL-based techniques in the field of computer science [25]. These primary findings expose an efficient alternative to solve the resource allocation problems in fog computing using the RL concept. In this regard, this chapter provides a significant review to channelize the state-of-the-art RL-based methods to solve the resource allocation problems in the fog computing environment.

The main contributions of the chapter are summarized as follows:

- We highlight key issues regarding fog resource management in fog computing for task offloading and task computation algorithms.
- We highlight key issues regarding fog resource management in fog computing for task offloading and task computation algorithms.
- We examine the RL concept as potential solutions to resource management issues.
- The state-of-the-art review of existing applications of RL in the fog computing environment is surveyed.
- We explore and discuss the challenges as well as associated open issues when using RL algorithms in the context of fog computing.

The rest of the chapter is structured as follows. Section 9.2 presents the key concept of fog computing and existing resource management issues of fog nodes. Section 9.3 overviews the principle of RL and key algorithms developed and used in practical applications. Section 9.4 presents a comprehensive review of existing works that apply RL algorithms in the context of fog computing. Section 9.5 discusses the challenges and open issues. Finally, Sect. 9.6 concludes the work.

9.2   Fog Computing Environment

9.2.1   System Model

A fog computing system is usually placed between an IoT layer and a cloud layer to form a three-tier architecture for the resulting IoT-fog-cloud system as illustrated in Fig. 9.1.

The first layer includes all IoT-enabled devices that generate IoT data, primarily process the data, and periodically report the raw and/or pre-processed data to the fog or cloud for further advanced processing and computing (i.e., data streaming applications). The fog computing devices (e.g., routers, switches, gateways, and cloudlets for mobile computing services) and servers distributed in the fog layer and cloud layer, respectively, are responsible for receiving, processing, and responding to the IoT computing service requests sent from the IoT layer. In contrast to the powerful servers in the cloud tier, fog devices have limited resources. In addition, they are heterogeneous in terms of computation, storage, and communication capability. Therefore, these resources require an efficient resource allocation strategy to

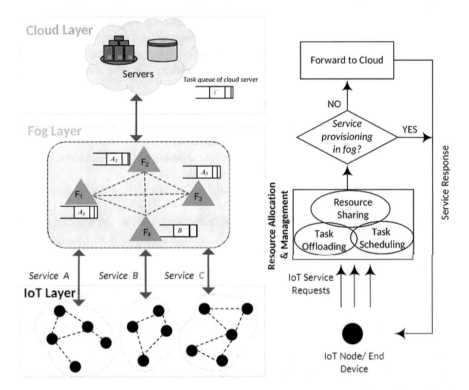

Fig. 9.1 A typical three-tier architecture of IoT-fog-cloud system, which provides specific kinds of IoT services (e.g., service A, B, C as examples) through either the fog layer or the cloud based on the adaptive resource allocation mechanism

Table 9.1 Resource state table of neighbors of fog node F_1

Node ID	Fog specification and resource status			
	M_r (MB)	Frequency (GHz)	RTT (ms)	W (ms)
F_2	200	10	2.5	350.2
F_3	100	5	3.1	500
F_4	400	2.5	4.8	239.1

improve the performance of fog computing tier in serving and delivering the services.

Depending on the specific objectives and scale of application system, the fog layer can be structured by three main architecture: centralized, distributed, and hierarchical form. In the first architecture, the computing system comprises of a fog controller and a set of fog nodes [26]. The controller is responsible for information aggregation and decision-makings, whereas the nodes work directly to serve as the supportive computing devices. Such architecture is widely applicable in software-defined networks. The second one is referred as to a network of fogs, which forms connectivity among fogs in a distributed manner. Task scheduling and resource allocation in the task offloading processes can be decided by fogs through distributed manners. Whereas in the hierarchical architecture, there exist clusters in which each cluster operates according to the master-slave operations. Especially, a fog node serves as a master to control and manage the operations of associated fog nodes known as slaves. The master is able to know the states of slaves regarding the resources and capacity; thus, it can derive optimal resource allocation and task scheduling in its cluster. In addition, a federation is enabled among the master fogs for further resource and load sharing.

Regardless of its architecture, the systems rely on available resource tables that contain the updated resource states of fogs in the systems to facilitate the resource allocation processes. Depending on the specific architecture of fog systems, the tables are maintained by different responsible fogs. For example, the controllers and fog masters are able to know the resource state of all fog devices and in their clusters, respectively, in the first two architecture. Also, in the distributed system, each fog maintains its own neighbor resource table containing updated information about the available resources of its colony [27, 28]. These tables are shared among the member of their colony to support the primary host to make offloading decisions, which ultimately aim at selecting the offloadees, the hosts, and the collaborative fogs. Table 9.1 shows an example of neighbor resource table stored by the fog node F_1, which records the resource states of neighbors with respect to residual memory (M), clock frequency (f), processor (i.e., CPU or GPU support), round-trip time (RTT), and expected waiting time in queue (W).

Each computing task k can be described with a tuple (A_k, B_k), where A_k and B_k are the vectors representing the input data features and required computing resources, respectively. Basically, A_k can include the following features: total size (in bits or bytes), splittable or non-splitable, and number of data types. The sizes of input data of tasks can be ranged from kilobytes to terabytes depending on the specific

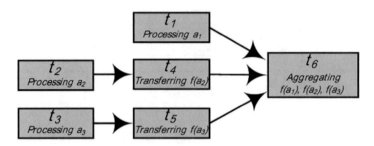

Fig. 9.2 Based on the data fragmentation concept, processing the input data (a bits) includes a set of tasks, which process the data subsets a_1, a_2, a_3 before completing the whole task by jointly processing the output data $f(a_1)$, $f(a_2)$, and $f(a_3)$ to achieve $f(a)$

applications [29]. Based on this feature, the tasks can be classified into light, medium, and heavy tasks as studied in many existing works [28, 30] for further analyzing the impact of task sizes on the performance of fog computing systems. The divisibility of tasks (i.e., input data) is also investigated in the literature. Accordingly, the whole input data can only be processed by a single fog device as it is unable to be divided into data subsets. Moreover, several existing works assumed that the task can be divided into subtasks with smaller data sizes. Such task division is employed to get benefit from parallel computing since the subtasks can be processed by different fog devices simultaneously. Figure 9.2 illustrates main subtasks for computing the input data a as it can be divided into three independent subsets $\{a_1, a_2, a_3\}$.

In particular, the outputs of subtasks (i.e., $f(a_1)$, $f(a_2)$, $f(a_3)$) are collected and jointly processed in the final stage to achieve the desired outcome (i.e., $f(a)$). This mechanism is called partial offloading as investigated in the existing works, such as [31]. The input data of a certain computing task can include multiple types of data such as text, image, video, and audio as studied in [27, 32]. Regarding the required computing resource, there are many attributes included in D_k to process the task. Some of the existing works just only consider B_k as the central processing units (CPU cycles) [33]. In another scenario, GPU and memory requirements are considered during resource allocation for executing heavy and complex tasks, such as the machine learning algorithms [34].

9.2.2   Resource Allocation Problems in Fog Computing Systems

The fog computing technology provides additional resources for executing the tasks and correspondingly providing various services with improved quality in the computing systems. However, the nature of fog computing environment exposes major challenges regarding the resource allocations for task execution to achieve the objective. This section explores and discusses such key challenges in fog computing,

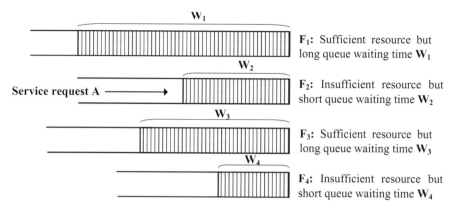

Fig. 9.3 The heterogeneity and unbalanced workload of fog environment in the IoT-fog-cloud systems expose issues in providing IoT services

which urge a need to develop alternative solutions beyond the existing heuristics propositions.

Firstly, the fog computing environment is complex and dynamically changing. Basically, fog computing devices like gateways, hubs, and switches are heterogeneous in terms of computation, storage, and communication capability. In many of the use cases, the complicated heterogeneity of fog environment represents a critical challenge for these systems to achieve the performance improvement objective. For instance, the presence of limited resource fogs results in the imbalance of workload distribution among the fogs, which in turn impacts negatively on the performance of system in terms of delay. Figure 9.3 illustrates such typical issue in the fog computing environment systems, in which a fog node F_2 is unable to process the whole input data of service request A due to lack of resources. Meanwhile, offloading the task to the fog neighbors F_1 and F_3 may lead to an extensive delay since there are high workloads in queues of these fog nodes.

In addition, the high rate of requests potentially prolongs the task queues in the powerful fog nodes since the limited resource fog nodes with respect to the computational capability and storage may be unable to process the whole input data of service. Furthermore, constrained by the cloud rental cost, the other objective of proposed framework is to maximize the usage of fog resources, thus minimizing the reliance on the cloud. All these perspectives lead to a direction to explore the task division concept that potentially can help in reducing the task execution delay through parallel subtask executions in the limited resources fogs. However, dividing tasks may not be effective in large-scale systems or high task request rate since it may increase the resource contention among the fogs, thus increasing the time and computation complexity of algorithms [27].

Secondly, the fog computing resource is dynamically changing due to mobility. In many practical applications, the presence of mobile fog nodes such as drones [35] and vehicles [36, 37] leads a dynamic change of fog computing resources over time. Moreover, leaving out and joining in the fog computing systems by fog devices are accounted for as causes for this change. Therefore, the resource allocation strategies must be designed in an adaptive and flexible way to cope with this situation.

Thirdly, the resource requirements for executing the tasks also change dynamically due to various types of tasks. The demand for resources varies according to specific applications, different time periods, and environmental condition. Generally, there are three major computing problems involving resource allocation in fog computing systems, which include resource sharing, task scheduling, and task offloading [12]. Basically, resource sharing is referred as to methods to share available resources among the fog devices to execute the computation demands of tasks [38, 39]. This algorithm is essential in the fog computing environment, where the heterogeneity of fog resources stress the need of multiple computing devices to complete a single task. As the fog computing system is considered a pool with a set of resource types, such as storage, CPU, and GPU, the resource sharing requires a cooperative among the nodes to execute the computational task demands. Therefore, mechanisms for fog-to-fog collaboration must be established within the fog computing domains to facilitate resource sharing [40]. However, to enable such the cooperative fog-to-fog is a challenging job since practical devices are different in terms of hardware, software, and functionalities such as gateways, routers, and hubs. Specially, task scheduling is usually performed without sufficient information support. Practically, there are no patterns to predict the arriving task profiles characterized by the number and size of tasks as well as arrival rate. Therefore, the algorithm has to schedule the tasks at once without any prior experience and prepared information. In addition, the scheduling algorithm needs automatically optimize resource utilization based on the changing demand. Task scheduling is a problem, which has a high impact on the performance of computing system, especially in terms of task execution delay. Generally, scheduling the tasks involves assigning which resources process which tasks within which expected time period. In large-scale systems including IoT layer, edge and fog layer, and cloud layer, possible resources for computation execution include IoT devices, edge devices, fog devices, and also server in the cloud tier. The heterogeneity of fog resources in terms of computation capabilities directly leads to the imbalance of workload distributed among the nodes. Concretely, more loads may be carried by powerful devices such as fast processing speed from greedy perspectives. As there exists a lack of management, the performance of computing systems can be degraded in the long run since a large number of available resources in the limited resource fogs are underutilized. Balancing the workload among the computing devices is a challenging problem to ensure a stable operation of computing systems in the long run. There are many factors needed to be considered during designing and developing efficient task offloading algorithms such as resource states of fog devices and task requirements, which dynamically change over time.

In order to solve the above problems, a lot of related studies are carried out. Most of them focus on some specific scenarios or rely on the acquired details of the incoming tasks in advance to derive efficient heuristics algorithms. In addition, most of the previous studies are single objective optimization-oriented (i.e., delay, energy consumption, and resource utilization). In particular, none of them have a generic framework to model and examine the above-mentioned challenges for further designing appropriate algorithms. In the next sections, we briefly introduce the principal concept of RL and conduct an analysis review on application of RL-based methods for solving the resource allocations in the fog computing environment.

9.3 Reinforcement Learning

9.3.1 Basic Concepts

Reinforcement learning (RL) is a method of supervised and unsupervised learning. It is not exclusively supervised because it does not depend just on training data, but it is not unsupervised because rewards or punishment is given to the agent in return of the optimization. In the RL algorithms, the agents are able to identify the best and right actions in any situations so as to achieve the overall goal based on the rewards and punishments. In other words, RL can be in simplest terms defined as the "*science of decision-making*" [41].

For the sake of clarity, Table 9.2 provides symbols mostly used in the RL frameworks.

In the standard RL model, the agent interacts with its environment to learn the characteristics of environment. The data perceived through the environment sensing serves as input for the agents for decision-making. The actions taken by the agent result in the change of environment, which is further communicated back to the agent for entire the process to start over again. Figure 9.4 illustrates the basic operation of RL.

Table 9.2 Symbols used in the work

Notation	Description
t	Time step t
a_t	Action that agent can take at t
s_t	State that agent is to be in at t
r_t	Immediate reward for agent to take a_t
A	Action space, $A = \{a_t\}$
S	State space, $S = \{s_t\}$
R	Return or cumulative reward
Q	Q value (function)
π	Policy
γ	Discount factor
P	Transition probability

Fig. 9.4 The fundamental operation of RL with agent, environment, reward, state, and action

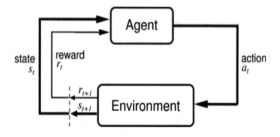

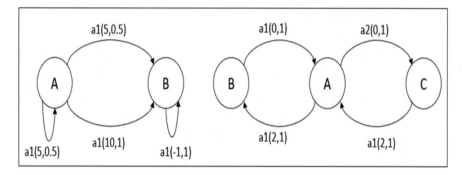

Fig. 9.5 Two simple MDP models that illustrate the underlying concepts and algorithms [46]

State Space

Interaction with the dynamic environment trains the RL system by trial and error as it learns mapping from situations to actions [42]. The RL system must be able to perfectly observe the information provided by the environment, which influences the action to be taken; thus, the true states of the environment affect the action taken by the RL system [43]. In most environment, the state transition is following a Markovian property that the current state s_t provides enough information to obtain an optimal decision. Therefore, a selection of an action will have the same probability distribution over the next states when this action is taken in the same state [44]. Markov decision process (MDP) is a mathematical framework used to model decision-making situations in the RL problem. MDPs consist of states, action, transition between states, and a reward function. The system is Markovian if the results of an action do not depend on the previous action and historical already visited states but only on the current state, that is, $P(s_{t + 1} | s_t, a_t, s_{t - 1}, a_{t - 1}) = P(s_{t + 1} | s_t, a_t)$ [45]. Often, MDPs are depicted as a state transition graph where the nodes correspond to states and (directed) edges denote transitions. Two simple MDPs as illustrated in Fig. 9.5 show the underlying concepts and algorithms, in which each transition is labeled with the action taken and a pair of numbers. The first number is immediate reward, and the second number represents the transition probability.

Action Space

An action taken by the agent is completely dependent on the environment; therefore, different environment results in different actions. The set of all valid actions in a given environment is called an action space, abbreviated as S [47]. Environments such as Atari and Go have discrete action spaces, where only a finite number of actions are available to the agent [48]. Other environments have continuous action spaces, such as where an agent controls a robot in a physical world [49].

Reward and Returns

As the agent performs an action a_t, it will immediately get a reward r_t. The immediate reward r_t is quantified by a numerical value (either positive or negative) to evaluate the desirability of action that the agent took. Therefore, the goal of agent is to maximize the total amount of rewards or the cumulative reward instead of immediate rewards. The return or commutative reward at time step t is defined as:

$$R_t = \sum_{k=0}^{\infty} r_{t+k+1}.$$

However, to account for the importance of immediate and future rewards, the return is discounted by a discount factor γ ($0 \leq \gamma \leq 1$), thus:

$$R_t = \sum_{k=0}^{\infty} \gamma^k r_{t+k+1}.$$

Policy

Policy is defined as the rule used by the agent to decide which action to take in each state. In other words, a policy is a function mapping states to actions. Therefore, the ultimate objective of RL algorithms is to derive the optimal policy that maximizes the return.

State Value and State-Action Value Function

A state value function ($V^\pi(s)$) is used to specify how good it is for an agent to be in a particular state (s) with a policy π. In the mathematical formulation, $V^\pi(s)$) is defined as:

$$V^{\pi}(s) = E_{\pi}\left[\sum_{k=0}^{\infty} \gamma^k r_{t+k+1} | s_t = s\right].$$

A state-action value function or Q-function ($Q^{\pi}(s, a)$) is used to specify how good it is for an agent to perform a particular action (a) in a state (s) following a policy π. The mathematical formulation of Q function is as follows:

$$Q^{\pi}(s) = E_{\pi}\left[\sum_{k=0}^{\infty} \gamma^k r_{t+k+1} | s_t = s, a_t = a\right].$$

Since the environment is stochastic, there is a probability denoted as $\pi(a|s)$ for a policy π to take an action a given the current state s. Certainly, $\sum_{a \in A} \pi(a|s) = 1$. The relationship between $V^{\pi}(s)$, $Q^{\pi}(s, a)$ is expressed by:

$$V^{\pi}(s) = \sum_a \pi(a|s) Q^{\pi}(s, a).$$

By denoting $P^a_{ss'}$ as transition probability to transit from a state s to a state s' as performing an action a, the relationship $V^{\pi}(s)$ and $Q^{\pi}(s, a)$ is also expressed by:

$$Q^{\pi}(s, a) = r(s, a) + \gamma \sum_{s' \in S} P^a_{ss'} V^{\pi}(s'),$$

where $r(s, a)$ is the immediate reward achieved after taking action a given the current state s.

Consequently, the state values can be formulated as:

$$Q^{\pi}(s, a) = r(s, a) + \gamma \sum_{s' \in S} P^a_{ss'} \sum_{a' \in A} \pi(a'|s') Q^{\pi}(s', a'),$$

where a' is next possible action of a.

In order to achieve the maximal return, the RL algorithms have to find the optimal policy that has an associated optimal state value function or state-action value function. Mathematically, the optimal policy π is found as:

$$V^*(s, a) = \max_{\pi} V^{\pi}(s),$$

$$\text{or } Q^*(s, a) = \max_{\pi} Q^{\pi}(s, a),$$

The next subsection is to review the key algorithms and taxonomies used in the literature to find the optimal policies for different scenarios.

9.3.2   Taxonomy of RL Algorithms

Broadly, RL can be classified into two categories including model-free and model-based methods [50]. A non-exhaustive list of RL-based algorithms in these two classes is presented in Fig. 9.6. In the model-based model, the agent is supported to make plan as it can see a range of future possibilities of choices, thus decide between its options well ahead. Thus, the agent can filter out the results into a learned policy. For example, the authors of [51] used this approach and called it as AlphaZero (AZ), wherein the sample efficiency improved significantly over other methods, which were also not having models. However, this approach exposes shortcomings, as the learning by the agent of the model is based only on the experience that itself creates many challenges. The biggest one is that of bias, which can be exploited by the agent, thereby forcing the agent to perform below par in real environment; secondly, it is very computation intensive, which can ultimately result in failure to pay sometime.

On the contrary, the model-free algorithms do not need "model"; as a result, the sample efficiency is lower, but they are easier in implementation and tuning, which makes them quite popular than its counterpart. The algorithms in this type can be further divided based on the learning to be carried out. Accordingly, there are two types of learning carried out. The first one is policy optimization in which the parameter θ is optimized for a policy $\pi_0(\cdot|s_t)$ based on the recent collection of the data.

Some key examples of this optimization are A2C/A3C [52], where performance is maximized by suing gradient ascent, and another is PPO [53], where a surrogate

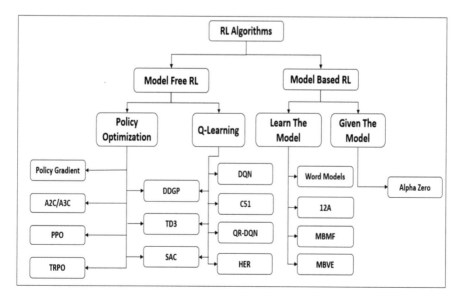

Fig. 9.6 Taxonomy of RL algorithms

objective function is used as an indirect measure of the performance. The second learning method is Q-Learning in which learning of an approximator $Q_\theta(s, a)$ gives an optimal function $Q_*(s, a)$. The objective function for Q-Learning approach is based on the Bellman equation [54]. Recently, this approach is used by in [55] called as DQN, which is a milestone for deep RL and [56] called C51, where the returns are learned leading to the policy expectation as Q_*. In particular, there are some certain algorithms used simultaneously such as policy optimization and Q-Learning to compromise the strengths and weaknesses of either sides. For example, the authors of [57] proposed DDPG, which simultaneously learns policy as well Q-function. In addition, the proposition in [58] proposed a combined approach of SAC and Q-learning with the help of stochastic policies and entropy regularization, thereby giving higher scores.

The model-based RL is not well-defined methods as models can be used in many orthogonal ways. Broadly, they can be classified, based on whether model is given or the model is learned. The learning of the model-based approach is used by [59] and called it as MBMF where pure planning technique and model predictive control are used in the selection of the action on some standard benchmark tasks for deep RL. The given model approach is used by [51], which is called as AZ in which explicit representation of the policy is learned with the pure planning, which produces an action that has strong influence as compared to when policy alone would have produced.

9.4   RL-Based Algorithms for Resource Allocation in FCS

This section summarizes key RL-based algorithms in the literature to address the resource allocation problems in the fog computing environment, which are discussed according to key types, namely, RL-based and DRL-based methods. In particular, the review analysis is conducted to emphasize on describing how the components of RL-based solutions in the fog computing systems such as state space, action space, MDP, and reward are formulated.

9.4.1   Resource Sharing and Management

Considering the fog computing systems as a resource pool with multiple kinds of resources (i.e., CPU, GPU, storage, and memory), resource sharing is an important mechanism to allocate the resource efficiently. In principle, the resource-sharing algorithms require the collaboration of fog entities for exchanging their available resource states, thus facilitating the resource allocation.

The work [60] studies the resource management for conserving energy consumption in the Fog Radio Access Networks (F-RAN), which can provide two main types of services: communication and computation. Considering the dynamic of edge and fog resource states, the network controller is able to make fast and intelligent decisions on the user equipment (UE) communication modes (i.e., C-RAN (Cloud-RAN) mode, D2D mode, and FAP (Fog Access Point) mode) and the on-off states of processors to minimize the long-term power consumption of systems. The well-trained DRL model is built on the system architecture to derive this optimal decision. In this model, the state space is defined as $S = \{s = (s^{\text{processor}}, s^{\text{mode}}, s^{\text{cache}})\}$, where $s^{\text{processor}}$ is a vector representing the current on-off states of all the processors, s^{mode} is a vector representing the current communication modes of all the UEs, and s^{cache} is a vector consisting of the cache state at each D2D transmitter. The network controller is able to control the on-off state of a processor and communication mode of a UE each time step. Thus, to reduce the number of action, the action space is defined as $A = \{a = \{a_{\text{processor}}, a_{\text{mode}}\}\}$, where $a_{\text{processor}}$ indicates "turn on" or "turn off" action for a processor and a_{mode} represents to change the communication mode for a UE (i.e., C-RAN, FAP, or D2D). To achieve the green F-RAN, the reward function is defined as the negative of system energy consumption, which is incurred by operation of processor in the cloud, front-haul transmission, and wireless transmission in the fog tier. To enhance the performance of proposed algorithm, multiple factors are developed and integrated in the DRL model. Firstly, the prioritized replay is proposed to reuse the experienced transition more effectively. Secondly, double DRL is used to overcome the optimistic Q-value estimation as well as improve the learning process in cases of environment change. In particular, transfer learning is integrated to accelerate the learning process, thus allowing the quick convergence of learning. These key factors result in the superiority of proposed algorithms compared to the related and baseline works.

Internet of Vehicles (IoV) where all vehicles are connected has emerged as a fundamental element of smart cities using real-time data to react instantly to user requests. Vehicular fog computing (VFC) has appeared as an emerging paradigm that facilitates the dynamic problems of networking, caching, and computing resources to enhance the efficacy of next-generation vehicular networks [61]. In these networks, vehicles both in movements or parked status are equally sever as fog nodes, which have limited resources for offering the services such as communication, computation, and storage. Considering the immense dynamic and highly complicated nature of VFC environment, enhancing QoS such as real-time response is a challenging job. This sort of problem in vehicular applications is investigated in [62], which aims at seeking efficient resource allocation strategies to minimize the service latency minimization. The Rl algorithm accordingly is developed to achieve the target that employed an LSTM-based DNN to predict the movement and parking status of vehicles, thus facilitating the resource assignment. In addition, the proposed RL technique uses the latest techniques, that is, proximal policy optimization technique, which has the ability to learn continuously the dynamic environment and therefore can adjust to decide the resource allocation correspondingly.

It is a significant challenge to present high-quality, low bit-rate variation and live streaming assistance for vehicles because of the dynamic characteristics of wireless resources and channels of IoV. The combination of a unique transcoding and streaming system for the maximization of video bit-rate and reduces bit-rate variance and time-delays in VFC powered IoV is a potential solution to the challenge. The scheme jointly optimizes the scheduling of vehicles, selection of bit-rate, and spectrum/computational resource allocation as an MDP problem. A deep RL algorithm, that is, soft actor-critic based on the highest entropy frame, is employed for the solution of MDP [63]. Moreover, an asynchronous advantage actor-critic (A3C) RL-based cooperative resource allocation and computation offloading frame for vehicular networks is presented [64].

In another VFC application, a resource-sharing scheme for supporting task offloading in terms of VFC is presented in [65]. In this model, the incentivization of vehicles is performed upon sharing the resource of idle computing over dynamic pricing. In this particular case, task priority, availability of service, and mobility of vehicles are comprehensively acknowledged. An MDP diagram is formulated for task offloading due to the dynamic vehicular environment that aims to maximize the average latency-aware use of tasks in a time. Based on the DRL method, a soft actor-critic is developed for the maximization of the policy of entropy and anticipated reward. Moreover, a mobile network operator (MNO) preference and switching problem are formed by simultaneously analyzing switching cost, various prices that can be charged by diverse MNOs and fog servers, and quality-of-service alterations within MNOs. A switching policy that is based on a double deep Q network (DQN) is presented proving to reduce each vehicle's long-term mean cost with promising reliability and latency performance [66]. Similarly, modeling of optimal computational offloading policy as MDP problem while considering ultra-dense system for mobile edge computing (MEC) is performed. A deep Q-network based on the RL algorithm as a computation offloading method is presented to overcome the large dimensionality that will determine the optimum policy for dynamic statistics and no prior knowledge [67]. A semi-MDP is formulated for the optimum and agile framework of resource slicing that simultaneously allocates the storage, radio resources, and computing of the network provider to various slice requests. Dual NN of deep Q-learning method is implemented that improves the performance by outperforming other RL-based approaches for network slicing management [68].

9.4.2 Task Scheduling

Overall, in the IoT-fog-cloud systems, task scheduling is referred to as making decisions on which tasks are processed by the IoT layer, the fog layer, or the cloud layer to achieve the target design objectives [12, 69]. In most applications, the main objective of scheduling algorithms is to minimize the task execution delay. However, an efficient scheduling design may improve other system performance indicators simultaneously such as reduced energy consumption and balanced workload distribution.

To minimize the long-term service delay and computation cost for the fog computing systems under task deadline and resource constraints, a double deep Q-learning (DDQL)-based scheduling algorithm is introduced in the work

[70]. Considering a fog-based IoT system with hierarchical architecture, the work aims at developing schedulers (also known as agents in the RL algorithm) each of which is embedded in a corresponding gateway (GW) to allocate resources (i.e., virtual machines (VM) embedded in the fog nodes and the cloud servers) for executing tasks. To reduce the dimension of RL-based algorithm, paths with the updated resource states are modeled as state space of system as $S = \left\{ s(t)_j^i = \left(\mu\text{CPU}_j^i, \mu\text{Memory}_j^i, \mu\text{Storage}_j^i \right) \right\}$. In this formula, three elements represent the resource utilization of $path_i$ in terms of CPU, memory, and storage, respectively, at the moment t that $task_j$ arrives at. The agent (i.e., scheduler) is responsible for assigning a certain resource (i.e., VM in fog or cloud) to process the task through the action. Thus, the action space is formulated as $A = \left\{ a_j^i | 1 \leq a_j^i \leq vmn_i \right\}$, where a_j^i is the action that is taken by the $agent_i$ and for a $task_j$ and vmn_i is the total number of VMs in $path_i$. To obtain the end-to-end (E2E) service delay, the immediate reward function is defined as $IR(a)_j^i = 1/nSD_j^i$, where $IR(a)_j^i$ is the immediate reward after taking action a for the $task_j$ in $path_i$ and nSD_j^i is the normalized service delay of $task_j$ in $path_i$. nSD_j^i accounts for waiting time delay in $path_i$ to get the objective to achieve the minimized E2E delay are enabled since the agent tries to maximize the cumulative reward through efficient action selection. In particular, to select the optimal action, the double DQL concept is introduced in the algorithm in which each agent is supported by two separate models as $Q1$ and $Q2$ for action selection and Q-value calculation, respectively. With two Q values, the agents are able to reduce the probability of taking valid and inefficient action, thus accelerating the learning process. For evaluating the performance of framework, the work first creates a simulation environment with multiple agents, state space, action space, and reward functions. Then the proposed DDQL-based scheduling algorithm is applied in this environment to assign appropriately which fog nodes will process the tasks in order to achieve the objectives. In particular, the target network and experience replay mechanisms are integrated into the DDQL-based scheduling policy to cease the fluctuation of results.

In data-driven IoT-based systems, the end devices or IoT sensors constantly generate online tasks, which requires the upper layer such as fog computing or cloud to process within the deadlines. The nature of online tasks exhibits critical challenges for the system to conduct task scheduling since there exists an inherent lack of prior information relating to task arrivals. The issues stress the need for adaptive scheduling solutions, which have been investigated and developed in the literature using the RL principle. In particular, the DRL-based approaches exhibit many effectiveness to deal with the situation of online task scheduling. For example, the work [22] designed an efficient scheduler based on a forward neural network (FNN), which is able to schedule n online tasks at a time to reduce the overall task slowdown. Although the algorithm is well performed in the case of predetermined n, it exposes the limitation in terms of flexibility since adjusting n may lead to adverse performance of system.

In the same method, the RL-based model in [24] is designed to make the scheduling decision for each arrival task. However, such a method is well applied in the cloud environment instead of fog computing since it can induce considerable overheads. The work presented in [71] reveals these aforementioned limitations and proposes a neural task scheduling (NTS) to release them. In principle, NTS adopts the model of recurrent neural network (RNN) based on the pointer network [72] to obtain more flexible output sequences. In addition, the network is integrated by the long short-term memory (LSTM) techniques and attention mechanism [73] to enhance the flexibility and learning efficiency when handling long sequences of tasks. From the RL design perspective, the space state S is modeled as the system state in time slot t represented by all n_t pending tasks with their characteristics (i.e., resource demands of tasks, and execution durations) and amount of remaining resources in future M time slots. In mathematical form, $S = \{s_t\}$, where s_t is a matrix of size $n_t \times (m + 1 + m \cdot M)$ and m is the number of resource types (e.g., CPU, storage, and memory). Regarding the action space, the action at time slot t is defined as $a_t = \{j_1, j_2, \ldots, j_{nt}\}$, which determines the order of resource allocation for the n_t pending tasks. The reward function is defined as $r_t = \sum_{j \in n_t} 1/l_j$, where l_j is the duration of task j execution. Thus, the average slowdown of task is minimized as the agent is aimed at maximizing the cumulative reward. Through extensive simulation, the algorithm is able to efficiently reduce the slowdown of an average task slowdown while ensuring the best QoS achieved.

Furthermore, a task scheduling issue is investigated in the edge computing situation, and various tasks are scheduled to virtual machines for the maximization of the long-term task satisfaction degree. The problem is expressed as MDP for which the state, action, state transition, and reward are created. For time scheduling and resource allocation, DRL is implemented, recognizing the heterogeneity of the tasks and the diversity of possible resources [74]. For the fairness of multi-resource considering diverse tasks, an online task scheduling system, that is, *FairTS* based on DRL techniques, is proposed. The systems learn undeviatingly from experience to efficiently reduce the mean task slowdown while guaranteeing multi-resource fairness among the tasks [75]. Moreover, in industrial applications, network traffic and computational offloading are explored using RL techniques for investigating the tradeoff within service delay and energy consumption. A cost minimization problem by employing the frame of MDP is formulated followed by the proposal of dynamic RL and scheduling algorithm algorithms to resolve the offloading determination problem [76].

Even though fog networking is an encouraging technology to handle the limitations of the cloud and the current networks, there are yet challenges that persist to be evaluated in the future. Most significantly, there is a necessity for a distributed intelligent platform at the edge that controls distributed computing, networking, and storage resources. Optimal distribution decision in fog networks faces several challenges because of contingencies linked with task requirements and available resources at the fog nodes and the extensive range of computing power capabilities of nodes [77]. Moreover, delay within nodes must be considered for the distribution decision that can result in increased processing time. Hence, the difficulties being encountered by the fog computing model are diverse and numerous; they include significant decisions about (i) whether offloading at fog nodes should be done or not, (ii) offloading of the optimal number of tasks, and (iii) given the corresponding resource limits, mapping of incoming tasks to possible fog nodes [78]. Considering the above challenges, the proposed algorithm expresses the offloading problem as an MDP subject to the fog node's behavior and dynamics of the system. MDP enables fog nodes to offload their computation-intensive tasks by choosing the most proper adjacent fog node in the presence of ambiguities on the task requirements and availability of resources at the fog nodes. Nevertheless, the system is unable to accurately predict the transition possibilities and rewards due to dynamically varying incoming task requirements and resource states. To resolve this dilemma, RL can be used to solve MDPs with unknown reward and transition functions by making observations from experience.

9.4.3   Task Offloading and Redistribution

The imbalance of workload among the fog resources mainly caused by the heterogeneity of fog computing environment can degrade the performance of computing systems in the long-term operation. This urges the need to develop efficient mechanisms to address the situation through offloading and redistributing the load.

The task offloading problem considering the uncertainties of mobility of end user (EU) devices, mobility of cloudlets, and the resource availability of cloudlets is studied in [79]. A deep Q-network (DQN) [80] is formulated to learn an efficient solution and then derive the optimal actions on how many tasks will be processed locally by end-user devices and how many task will be offloaded by the cloudlets. In this proposed model, the state space is defined as a $S = \{s = (Q^u, Q^C, D)\}$, where Q^u, Q^C, and D denote the queue state of EU device, the queue state of cloudlets, and the distance state of cloudlets, respectively. The mobility of devices and cloudlets affect the performance of their communication; thus, the distance state is used to capture the change of computing system. To determine the optimal offloading decision, the action space is defined as $A = \{a = (a_0, \ldots, a_i, \ldots, a_N)\}$, where a_0 and a_i are the number of tasks to be processed locally or by cloudlet i, respectively. The immediate reward function is defined as $R(s, a) = U(s, a) - C(s, a)$, where $U(s, a)$ and $C(s, a)$ are immediate utility and cost function, which are calculated as following equations:

$$U(s,a) = \rho \sum_{i=0}^{N} \log(1 + a_i).$$

$$C(s,a) = w_1 I(s,a) + w_2 E(s,a) + w_3 D(s,a) + w_4 \Gamma(s,a).$$

Recall that ρ is a utility constant and N is the number of cloudlets deployed in the systems for assisting the offloading processes. $I(s, a)$, $E(s, a)$, $D(s, a)$, and $\Gamma(s, a)$ are immediate required payment, energy consumption, delay, and task loss probability, respectively. Therefore, by maximizing the cumulative reward, the algorithm enables to obtain the maximized utility as well as minimized operation cost. The Q-network can be considered as a neural network approximator with an approximate action-value function $Q(s, a, \theta)$ with weights θ. At each decision period, the user first takes the state vector $s = (Q^u, Q^c, D)$ as the input of the Q-network and obtains the Q-values $Q(s, a)$ for all possible action as outputs. Then, the user selects the action according to the ε-greedy method. Furthermore, the Q-network is trained by iteratively adjusting the weights θ to minimize a sequence of the loss functions, where the loss function at time-step t is defined as

$$L_t(\theta_t) = E\left[\left(r_t + \gamma \max_{a'} Q(s_{t+1}, a'; \theta_{t-1}) - Q(s_t, a_t; \theta_t)\right)^2\right].$$

Although the DQN-based algorithms are able to achieve excellent performance in high-dimensional decision-making problems [80], the proposed algorithm is evaluated in the simulation environment with only four cloudlets. The task arrival rate is varied to analyze the impact on the queue states of EU devices and cloudlets. In addition, no comparative analysis is performed in the work to compare with baseline or related works; thus, the feasibility of performance improvement is unexplored.

Balancing the workload among nodes and simultaneously minimizing the task processing delay are studied in [26]. In an SDN-based fog computing system, an SDN fog controller is able to know the global information relating to the system states (e.g., task profiles and queue states of fog devices), thus deriving the optimal task offloading. Using the DRL-based approach, the fog controller serves as the agent to make the decision. In this model, the state space is defined as $S = \{s = (n^l, w, Q)\}$ where n^l is the fog node, w is the number of tasks to be allocated per unit time, and $Q = \{(Q_1, \ldots, Q_N)\}$ is a vector indicating the number of tasks currently remaining in the queues of N fog nodes. The action space is in form $A = \{a = (n^0, w^0)\}$, in which n^0 is a neighbor node of n^l and w^0 is the number of tasks to be offloaded by n^0. Aiming at maximizing the utility and simultaneously minimizing the task processing delay and overload probability, the immediate reward function is modeled as $R(s, a) = U(s, a) - (D(s, a) + O(s, a))$, where $U(s, a)$ is the immediate utility, $D(s, a)$ is immediate delay accounting for waiting delay in queues, communication delay for offloading, and execution delay at local device and offloading neighbor node, and $O(s, a)$ is overloaded probability averaging for n^0 and n^l. Q-learning with ε-greedy algorithm is applied in the RL-based model to derive the optimal action selection.

The benefit of task offloading becomes prominent in the case of fog nodes by the selection of the appropriate nodes and suitable resource management while assuring the QoS requirements of the users [81]. An efficient solution is proposed accordingly in the case of heterogeneous service tasks within the multi-fog nodes where both joint tasks offloading and resource allocation management is considered. The problem formulation is based on a partly visible stochastic game where cooperation of each node is performed resulting in the maximization of combined local rewards. A deep recurrent Q-network (DRQN) method is applied to cope with partial visibility and to guarantee the accuracy and convergence of NN, and adaptive exploration-exploitation approach is utilized [81]. Furthermore, for IoT applications, sequential allocation of the fog nodes restricted resources in the case of heterogeneous latency needs is considered. The problem formulation of the Fog radio access network is made as MDP followed by different RL approaches such as Q-learning, Monte Carlo, SARSA, and Expected SARSA to make optimal decision-making policies [82].

In some of the fog-enabled networks, the task nodes that are fog nodes having tasks in queues to be processed are unknown about the resource information of their neighbors. Therefore, offloading decisions require a tradeoff between exploiting the empirically best nodes and exploring other nodes to find more beneficial actions, which is simply addressed by ε-greedy algorithm [83, 84]. However, this low-complexity solution is time-consuming for approaching convergence and nonoptimal [85]. In this context, multi-armed bandit (MAB)-based solutions are developed to address these kinds of shortcomings [86]. In particular, the upper-confidence bound (UCB) mechanism is integrated for obtaining guaranteed performance and low complexity [87, 88]. Accordingly, the work [87] introduced Bandit learning-based Offloading of Tasks (BLOT) algorithm to offloading non-splitable tasks. Meanwhile, D2CIT—a decentralized computation offloading—is proposed in [88] to offloading the subtasks, which are constituted of high-complexity tasks.

For the sake of clarity, Table 9.3 summarizes the notable applications of RL in the fog computing resource allocations proposed in the literature.

9.5 Challenges and Open Issues of RL-Based Resource Allocations

Although RL is a powerful approach to introduce intelligence to fog computing-based systems, however, there are still many challenges and open issues that need to be addressed and overcome to fully exploit the potential of RL in assisting the fog paradigm. This section enumerates key challenges and correspondingly explores the open issues regarding the utilization of RL-based approaches for solving resource allocation problems in the fog computing environment. We identify and discuss them according to three key classes relating to the RL, the fog computing environment, and the computing tasks.

Table 9.3 The summary of key RL-based algorithms in the resource allocation problems

Resource allocation problem	References	RL algorithms and feature	Objective
Resource sharing	[60]	DRL Integrating prioritized replay Using transfer learning	Minimizing the energy consumption
	[62]	DRL Integrating LST-based DNN to predict vehicle movements Using proximal policy optimization	Minimizing the service latency
	[63, 64]	DRL Soft actor-critic technique Using the highest entropy frame	Maximizing the video bit rate Reducing the bit rate variance Reducing the time delays of streaming services
	[65]	DRL Soft actor-critic technique Using dynamic pricing	Maximizing the resource utilization Reducing the time delays of VFC services
	[66]	DQN Adaptive switching policies	Minimizing the long-term cost Ensuring the guaranteed latency Guaranteed operation reliability
Task scheduling	[70]	Double deep Q-Learning Using multi-agent for multi-scheduler Using double Q for action selection and evaluation Integrating the target network and experience replay technique	Reducing the average delay Minimizing the computational cost
	[34]	DRL Modeling RNN with pointer network Integrating LSTM and attention mechanism	Reducing average task slowdown Ensuring the best QoS
	[75]	DRL	Reducing average task slow down Multi-resource fairness
	[74]	DRL Integrating policy-based REINFORCE algorithm Using fully connected NN (FCN) to extract the features	Average task satisfaction degree Increasing the task success ratio
	[76]	Dynamic RL scheduling (DRLS) Deep dynamic scheduling (DDS)	Saving energy consumption Reducing task execution delay

(continued)

Table 9.3 (continued)

Resource allocation problem	References	RL algorithms and feature	Objective
Task offloading	[79]	DQN	Saving energy consumption Reducing task execution delay Minimizing task lost probability
	[26]	DRL Q-learning ε-greedy	Load balancing Minimizing computational cost
	[81]	Q-learning SARSA and Expected SARSA Monte Carlo	Load balancing Minimizing computational cost
	[82]	DRQN Q-learning ε-greedy	Maximizing the total served utility Minimizing the fog resource idle time
	[87, 88]	MBA Using the bandit learning technique Integrating Upper Confidence Bound (UCB)	Reducing the task execution delay Minimizing the energy and computation cost

9.5.1 RL-Related Challenges

Nature of RL-Based Algorithms

Naturally, the RL-based algorithms are time- and resource-consuming since they require a large volume of data collected through exploration and exploitation processes to derive the effectiveness of learning model. Meanwhile, fog computing resources are heterogeneous and limited in terms of computation, storage, and energy compared to cloud computing servers. Therefore, running the RL-based algorithms on the fog devices in the long-term operation is a challenging job that calls for appropriate and lightweight algorithm designs to tackle this challenge.

Load Balancing in RL-Enabled Fog Computing

The RL approaches can be helpful for nodes to find the optimal policies (i.e., the number of tasks and size of tasks, offloadees in both the fog stratum and cloud stratum) to offload their requested tasks. If the overload probability and processing time is minimal, the action selection is considered optimal [89]. However, the action selection in most reviewed works is mainly dependent on the exploration policy.

This situation probably leads to greedy and optimistic decisions, which choose the more powerful fog resources to offload the tasks, thus resulting in the imbalance of workload consequently. To strike the imbalance situation from RL perspective, merging model-free RL learning with a model-based learning method can provide bias-free results having less dependency on exploration policy.

Task Scheduling in RL-Enabled Fog Computing

Even though the fog node is equipped with better storage and computing power, however, it still possesses resources much lesser than cloud servers. Due to network heterogeneity, complexity, and uncertainty of the wireless environment, task scheduling in the fog computing environment has been categorized as a complex problem [70]. The RL algorithm can model complex problems; however, by increasing the state and action space dimensions, the hardware requirements of the scheduler will also need to increase. If we consider deep RL solutions for multidimensional problems, we would require multiple deep learning solutions that will add to computational power, storage, and memory requirements. The RL should provide a lightweight but efficient solution to a complex task scheduling problem.

Energy-Efficiency Tradeoff in RL-Enabled Fog Computing

In time-critical IoT applications, RL-assisted fog computing systems could bring intelligence features to utilize readily available data and computing resources. Minimizing delay and energy consumption simultaneously has been a key challenge for RL algorithms [90]. First, the training of learning model requires high-energy consumption, and similarly, fast learning on time-critical systems given limited samples is a complex problem for RL-enabled fog systems. Thus, there are many open challenges in deploying large-scale state-action space RL models for resource-constrained fog systems.

Real-Time Responsiveness in RL-Enabled Fog

Ultra-reliable and low latency communication (URLLC) and real-time interaction are one of the main enablers of IoT and 5G communication [91]. Fog computing can support computation tasks with low latency, thus enabling to provide some kinds of real-time applications. In the case of a heterogeneous IoT network, some applications are delay-tolerant, while others are delay-sensitive. The RL algorithm provides intelligent utilization of resource capability to fog nodes; however, RL algorithms also consume time to process large-scale state-action-reward tuple [92]. In the case of multidimensional states and action space, the processing time further increases. Therefore, one of the critical challenges of the RL-enabled fog network is to intelligently satisfy time-critical IoT applications. The deep RL system can learn more quickly and efficiently through episodic memory and meta-learning technique, which have been not explored in the literature [92].

Advance of Optimization Algorithms

In fact, reinforcement learning algorithms are kinds of time-consuming works since it requires extensive time dedicated to the learning process. Therefore, the RL-based algorithms should be advanced to reduce the convergence time, thus accelerating the decision-making. In addition, the performance of RL-based algorithms is dependent on the complexity of fog networks and arrival rate of tasks. Thus, for achieving a good tradeoff of the training time cost and the performance, it is strongly recommended to prepare the sample data set to a reasonable scale with sampling technology to reduce the complexity of scheduling model. Advancing algorithms is required to improve the speed and effectiveness of learning process. How to reduce the dimension of problems (i.e., state space and action space) to accelerate the learning process is an open issue.

9.5.2 Fog Computing Environment-Related Challenges

The presence of fog computing tier is increasingly essential in IoT-enabled systems to meet any application requirement. However, various applications require different designs of fog computing architecture (i.e., either specific or agnostic), which totally can contribute as a challenging factor to use RL in this context. This is because there is no common RL-based solutions which can be used for different fog computing architectures and applications.

RL-Based Resource Allocation in F-RAN

For densely deployed IoT devices, cloud radio access network (C-RAN) architecture is proposed. C-RAN improves spectral efficiency and reduces energy consumption. However, the demand for IoT devices and applications is increasing, placing a high burden on centralized cloud computing. Busy cloud servers and limited front-haul capacity cause large computation and transmission delays. Some IoT applications are delay-sensitive and cannot tolerate such delays. To handle this problem, F-RAN is a critical solution for the fifth-generation (5G) communication to support the URLLC requirement for IoT devices and applications [95]. The fog nodes are capable of performing signal processing, computation, and RF functionalities. IoT environment is heterogeneous in nature with various traffic transmission rates and latency needs. The fog nodes are expected to allocate resources in Fog-RAN efficiently. RL method provides a solution for efficient resource utilization along with satisfying low-latency requirements for various IoT applications. Multi-agent RL is utilized to enhance network resource utilization in heterogeneous environments. Similarly, the model-free RL technique is used for user scheduling in heterogeneous networks for network energy efficiency [96]. Various RL methods such as Q-learning, SARSA, Expected SARSA (E-SARSA), and Monte Carlo (MC) are used for resource allocation problems. However, there are still open issues such as providing dynamic resource allocation framework with heterogeneous service time. Similarly, collaborative resource allocation mechanism with multiple fog nodes is one of the future directions.

RL-Based Power Consumption Optimization for F-RAN

F-RAN with 5G support is well suited to provide various IoT services including healthcare, industrial IoT, and autonomous vehicles. In F-RAN, each device can operate in different communication modes including D2D, C-RAN, or FAP. In resource management mechanism, communication mode selection problem is considered NP-hard due to network dynamics and a continuously changing environment. Nevertheless, applying deep reinforcement learning (DRL) has shown considerable benefits for complex environment with high-dimensional raw input data. The devices can obtain the desired information locally without accessing base station due to the caching capabilities of D2D transmitters. In this way, the burden on front-haul can be reduced by traffic offloading and turning off some processors in the cloud for energy optimization. The dynamics of cache state of D2D transmitter can be modeled as MDP [97]. In such an MDP problem, the network controller learns to minimize the system power consumption by adjusting devices communication modes and processors on-off states at each learning step. However, in the DRL-based resource allocation mechanism, further research is required to utilize power control of D2D communicating devices, sub-channel allocation, and front-haul resource allocation for improving the F-RAN performance.

RL for Ultra-dense Fog Network

An ultra-dense network with an assistant of fog computing is a promising solution to sustain the increasing traffic demand in wireless networks. Network densification brings a number of challenges including resource management [98]. Machine learning particularly RL has been proven to solve resource management challenges effectively. In an ultra-dense fog network scenario, RL algorithms need to enable the parallelism and partition of large-scale networks to manage the computational load of fog devices. Similarly, in the case of wired and wireless backhaul networks, bandwidth allocation must be considered since it is an important factor affecting the performance. The powerful capability of deep learning and neural networks can enhance the performance of resulting DRL-based methods to solve high-dimensional problems. Many proposed models have reduced the dimension by efficiently configuring the state and action spaces. However, none of the existing works has been investigated and developed the RL-based algorithms for the large-scale fog computing systems, which basically contain a large number of fog nodes. Practically, this is an open issue.

Reliability of Fog Networks

The complex nature of fog computing environment may cause the reliability problem for the fog network. For example, the dynamic mobility of fog nodes that strongly impacts on the fog resource status must be taken into account in designing the algorithms. In addition, the outdated channel probably blocks the communication between the fog nodes [99]. Moreover, VMs in both fog stratum and cloud may fail and lead to QoS degradation [100]. Hence, reliability of VMs should also be considered when addressing the fog resource provisioning problem. None of the reviewed algorithms cover and consider the reliability of fog network, thus opening the issue for future studies.

Security and Trust in Fog Network

A fog node is responsible to ensure the security and trust for other devices. Fog node must ensure the global concealing process on the released data. Fog nodes must ensure a mechanism for all nodes to have a certain level of trust in each other [93]. The fog node handles the workload for other nodes in real time. Protecting the integrity in case of a malicious attack is one of the challenges of fog computing. Similarly, authentication is essential to provide a secure connection between the fog node and other devices. Authentication is needed to provide real-time data communication, particularly in a scenario where nodes are moving from one coverage area to another. The user must experience a minimum delay in real-time services while traveling. The latency is caused by the authentication process performed in the fog node. During the authentication process, there is a possibility of user identity exposure to attackers [94]. Authorization and authentication in fog networks are one of the major concerns. Providing real-time services in a fog computing environment with secure authentication is one of the priority research areas.

9.5.3 Computing Task-Related Challenges

In the IoT-based context, requesting computing tasks is varied in a wide range in terms of profiles, complexity levels, and resource requirements for computation. These property variations serve as a challenging factor to apply RL-based algorithms.

Big Data Analytics

The IoT and end user devices increasingly produce a huge amount of high-dimensional big data to be processed at the fog nodes [101]. A selection of appropriate prediction model and RL parameters, for example, learning rate and discount factor, needs to be considered carefully to obtain an optimized model for big data analytics. A proper analytic model can produce accurate results and can learn from heterogeneous data sources. In big data analytics, one of the challenges a learning algorithm faces is how to distribute big data among resources constrained fog devices fairly.

Data Fragmentation for Parallel Computing Exploitation

Besides big data analytics-related tasks, some of the tasks in the IoT-enabled systems can be complex in terms of size and data structure. For example, the input data of a ML computing task can contain four types of data: text, image, video, and audio, which require many kinds of resources to process. However, the limitation of fog computing resource causes imbalance of workload among the fog nodes since many of them with insufficient available resources is unable to process a single task. Data division is a key approach to solve these issues in the complicated heterogeneous fog environment [27]. However, the diversity of input data structure in practical application requires alternative division solutions for improving or optimizing the system performance. For instance, as the data dependency constraints among the subtasks are taken into account in the associated workflow model, the collaborative task offloading mechanism must be adapted to such a change accordingly. In addition, the data can be divided according to different features such as by size explicitly. In this way, an optimization can be formulated to find the optimal number of data subsets and associated sizes of data subset for optimizing the system performance. Although the input data of tasks can be divided to take the benefit of parallel computing, it may raise the large space as applying RL models. Therefore, to achieve the efficient tradeoff between the performance and time-consuming training, it requires to search for an optimal number of data subsets divided from the input data.

9.6　Conclusions

Fog computing has been integrated in a wide range of IoT-enabled systems as a support computing resource to cure the pressure of cloud computing resources, thus improving the operation performance of systems. However, the fog computing environment is a complex resource pool in terms of heterogeneity, mobility, and dynamic change, which serve as critical barriers for achieving efficient and effective resource allocation strategy. In addition, the computing tasks are varied with respective to task characteristics and resource demands. Moreover, most of the efficient heuristics algorithms in the literature lack the adaptivity and flexibility to respond to the uncertainties of fog computing environment. These aforementioned challenges stress a need to develop an alternative for resource allocation solutions to flexibly deal with the complexity of fog computing environment.

This chapter surveys the literature on the applications of RL in the fog computing environment to allocate computing resources for task computation and execution. The concept of RL is briefly introduced to highlight accordingly the role and algorithmic model to support deriving the optimal decision makings in many practical applications (e.g., game, robotics, and finance). The start-of-the art literature review is conducted to describe intensively the key RL-based solutions for the resource allocation problems in the fog computing environment. We identify and analyze these algorithms according to three major problems, namely, resource sharing, task scheduling, and task offloading. Finally, the work also explored and discussed the key challenges faced by the nature of RL-based algorithms, the fog computing environment, and the computing tasks in a variety of practical applications. The corresponding open issues are also presented for further studies.

References

1. Zanella A, Bui N, Castellani A, Vangelista L, Zorzi M (2014) Internet of things for smart cities. IEEE Internet Things J 1(1):22–32
2. Saleem Y, Crespi N, Rehmani MH, Copeland R (2019) Internet of things-aided smart grid: technologies, architectures, applications, prototypes, and future research directions. IEEE Access 7:62962–63003
3. Chekired DA, Khoukhi L, Mouftah HT (2018) Industrial IoT data scheduling based on hierarchical fog computing: a key for enabling smart factory. IEEE Trans Industr Inform 14(10):4590–4602
4. Jin J, Gubbi J, Marusic S, Palaniswami M (2014) An information framework for creating a smart city through internet of things. IEEE Internet Things J 1(2):112–121
5. Tran-Dang H, Kim D (2018) An information framework for internet of things services in physical internet. IEEE Access 6:43967–43977
6. Botta A, de Donato W, Persico V, Pescape A (2016) Integration of cloud computing and internet of things: a survey. Futur Gener Comput Syst 56:684–700
7. Dastjerdi AV, Buyya R (2016) Fog computing: helping the internet of things realize its potential. Computer 49(8):112–116
8. Sarkar S, Chatterjee S, Misra S (2018) Assessment of the suitability of fog computing in the context of internet of things. IEEE Trans Cloud Comput 6(1):46–59
9. Aazam M, Zeadally S, Harras KA (2018) Offloading in fog computing for IoT: review, enabling technologies, and research opportunities. Futur Gener Comput Syst 87:278–289
10. Patil-Karpe S, Brahmananda SH, Karpe S (2020) Review of resource allocation in fog computing. In: Smart intelligent computing application. Springer Singapore, pp 327–334. [Online]. Available https://doi.org/10.1007/978-981-13-9282-530
11. Yin L, Luo J, Luo H (2018) Tasks scheduling and resource allocation in fog computing based on containers for smart manufacturing. IEEE Trans Industr Inform 14(10):4712–4721
12. Mouradian C et al (2018) A comprehensive survey on fog computing: state-of-the-art and research challenges. IEEE Commun Surv Tutor 20(1):416–464

13. Sutton RS, Barto AG (2018) Reinforcement learning: an introduction. MIT Press
14. Szepesvari C (2010) Algorithms for reinforcement learning. Synth Lect Artif Intell Mach Learn 4(1):1–103
15. Gedeon J, Brandherm F, Egert R, Grube T, Muhlhauser M (2019) What is the fog? Edge computing revisited: promises, applications and future challenges. IEEE Access 7:152847–152878
16. Liu X, Qin Z, Gao Y (2019) Resource allocation for edge computing in IoT networks via reinforcement learning. In: Proceedings of the IEEE ICC
17. Dutreilh X et al (2011) Using reinforcement learning for autonomic resource allocation in clouds: towards a fully automated workflow. In: Proceedings of the ICAS
18. Lin X, Wang Y, Pedram M (2016) A reinforcement learning-based power management framework for green computing data centers. In: Proceedings of the IEEE IC2E
19. Yuan J, Jiang X, Zhong L, Yu H (2012) Energy aware resource scheduling algorithm for data center using reinforcement learning. In: Proceeding on ICICTA
20. Li Y, Wen Y, Tao D, Guan K (2020) Transforming cooling optimization for green data center via deep reinforcement learning. IEEE Trans Cybern 50(5):2002–2013
21. Arulkumaran K, Deisenroth MP, Brundage M, Bharath AA (2017) Deep reinforcement learning: a brief survey. IEEE Signal Process Mag 34(6):26–38
22. Mao H, Alizadeh M, Menache I, Kandula S (2016) Resource management with deep reinforcement learning. In: Proceedings of the ACM HotNets
23. Che H, Bai Z, Zuo R, Li H (2020) A deep reinforcement learning approach to the optimization of data center task scheduling. Complexity 2020:1–12. [Online]. Available: https://doi.org/10.1155/2020/3046769
24. Wei Y, Pan L, Liu S, Wu L, Meng X (2018) Drl-scheduling: an intelligent qos-aware job scheduling framework for applications in clouds. IEEE Access 6:55112–55125
25. Shyalika C, Silva T, Karunananda A (2020) Reinforcement learning in dynamic task scheduling: a review. SN Comput Sci 1(6):306
26. Baek J-y, Kaddoum G, Garg S, Kaur K, Gravel V (2019) Managing fog networks using reinforcement learning based load balancing algorithm. In: Proceedings of the IEEE WCNC
27. Tran-Dang H, Kim D-S (2021) Task priority-based resource allocation algorithm for task offloading in fog-enabled IoT systems. In: Proceedings of the IEEE ICOIN
28. Yousefpour A, Ishigaki G, Gour R, Jue JP (2018) On reducing IoT service delay via fog offloading. IEEE Internet Things J 5(2):998–1010
29. Ahmed A et al (2019) Fog computing applications: taxonomy and requirements. arXiv preprint arXiv:190711621
30. Liu Z, Yang X, Yang Y, Wang K, Mao G (2019) Dats: dispersive stable task scheduling in heterogeneous fog networks. IEEE Internet Things J 6(2):3423–3436
31. Liu Z, Yang Y, Wang K, Shao Z, Zhang J (2020) Post: parallel offloading of splittable tasks in heterogeneous fog networks. IEEE Internet Things J 7(4):3170–3183
32. Tran-Dang H, Kim D-S (2021) Frato: fog resource based adaptive task offloading for delay-minimizing IoT service provisioning. IEEE Trans Parallel Distrib Syst 32(10):2491–2508
33. Guo K, Sheng M, Quek TQ, Qiu Z (2019) Task offloading and scheduling in fog ran: a parallel communication and computation perspective. IEEE Wireless Commun Lett 9(2):215–218
34. Bian S, Huang X, Shao Z, Yang Y (2019) Neural task scheduling with reinforcement learning for fog computing systems. In: Proceedings of the IEEE GLOBECOM
35. Fernando N et al (2019) Opportunistic fog for IoT: challenges and opportunities. IEEE Internet Things J 6(5):8897–8910
36. Xiao Y, Zhu C (2017) Vehicular fog computing: vision and challenges. In: Proceedings of the IEEE PerCom workshops
37. Khattak HA, Islam SU, Din IU, Guizani M (2019) Integrating fog computing with vanets: a consumer perspective. IEEE Commun Stand Mag 3(1):19–25

38. Nishio T, Shinkuma R, Takahashi T, Mandayam NB (2013) Service oriented heterogeneous resource sharing for optimizing service latency in mobile cloud. In: Proceedings of the ACM MobiHoc
39. Oueis J, Strinati EC, Sardellitti S, Barbarossa S (2015) Small cell clustering for efficient distributed fog computing: a multi-user case. In: 2015 IEEE 82nd vehicular technology conference (VTC2015-Fall), pp 1–5
40. Masri W, Ridhawi IA, Mostafa N, Pourghomi P (2017) Minimizing delay in IoT systems through collaborative fog-to-fog (f2f) communication. In: 2017 ninth international conference on ubiquitous and future networks (ICUFN), pp 1005–1010
41. Lindelauf R (2021) Nuclear deterrence in the algorithmic age: game theory revisited. In: NL ARMS, p 421
42. Kim C (2020) Deep reinforcement learning by balancing offline Monte Carlo and online temporal difference use based on environment experiences. Symmetry 12(10):1685
43. Kovari B, Hegedus F, Becsi T (2020) Design of a reinforcement learning-based lane keeping planning agent for automated vehicles. Appl Sci 10(20):7171
44. Mousavi SS, Schukat M, Howley E (2016) Deep reinforcement learning: an overview. In: Proceedings on intelligent system, pp 426–440
45. Costa OLV, Assumpc E, Filho AO, Boukas E, Marques R (1999) Constrained quadratic state feedback control of discrete-time Markovian jump linear systems. Automatica 35(4):617–626
46. Mahadevan S (1996) Average reward reinforcement learning: foundations, algorithms, and empirical results. Mach Learn 22(1):159–195
47. Chandak Y, Theocharous G, Kostas J, Jordan S, Thomas P (2019) Learning action representations for reinforcement learning. In: International conference on machine learning. PMLR, pp 941–950
48. Kanervisto A, Scheller C, Hautamaki V (2020) Action space shaping in deep reinforcement learning. In: 2020 IEEE conference on games (CoG), pp 479–486
49. Kumar A, Buckley T, Lanier JB, Wang Q, Kavelaars A, Kuzovkin I (2019) Offworld gym: open-access physical robotics environment for real-world reinforcement learning benchmark and research. arXiv preprint arXiv:191008639
50. Moerland TM, Broekens J, Plaat A, Jonker CM (2023) Model-based reinforcement learning: a survey. Found Trends Mach Learn 16(1):1–118
51. Silver D, Hubert T, Schrittwieser J, Antonoglou I, Lai M, Guez A, Lanctot M et al (2017) Mastering chess and shogi by self-play with a general reinforcement learning algorithm. arXiv preprint arXiv:171201815
52. Mnih V, Badia AP, Mirza M, Graves A, Lillicrap T, Harley T, Silver D, Kavukcuoglu K (2016) Asynchronous methods for deep reinforcement learning. In: International conference on machine learning. PMLR, pp 1928–1937
53. Schulman J, Wolski F, Dhariwal P, Radford A, Klimov O (2017) Proximal policy optimization algorithms. arXiv preprint arXiv:170706347
54. Serrano JB, Curi S, Krause A, Neu G (2021) Logistic Q-learning. In: International conference on artificial intelligence and statistics. PMLR, pp 3610–3618
55. Mnih V, Kavukcuoglu K, Silver D, Graves A, Antonoglou I, Wierstra D, Riedmiller M (2013) Playing atari with deep reinforcement learning. arXiv preprint arXiv:13125602
56. Bellemare MG, Dabney W, Munos R (2017) A distributional perspective on reinforcement learning. In: International conference on machine learning. PMLR, pp 449–458
57. Lillicrap TP, Hunt JJ, Pritzel A, Heess N, Erez T, Tassa Y, Silver D, Wierstra D (2015) Continuous control with deep reinforcement learning. arXiv preprint arXiv:150902971
58. Haarnoja T, Zhou A, Abbeel P, Levine S (2018) Soft actor-critic: off-policy maximum entropy deep reinforcement learning with a stochastic actor. In: International conference on machine learning. PMLR, pp 1861–1870
59. Nagabandi A, Kahn G, Fearing RS, Levine S (2018) Neural network dynamics for model-based deep reinforcement learning with model-free fine-tuning. In: 2018 IEEE international conference on robotics and automation (ICRA), pp 7559–7566

60. Sun Y, Peng M, Mao S (2019) Deep reinforcement learning-based mode selection and resource management for green fog radio access networks. IEEE Internet Things J 6(2): 1960–1971
61. He Y, Zhao N, Yin H (2017) Integrated networking, caching, and computing for connected vehicles: a deep reinforcement learning approach. IEEE Trans Veh Technol 67(1):44–55
62. Lee S-S, Lee S (2020) Resource allocation for vehicular fog computing using reinforcement learning combined with heuristic information. IEEE Internet Things J 7(10):10450–10464
63. Fu F, Kang Y, Zhicai Zhang F, Richard Y, Tuan W (2020) Soft actor–critic DRL for live transcoding and streaming in vehicular fog-computing-enabled IoV. IEEE Internet Things J 8(3):1308–1321
64. Feng J, Richard Yu F, Pei Q, Chu X, Jianbo D, Zhu L (2019) Cooperative computation offloading and resource allocation for blockchain-enabled mobile-edge computing: a deep reinforcement learning approach. IEEE Internet Things J 7:6214–6228
65. Shi J, Du J, Wang J, Wang J, Yuan J (2020) Priority-aware task offloading in vehicular fog computing based on deep reinforcement learning. IEEE Trans Veh Technol 69(12): 16067–16081
66. Zhang X, Xiao Y, Li Q, Saad W (2020) Deep reinforcement learning for fog computing-based vehicular system with multi-operator support. In: ICC 2020 IEEE international conference on communications (ICC), pp 1–6
67. Chen X, Zhang H, Wu C, Mao S, Ji Y, Bennis M (2018) Performance optimization in mobile-edge computing via deep reinforcement learning. In: 2018 IEEE 88th vehicular technology conference (VTC-Fall), pp 1–6
68. Van Huynh N, Hoang DT, Nguyen DN, Dutkiewicz E (2019) Optimal and fast real-time resource slicing with deep dueling neural networks. IEEE J Sel Areas Commun 37(6): 1455–1470
69. Guevara JC, da Fonseca NLS (2021) Task scheduling in cloud-fog computing systems. Peer Peer Netw Appl 14(2):962–977
70. Gazori P, Rahbari D, Nickray M (2020) Saving time and cost on the scheduling of fog-based IoT applications using deep reinforcement learning approach. Futur Gener Comput Syst 110: 1098–1115
71. Bian S, Huang X, Shao Z, Yang Y (2019) Neural task scheduling with reinforcement learning for fog computing systems. In: 2019 IEEE global communications conference (GLOBECOM), pp 1–6
72. Vinyals O, Fortunato M, Jaitly N (2015) Pointer networks. In: NIPS, pp 2692–2700. [Online]. Available https://arxiv.org/pdf/1506.03134.pdf
73. Sutskever I, Vinyals O, Le QV (2014) Sequence to sequence learning with neural networks. In: Proceedings of the 27th international conference on neural information processing systems – volume 2, ser. NIPS'14. MIT Press, Cambridge, MA, pp 3104–3112
74. Sheng S, Chen P, Chen Z, Wu L, Yao Y (2021) Deep reinforcement learning-based task scheduling in IoT edge computing. Sensors 21(5):1666
75. Bian S, Huang X, Shao Z (2019) Online task scheduling for fog computing with multi-resource fairness. In: 2019 IEEE 90th vehicular technology conference (VTC2019-Fall), pp 1–5
76. Wang Y, Wang K, Huang H, Miyazaki T, Guo S (2018) Traffic and computation co-offloading with reinforcement learning in fog computing for industrial applications. IEEE Trans Industr Inform 15(2):976–986
77. Yu L, Chen L, Cai Z, Shen H, Liang Y, Pan Y (2016) Stochastic load balancing for virtual resource management in datacenters. IEEE Trans Cloud Comput 8(2):459–472
78. Lee G, Saad W, Bennis M (2019) An online optimization framework for distributed fog network formation with minimal latency. IEEE Trans Wirel Commun 18(4):2244–2258
79. Van Le D, Tham C-K (2018) A deep reinforcement learning based offloading scheme in ad-hoc mobile clouds. In: IEEE INFOCOM 2018-IEEE conference on computer communications workshops (INFOCOM WKSHPS), pp 760–765

80. Mnih V, Kavukcuoglu K, Silver D, Rusu AA, Veness J, Bellemare MG, Graves A, Riedmiller M, Fidjeland AK, Ostrovski G, Petersen S, Beattie C, Sadik A, Antonoglou I, King H, Kumaran D, Wierstra D, Legg S, Hassabis D (2015) Human-level control through deep reinforcement learning. Nature 518(7540):529–533

81. Baek J, Kaddoum G (2021) Heterogeneous task offloading and resource allocations via deep recurrent reinforcement learning in partial observable multifog networks. IEEE Internet Things J 8(2):1041–1056

82. Nassar A, Yilmaz Y (2019) Reinforcement learning for adaptive resource allocation in fog ran for IoT with heterogeneous latency requirements. IEEE Access 7:128014–128025

83. Min M, Wan X, Xiao L, Chen Y, Xia M, Wu D, Dai H (2018) Learning-based privacy-aware offloading for healthcare IoT with energy harvesting. IEEE Internet Things J 6(3):4307–4316

84. Min M, Xiao L, Chen Y, Cheng P, Wu D, Zhuang W (2019) Learning-based computation offloading for IoT devices with energy harvesting. IEEE Trans Veh Technol 68(2):1930–1941

85. Auer P, Cesa-Bianchi N, Fischer P (2002) Finite-time analysis of the multiarmed bandit problem. Mach Learn 47(2):235–256

86. Berry DA, Fristedt B (1985) Bandit problems: sequential allocation of experiments (monographs on statistics and applied probability), vol 5. Chapman and Hall, London, pp 71–87

87. Zhu Z, Liu T, Yang Y, Luo X (2019) Blot: bandit learning-based offloading of tasks in fog-enabled networks. IEEE Trans Parallel Distrib Syst 30(12):2636–2649

88. Misra S, Rachuri SP, Deb PK, Mukherjee A (2021) Multi-armed bandit-based decentralized computation offloading in fog-enabled IoT. IEEE Internet Things J 8(12):10010–10017

89. Talaat FM, Saraya MS, Saleh AI, Ali HA, Ali SH (2020) A load balancing and optimization strategy (LBOS) using reinforcement learning in fog computing environment. J Ambient Intell Humaniz Comput 11:4951–4966

90. La QD, Ngo MV, Dinh TQ, Quek TQ, Shin H (2019) Enabling intelligence in fog computing to achieve energy and latency reduction. Digit Commun Netw 5(1):3–9

91. Naha RK et al (2018) Fog computing: survey of trends, architectures, requirements, and research directions. IEEE Access 6:47980–48009

92. Botvinick M et al (2019) Reinforcement learning, fast and slow. Trends Cogn Sci 23(5): 408–422

93. Illy P, Kaddoum G, Moreira CM, Kaur K, Garg S (2019) Securing fog-to-things environment using intrusion detection system based on ensemble learning. In: 2019 IEEE wireless communications and networking conference (WCNC), pp 1–7

94. Abeshu A, Chilamkurti N (2018) Deep learning: the frontier for distributed attack detection in fog-to-things computing. IEEE Commun Mag 56(2):169–175

95. Khumalo NN, Oyerinde OO, Mfupe L (2018) Reinforcement learning-based resource management model for fog radio access network architectures in 5g. IEEE Access 9:12706–12716

96. Nassar A, Yilmaz Y (2019) Resource allocation in fog ran for heterogeneous IoT environments based on reinforcement learning. In: ICC 2019 IEEE international conference on communications (ICC), pp 1–6

97. Sun Y, Peng M, Mao S (2018) Deep reinforcement learning-based mode selection and resource management for green fog radio access networks. IEEE Internet Things J 6(2): 1960–1971

98. Mukherjee M, Shu L, Wang D (2018) Survey of fog computing: fundamental, network applications, and research challenges. IEEE Commun Surv Tutor 20(3):1826–1857

99. Dinh THL, Kaneko M, Fukuda EH, Boukhatem L (2021) Energy efficient resource allocation optimization in fog radio access networks with outdated channel knowledge. IEEE Trans Green Commun Netw 5(1):146–159

100. Yao J, Ansari N (2019) Fog resource provisioning in reliability-aware IoT networks. IEEE Internet Things J 6(5):8262–8269

101. Prabhu C (2019) Fog computing, deep learning and big data analytics-research directions. Springer

Chapter 10
Bandit Learning and Matching-Based Distributed Task Offloading in Fog Networks

This chapter proposes an algorithm called BLM-DTO, which allows each fog node (FN) to implement the task offloading operations in a distributed manner in the fog computing networks (FCNs). Fundamentally, BLM-DTO leverages the principle of matching game theory to achieve a stable matching outcome based on preference relations of two sides of the game. Due to the dynamic nature of fog computing environment, the preference relation of one-side game players is unknown a priori and achieved only by iteratively interacting with the other side of players. Thus, BLM-DTO further incorporates multi-armed bandit (MAB) learning using Thompson sampling (TS) technique to adaptively learn their unknown preferences. Extensive simulation results demonstrate the potential advantages of the proposed TS-type offloading algorithm over the ε-greedy and upper-bound confidence (UCB)-type baselines.

10.1 Introduction

Fog computing has been introduced and integrated widely in the practical IoT and cyber-physical systems (CPS). As an extension of cloud computing, fog computing placed between the cloud layer and user equipment (UE) layer in the systems also provides the cloud-like services (i.e., IaaS, PaaS, SaaS) to the UEs. In this context, fog computing platforms can process and offload most tasks requested by the UEs on behalf of the cloud servers [1], thereby allowing the systems to achieve improved performances in terms of service delay, energy saving, and service cost [2]. However, to realize these benefits of fog computing paradigm, it requires efficient task offloading operations to overcome inherent challenges in the fog computing environment such as the heterogeneity of computing devices and various types of computational tasks with different requirements [3].

There are a large number of centralized optimization techniques and algorithms proposed in the literature to provide optimal offloading solutions [4]. These

© The Author(s), under exclusive license to Springer Nature Switzerland AG 2023
H. Tran-Dang, D.-S. Kim, *Cooperative and Distributed Intelligent Computation in Fog Computing*, https://doi.org/10.1007/978-3-031-33920-2_10

approaches require a centralized control to gather the global system information, thus incurring a significant overhead and computation complexity of algorithms, especially in the case of density and heterogeneity of FCNs [5]. The aforementioned limitations of optimization have led to a second class of game theory-based offloading solutions that can avoid the cost-intensive centralized resource management as well as substantially reduce the complexity of algorithms [6]. However, classical game theoretical algorithms such as best response require some information regarding actions of other players [7]. Correspondingly, many assumptions are introduced in the game theory-based algorithms to simplify the system models that, in some cases, are impractical. In addition, most game-theoretic solutions, for example, Nash equilibrium, investigate one-sided stability notions in which equilibrium deviations are evaluated unilaterally per player.

Recently, matching theory has emerged as a promising technique applied to derive distributed task offloading algorithms [8] that significantly can reduce the service latency in fog-based systems. More importantly, the matching-based approaches have potential advantages over the optimization and game theory-based solution owing to the distributed and low computational complexity algorithm. However, most of them assume the full preferences of players are known a priori, which is not realistic in many practical applications. For example, the resource supply-side FNs are likely to be uncertain about the types and requirement of tasks requested from the EU. Therefore, to produce the preference relation of tasks, the players of two sides must interact iteratively to learn their unknown preferences. Multi-armed bandit (MAB) is a common approach to modeling this type of learning process, which aims to solve the exploitation and exploration dilemma. In the era of fog computing, ϵ-greedy and UCB techniques have been used to design decentralized offloading solutions [9, 10]. In this paper, we apply Thompson sampling (TS) technique [11] for bandit learning and investigate its performance in the dynamic fog computing environment. To the best of our knowledge, this work presents the first combination of the matching theory and TS-based bandit learning technique to design a distributed algorithm for task offloading that is able to minimize the overall task execution delay in the fog-enabled systems.

10.2   Background and Related Works

10.2.1   One-to-One Matching-Based Computation Offloading Algorithms

The most prominent model of OTO matching is the marriage model. In this model, there are two distinct sets of agents represented by $X = \{x_1, x_2, \ldots, x_n\}$ and $Y = \{y_1, y_2, \ldots, y_n\}$, as illustrated in Fig. 10.1.

Each agent has a complete PL over the agents on the other side. Assume that an arbitrary agent x in X has a PL denoted as $P(x) = \{y_2, y_4, x, y_1, y_3, \ldots\}$. This means

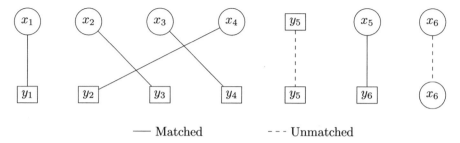

Fig. 10.1 An example of OTO matching between agents of two sets, X and Y

that x prefers agent y_2 to y_4 and prefers remaining single (x) over matching with y_1 or y_3. Denote $y_i >_x y_j$ to express that an agent x prefers agent y_i to y_j in the matching game. In particular, as $y_i \geq_x y_j$, there exists a tie in the PL of agent x. In summary, the OTO matching model is defined as follows:

Definition 10.1 The outcome of the OTO matching model is a matching function $M : X \cup Y \rightarrow X \cup Y$ such that the three following constraints are satisfied:

- For any $x \in X$, $M(x) \in Y \cup \{x\}$.
- For any $y \in Y$, $M(y) \in X \cup \{y\}$.
- For any $x \in X$ and $y \in Y$, $x = M(y)$ if and only *if* $y = M(x)$.

In the one-to-one matching model, each agent x can only be matched with one agent y, and x remains unmatched if $M(x) = x$. The objective of matching is to reach a stable status for all pairs.

Definition 10.2 A matching M is pairwise stable if there is no block pair (x, y).

Definition 10.3 (x, y) is a block pair for a matching M if the three following conditions are satisfied:

- $M(x) \neq y$.
- $y >_x M(x)$,
- $x >_y M(y)$.

In the fog computing applications, the recent work [8] provided a comprehensive survey of the state-of-the art algorithms using matching theory for task offloading problems. The basic task offloading problems can be interpreted as a matching problem between the set of computing resources including FNs and cloud and the set of computation tasks. The main goal of matching is to optimally match resources and tasks given their individual, often different, objectives and exchanged information. Each resource (task) builds a ranking of the tasks (resources) using a preference relation. In its basic form, a preference can simply be defined in terms of an objective utility function that quantifies the QoS achieved by a certain resource-task matching. In most works in the literature, the utility function is used to construct the PLs of agents.

10.2.2   Bandit Learning-Based Computation Offloading Algorithms

Task offloading has recently gained popularity as a potential approach to efficiently use distributed computing resources, and several studies conducted in this area have proposed efficient offloading solutions using different methodologies.

The work presented in [12] developed a code offloading architecture with on-demand computing resource allocation and concurrent task execution. The task offloading was represented as a deterministic optimization problem in [13, 14]. To enhance the total energy efficiency in homogeneous fog networks, the authors in [15] specifically made the assumption that they had complete knowledge of the system status. The offloading decision of which node to offload optimally becomes an integer programming problem and is challenging to solve under the supposition that the tasks could not be divided arbitrarily [16]. Real-time information collection and response are essential for making intelligent offloading decisions in a fog-enabled network [17]. Using the real-time statuses of the users and the servers, such as the sizes of the compute queues, one efficient task offloading technique should be able to quickly adapt to the demanding dynamics in the environments. As a result, task offloading is frequently a stochastic programming issue, and the abovementioned traditional optimization techniques with deterministic parameters are no longer appropriate. Utilizing the Lyapunov optimization approach like in [18, 19] is one option to resolve this conundrum. Additionally, a game-theoretic decentralized strategy was offered in [20] to provide independent offloading decisions from each user. Accordingly, the task offloading is structured as a game and followed the Nash equilibrium rather than attempting to solve a challenging integer programming problem.

All of the computation offloading strategies listed above presupposed complete knowledge of the system characteristics. In practice, these factors are sometimes unknown or just partially known to the user. As an example, some values (also known as bandit feedback) are only disclosed for the nodes that are queried. The authors in [21] specifically considered the calculation and communication delays of each task as a posteriori. Each device's movement was thought to be unpredictable in [22]. Offloading feedback are used in reinforcement learning-based offloading methods, such as those in [23, 24], to learn characteristics like latency and energy cost. There will be a tradeoff between using the empirically best node as frequently as possible and researching other nodes to uncover more lucrative activities when the number of nodes that can be queried is constrained owing to the limiting amount of resources that are available. To tackle this tradeoff, the ϵ-greedy approach, which is commonly used in reinforcement learning [23–25], should be used. This strategy, nevertheless, converges slowly and is nonoptimal [26].

The authors in [9] introduced D2CIT—a two-tier distributed strategy for offloading computing in an IoT context with fog. They took into account SNs with time-sensitive tasks that needed to be computed within the predefined deadlines. The high-level tasks will be divided into more manageable subtasks by D2CIT, which will then create a DATG. For the FN selection, they provided a greedy solution that separates the job from the appropriate SNs. In a dynamic setting, they develop a ε-greedy nonstationary MAB-based strategy for automated subtask redistribution. Additionally, they contrasted D2CIT with already existing solutions and demonstrated how the suggested algorithm performs better in terms of latency and speedup.

The study [10] examined a performance guarantee for an effective online task offloading approach in a fog-enabled network. A stochastic programming with delayed bandit feedback was defined and formulated since the expectations for processing speeds vary rapidly at unknown time instants and the system information is only accessible after completing the related tasks. BLOT, an effective online task offloading method based on the UCB policy, is developed to address this issue. The simulation results show that the proposed BLOT algorithm is capable of learning and selecting the appropriate node to offload tasks in an online manner under nonstationary conditions.

10.3 System Model

10.3.1 Fog Computing Networks

As illustrated in Fig. 10.2, a fog computing network includes a set F of N FNs ($F = \{F_1, F_2, \ldots, F_N\}$) connected to a cloud data center C with M virtual machines (VMs).

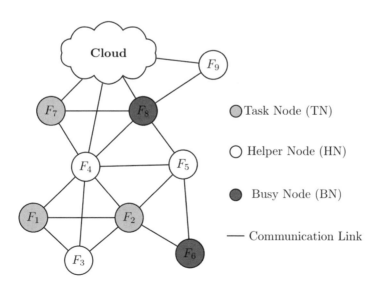

Fig. 10.2 An illustrative model of FCN includes three TNs (F_1, F_2, F_7), two BNs (F_6, F_8), and four HNs (F_3, F_4, F_5, F_9), which can connect to the cloud to request the cloud services

FNs can connect together through wired and wireless links for further cooperative offloading. At the beginning of every time slot, a FN can be in one of three modes: (i) a task node (TN) that has tasks in its queue, (ii) a busy node (BN) that is busy processing tasks, and (iii) a helper node (HN) that has the available resource to offload tasks. These states of nodes are reported to their neighbors at the beginning of time slot. We use β as notation to denote the percentage of TNs in each scheduling time. To design an efficient offloading policy, TNs are based on a table of neighbor resources that contains the updated information about the state and computing capabilities of neighbor HNs. The FNs are able to connect together to share these information for facilitating the offloading decisions. The computing capability of a FN is represented through CPU frequency (f (cycles/s)) and CPU processing density (γ (cycles/bit)).

10.3.2 Computation Offloading Model

Computation tasks from the end user devices such as IoT sensors and smartphones arriving at the queues of FNs follow a certain distribution. At a certain time slot τ, the FCN has a set $T = \{T_1, T_2, \ldots, T_K\}$ including K computational tasks resided in the queues of $F_1, F_2, \ldots, F_K$, respectively. A single task T_i of TN F_i can be processed locally by F_i or fully offloaded by a neighbor HN F_k.

When the offloading is needed, TNs send their offloading requests to their neighbor HNs. Typically, the offloading request is represented by a tuple $R_{\text{off}} = \{Task\text{-}ID, Task\text{-}Size, Task\text{-}Type, Deadline\}$ containing the features and requirements of tasks. When the request is accepted, the task data is immediately sent from TN to HN.

Considering a task T_i arriving at the request queue of F_i at the beginning of time slot, delay D_i to finish the task is estimated as follow.

A. Local Computing When T_i is computed locally by F_i, the delay is $D_i^{lc} = D_i^q + D_i^e$, where D_i^q and D_i^e are queuing delay of F_i and execution delay by F_i. Basically, $D_i^e = A_i \gamma_i / f_i$, where A_i is task size of T_i.

B. Offloading by a HN When T_i is offloaded by a H_j, the delay is $D_i^{off} = D_{ij}^{tx} + D_{ij}^e$, where D_{ij}^{tx} and D_{ij}^e are transmission delay from F_i to H_j and execution delay at F_j. Basically, $D_{ij}^t = A_i / r_{ij}$, where r_{ij} is the transmission rate of communication link ij and $D_{ij}^e = A_i \gamma_j / f_j$.

C. Cloud Computing Similarly, when T_i is offloaded by the cloud, the delay is $D_i^c = D_{ic}^{tx} + D_{ic}^e$, where D_{ic}^{tx} and D_{ic}^e ic are transmission delay from F_i to cloud and execution delay at cloud. Basically, D_{ic}^{tx} is achieved based on the number of hops from F_i to the cloud, and $D_{ic}^e = A_i \gamma_c / f_c$.

10.4 Design of BLM-DTO Algorithm

10.4.1 OTO Matching Model for Computation Offloading

We assume that each HN is able to offload only one single task, and a task is processed only by a single FN. Thus, at the beginning of each time slot, the task offloading problem can be modeled as an OTO matching model between the set T and the set H. In this matching model, while each TN can achieve a full preference relation over its HNs before sending the offloading request, each HN only builds its PL after receiving all possible requests because the task types are varied over time.

A. PLs of TNs The preference relations of TNs are based on the delay offered by their HNs. Basically, for each $T_k \in T$ and two connected H_i and $H_i \in H$, the preference relation is expressed by $H_i >_{T_k} H_j$ if and only if $D_{ki} \leq D_{kj}$.

B. PLs of HNs Practically, the FN is operated under the management of providers whose objective is to maximize the revenue by providing the best services (PaaS, IaaS, and SaaS). Therefore, the preference relation of HN is based on the cost that it receives to process the tasks. In the context of computation tasks, we consider two types of tasks in this paper. The first type includes tasks with deadline abbreviated as T_i and the rest without deadline termed as $\overline{T}_i$. For each HN, the priority of tasks with deadlines is higher than the one of the others. Denote $c_k(T_i)$ and $c_j(\overline{T}_i)$ as the cost to process a bit of task T_i and T_j, respectively, and $c_k(T_i) > c_j(\overline{T}_i)$. The total costs to offload T_i and T_j are $C_k(T_i) = c_k(T_i)A_i$ and $C_k(\overline{T}_j) = c_j(\overline{T}_j)A_j$. For any two tasks T_i and T_j requested to be offloaded by a HN H_k, the preference relation is configured as follow formula: $Ti >_{H_k} Tj$ if and only if $C_{ki} > C_{kj}$.

10.4.2 Multi-player Multi-armed Bandit with TS

The interaction between the set T of TNs and the set H of HNs can be modeled as MAB with multi-player, in which TNs and HNs play roles as players and arms, respectively. At each round $t = 1, 2, \ldots, T$, each player $T_i \in T$ attempts to pull an arm $H_i(t) \in H$. When multiple players attempt to pull the same arm, there will be a conflict, and only the player preferred most by this arm is accepted.

The idea behind TS is the so-called probability matching. At each round, we want to pick a bandit with probability equal to the probability of it being the optimal choice. We emulate this behavior in a very simple way. At each round, we calculate the posterior distribution of θ_k, for each of the bandits. Then, we draw a single sample of each of our θ_k and pick the one with the largest value as shown in Algorithm 10.1.

Algorithm 10.1: BLOM-DTO Algorithm

Input: Player set $\mathbf{T}$, arm set $\mathbf{H}$, parameter $\lambda \in (0, 1)$;
Output: A stable matching $\mathbf{M}$
Data: Initialize: $\forall i \in [\mathbf{T}], j \in [\mathbf{H}]$, $a_{ij} = b_{ij} = 1$

1 **for** $t = 1, 2, ..., T$ **do**
2   **for** $T_i \in \mathbf{T}$ **do**
3          $\forall \mathbf{H}_j$, sample $\theta_{i,j}(t) \in BETA(a_{ij}, b_{ij})$
4   Independently draw $D_i(t) \in Bernoulli(\lambda)$
5   **if** $D_i(t) = 0$ **then**
6   Construct a achievable set
7              $S_i(t) := \{j : \mathbf{C}_{j,i} \geq \mathbf{C}_{j,i'}\}$ where
                $\overline{H}_{i'}(t - 1) = j$
8   Pull $H_i(t) \in \arg\max_{j \in S_i(t)} \theta_{i,j}(t)$
9   **else**
10   Pull $H_i(t) = H_i(t - 1)$
11   **if** T_i *wins confict* **then**
12             $\overline{H}_i(t) = H_i(t)$
13             $Y_i(t) \in Bernoulli(X_{i,H_i(t)}(t))$
14   Update $a_{i,H_i(t)} = a_{i,H_i(t)} + Y_i(t)$
15             $b_{i,H_i(t)} = b_{i,H_i(t)+(1-Y_i(t))}$
16   **else**
17             $\overline{H}_i(t) = -1$

10.5   Simulation Results and Evaluation Analysis

10.5.1   *Simulation Environment Configuration*

The event-driven framework supported SimPy library in Python is used to conduct the simulation scenarios, which investigate the performance of algorithms. Table 10.1 summarizes the important parameters and values for the simulation scenario, where $U[x, y]$ indicates the uniform distribution on interval $[x, y]$.

Table 10.1 Parameters for simulation analysis

Parameters	Values
Number of FNs, N	100
Number of VMs provided by cloud, M	50
Size of task T_i, a_i	{5, 10, 15} (MB)
Active ratio of TNs, β	{0.1, 0.2, 0.3, 0.4, 0.5, 0.6, 0.7, 0.8, 0.9}
Processing density of FNs, γ	U[500, 1000] (cycles/bit)
CPU frequency of FNs, f	{1.0, 1.5, 2.0, 2.5} (GHz)
Processing density of each VM, γ_c	100 (cycles/bit)
CPU frequency of each VM, f_c	10 (GHz)

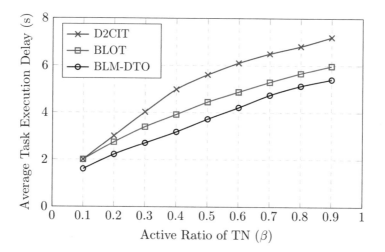

Fig. 10.3 The delay reduction ratio offered by D2CIT, BLOT, and BLM-DTO

10.5.2   Comparative Evaluation and Analysis

Figure 10.3 depicts the average delay achieved by D2CIT, BLOT, and BLM-DTO when β is varied.

When there is a large percentage of HNs in the network (i.e., β is small (0.1, 0.2)), the three algorithms have a similar performance. With this scenario, there are abundant resources to offer the optimal solutions for offloading tasks. When β increases, the performance gap between BLM-DTO and D2CIT and BLOT is larger. When $\beta = 0.9$, there presents a high workload in the network and a small percentage of available resources (HNs). Therefore, it is likely to have more tasks computed locally by TNs. That leads to a considerable increase of delay for the three algorithms. However, BLMDTO still outperforms the other algorithms because it can allocate the resources better through stable matching. Concretely, D2CIT and BLOT assign the best HNs to tasks in a greedy manner. Meanwhile, BLM-DTO uses the principles of stability in the matching theory to allocate the resource fairly.

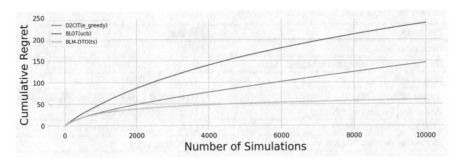

Fig. 10.4 Commutative regrets obtained by different bandit learning policies used in the three task offloading solutions

The outperformance of the proposed algorithm is enabled by TS-based learning technique. Figure 10.4 shows the comparison of commutative regret obtained by three algorithms.

The ϵ-greedy strategy uses a constant to balance exploration and exploitation. This is not ideal when the hyperparameter may be hard to tune. Also, the exploration is done 100% randomly, such that we explore bandits equally (on average), irrespective of how promising they may look. The UCB strategy, unlike the ϵ-greedy, uses the uncertainty of the posterior distribution to select the appropriate bandit at each round. It supposes that a bandit can be as good as it is reward distribution UCB. Finally, TS uses a very elegant principle: to choose an action according to the probability of it being optimal. In practice, this makes for a very simple algorithm by taking one sample from each reward distribution and choose the one with the highest value. Despite its simplicity, TS achieves state-of-the-art results, greatly outperforming the other algorithms. That is because TS promotes efficient exploration: it explores more where it is promising and quickly discards bad actions.

10.6   Conclusions

This chapter introduced TS-DTO algorithm enabling the FNs in the fog network to implement the task offloading operation in an online and distributed manner. Firstly, we modeled the task offloading between TNs and HNs as an OTO matching model, and the objective is to achieve stable matching. Given the dynamic nature of fog computing environment in terms of computation tasks and roles of FNs, the preference relations are only known by TN side, and they can be achieved by HN side after interaction between them. Therefore, we further modeled the selection of best HN as an MAB problem and solving it using TS technique. The simulation results show that the proposed algorithm outperforms the baselines in terms of delay and commutative regret.

References

1. Bonomi F, Milito R, Zhu J, Addepalli S (2012) Fog computing and its role in the internet of things. In: Proceedings of the first edition of the MCC workshop on Mobile cloud computing – MCC 2012. ACM Press
2. Tran-Dang H, Kim D-S (2021) FRATO: fog resource based adaptive task offloading for delay-minimizing IoT service provisioning. IEEE Trans Parallel Distrib Syst 32(10):2491–2508
3. Aazam M, Zeadally S, Harras KA (2018) Offloading in fog computing for IoT: review, enabling technologies, and research opportunities. Futur Gener Comput Syst 87:278–289
4. Liu L, Chang Z, Guo X, Mao S, Ristaniemi T (2018) Multiobjective optimization for computation offloading in fog computing. IEEE Internet Things J 5(1):283–294
5. Lee G, Saad W, Bennis M (2019) An online optimization framework for distributed fog network formation with minimal latency. IEEE Trans Wirel Commun 18(4):2244–2258
6. Yang Y, Liu Z, Yang X, Wang K, Hong X, Ge X (2019) Pomt: paired offloading of multiple tasks in heterogeneous fog networks. IEEE Internet Things J 6(5):8658–8669
7. Durand S, Gaujal B (2016) Complexity and optimality of the best response algorithm in random potential games. In: Symposium on algorithmic game theory (SAGT), pp 40–51
8. Tran-Dang H, Kim D-S (2022) A survey on matching theory for distributed computation offloading in IoT-fog-cloud systems: perspectives and open issues. IEEE Access 10:118353–118369
9. Misra S, Rachuri SP, Deb PK, Mukherjee A (2020) Multi armed bandit-based decentralized computation offloading in fog-enabled IoT. IEEE Internet Things J 8(12):10010–10017
10. Zhu Z, Liu T, Yang Y, Luo X (2019) Blot: bandit learning-based offloading of tasks in fog-enabled networks. IEEE Trans Parallel Distrib Syst 30(12):2636–2649
11. Chapelle O, Li L (2011) An empirical evaluation of Thompson sampling. In: Advances in neural information processing systems, vol 24, pp 2249–2257
12. Kosta S, Aucinas A, Hui P, Mortier R, Zhang X (2012) Thinkair: dynamic resource allocation and parallel execution in the cloud for mobile code offloading. In: 2012 proceedings IEEE INFOCOM, pp 945–953
13. You C, Huang K, Chae H, Kim B-H (2016) Energy-efficient resource allocation for mobile-edge computation offloading. IEEE Trans Wirel Commun 16(3):1397–1411
14. Wang F, Xu J, Wang X, Cui S (2017) Joint offloading and computing optimization in wireless powered mobile-edge computing systems. IEEE Trans Wirel Commun 17(3):1784–1797
15. Yang Y, Wang K, Zhang G, Chen X, Luo X, Zhou M-T (2018) Meets: maximal energy efficient task scheduling in homogeneous fog networks. IEEE Internet Things J 5(5):4076–4087
16. Dinh TQ, Tang J, La QD, Quek TQS (2017) Offloading in mobile edge computing: task allocation and computational frequency scaling. IEEE Trans Commun 65(8):3571–3584
17. Yang P, Zhang N, Bi Y, Yu L, Shen XS (2017) Catalyzing cloudfog interoperation in 5g wireless networks: an SDN approach. IEEE Netw 31(5):14–20
18. Yang Y, Zhao S, Zhang W, Chen Y, Luo X, Wang J (2018) Debts: delay energy balanced task scheduling in homogeneous fog networks. IEEE Internet Things J 5(3):2094–2106
19. Pu L, Chen X, Xu J, Fu X (2019) D2d fogging: an energy-efficient and incentive-aware task offloading framework via network-assisted d2d collaboration. IEEE J Select Areas Commun 34(12):3887–3901
20. Chen X (2014) Decentralized computation offloading game for mobile cloud computing. IEEE Trans Parallel Distribut Syst 26(4):974–983
21. Chen T, Giannakis GB (2019) Bandit convex optimization for scalable and dynamic IoT management. IEEE Internet Things J 6(1):1276–1286
22. Tekin C, van der Schaar M (2014) An experts learning approach to mobile service offloading. In: 2014 52nd annual Allerton conference on communication, control, and computing (Allerton), pp 643–650

23. Min M, Wan X, Xiao L, Chen Y, Xia M, Wu D, Dai H (2018) Learning-based privacy-aware offloading for healthcare IoT with energy harvesting. IEEE internet things J 6(3):4307–4316
24. Min M, Xiao L, Chen Y, Cheng P, Wu D, Zhuang W (2019) Learning-based computation offloading for IoT devices with energy harvesting. IEEE Trans Veh Technol 68(2):1930–1941
25. Sutton R, Barto A (2015) Reinforcement learning: an introduction. IEEE Trans Neural Netw 9(5):1054–1054
26. Auer P, Cesa-Bianchi N, Fischer P (2002) Finite-time analysis of the multiarmed bandit problem. Mach Learn 47(2):235–256

Printed in the United States
by Baker & Taylor Publisher Services